A Student's Guide to Education

CW01024081

This new edition of *A Student's Guide to Education Studies* is an essential resource for any undergraduate making their first explorations into the fascinating world of education. It explores a wide range of alternative visions of education encouraging students to challenge the perceived notions about learning and knowledge.

Offering new perspectives and powerful ideas for discussion on a variety of long-standing topics such as class, race and gender, the book is organised around five enduring themes: Policy and Politics, Global and Environmental Education, Knowledge and Learning, Childhood and Youth, Professionalism and Employment. With a distinctive international and global focus, this new edition has been extensively updated to reflect the latest research and thinking in the field and features new chapters on:

- The sociology of education and the philosophy of education
- Inclusion
- Childhood and youth
- Professionalism and work-based learning
- Populism in politics

Including summary points, questions for discussion and annotated suggestions for further reading, this book provides the theoretical background needed to carry out a critical analysis of education policy and practice and is an essential resource for all students of Education Studies.

Catherine A. Simon is a principal lecturer in Education Studies at Bath Spa University, UK.

Stephen Ward is Professor Emeritus of Education at Bath Spa University, UK.

A Student's Guide to Education Studies

Fourth edition

Edited by Catherine A. Simon
and Stephen Ward

LONDON AND NEW YORK

Fourth edition published 2020
by Routledge
2 Park Square, Milton Park, Abingdon, Oxon, OX14 4RN

and by Routledge
52 Vanderbilt Avenue, New York, NY 10017

Routledge is an imprint of the Taylor & Francis Group, an informa business

© 2020 selection and editorial matter, Catherine A. Simon and Stephen Ward;
individual chapters, the contributors

The right of Catherine A. Simon and Stephen Ward to be identified as the
authors of the editorial material, and of the authors for their individual
chapters, has been asserted in accordance with sections 77 and 78 of the
Copyright, Designs and Patents Act 1988.

All rights reserved. No part of this book may be reprinted or reproduced or utilised
in any form or by any electronic, mechanical, or other means, now known or
hereafter invented, including photocopying and recording, or in any information
storage or retrieval system, without permission in writing from the publishers.

Trademark notice: Product or corporate names may be trademarks or registered
trademarks, and are used only for identification and explanation without intent to infringe.

First edition published by Routledge 2004
Third edition published by Routledge 2013

British Library Cataloguing-in-Publication Data
A catalogue record for this book is available from the British Library

Library of Congress Cataloging-in-Publication Data
Names: Simon, Catherine A., editor. | Ward, Stephen, editor. |
Routledge (Firm)
Title: A student's guide to education studies /
edited by Catherine A. Simon and Stephen Ward.
Identifiers: LCCN 2019042564 (print) | LCCN 2019042565 (ebook) |
ISBN 9780367276683 (Hardback) | ISBN 9780367276690 (Paperback) |
ISBN 9780429297212 (eBook)
Subjects: LCSH: Education. | Teaching. | Learning.
Classification: LCC LB1025.3 .E334 2020 (print) |
LCC LB1025.3 (ebook) | DDC 370.71/1–dc23
LC record available at https://lccn.loc.gov/2019042564
LC ebook record available at https://lccn.loc.gov/2019042565

ISBN: 978-0-367-27668-3 (hbk)
ISBN: 978-0-367-27669-0 (pbk)
ISBN: 978-0-429-29721-2 (ebk)

Typeset in Bembo
by Newgen Publishing UK

Contents

Acknowledgement

The ideas in these chapters were developed with Education Studies students in several universities. We learned from their enthusiastic and critical responses and they were the inspiration for this book.

Abbreviations

ASCL	Association of School and College Leaders
AI	artificial intelligence
ANT	actor–network theory
APPG	All Party Parliamentary Group
AR	augmented reality
ASCL	Association of School and College Leaders
BAME	black, Asian and minority ethnic
BBC	British Broadcasting Corporation
BEd	Bachelor of Education (degree)
BITC	Business in the Community
BSA	British Social Attitudes (survey)
BSF	Building Schools for the Future
CAT	Centre for Alternative Technology
CLA	Cultural Learning Alliance
CO_2	carbon dioxide
CofE	Church of England
CoP	*Code of Practice*
CoRE	Commission on Religious Education in England
CPD	continuing professional development
DBS	Disclosure and Barring Service
DCSF	Department for Children, Schools and Families
DES	Department of Education and Science
DfE	Department for Education
DfEE	Department for Education and Employment
DfES	Department for Education and Skills
DWP	Department for Work and Pensions
EBacc	English Baccalaureate
ECEC	Early Childhood Education and Care
ECM	Every Child Matters
ECS	Early Childhood Studies
EDI	Education Development Index

EEF	Educational Endowment Foundation
EHRC	Equality and Human Rights Commission
ESD	Education for Sustainable Development
EU	European Union
FAANG	Facebook, Apple, Alphabet, Amazon, Netflix and Google
FE	further education
FSM	Free School Meals
FTSE	Financial Times Stock Exchange (100 Index)
GCSE	General Certificate of Secondary Education
HE	higher education
HMI	Her Majesty's Inspector
ICDS	Indian Integrated Child Development Service
IMF	International Monetary Fund
INC-CO	Inclusion Co-ordinator
IQ	Intelligence Quotient
JRF	Joseph Rowntree Foundation
KS	Key Stage
LA	local authority
LEA	local education authority
LGBT	lesbian, gay, bisexual, and transgender
LMS	local management of schools
MAT	multi-academy trust
MDG	Millennium Development Goals
MFI	monetary financial institutions
MOOC	Massive Open Online Course
MR	mixed reality
NACCCE	National Advisory Committee on Creative and Cultural Education
NCIHE	National Committee of Inquiry into Higher Education
NGO	Non-Government Organisations
NHS	National Health Service
NS-SEC	National Statistics Socio-Economic Classification Analytic Classes
OECD	Organisation for Economic Cooperation and Development
Ofsted	Office for Standards in Education
ONS	Office for National Statistics
PC	personal computer
PFI	Private Finance Initiative
PISA	Programme for International Student Assessment
PRP	Penn Resiliency Program
PSE	pre-school education
PSHE	Personal, Social and Health Education
QCA	Qualifications and Curriculum Authority
QTS	Qualified Teacher Status
RE	Religious Education

REC	Religious Education Council of England and Wales
RSC	Regional School Commissioner
SACRE	Standing Advisory Council on Religious Education
SAT	Statutory Assessment Test
SCAA	Schools Curriculum and Assessment Authority
SEEd	Sustainability and Environmental Education
SENCO	Special Educational Needs Co-ordinator
SEND	Special Educational Needs and Disabilities
SENDCO	Special Educational Needs and Disabilities Co-ordinator
SES	socio-economic status
SMSC	spiritual, moral, social and cultural
SPL	shared parental leave
STEM	science, technology, engineering and mathematics
TA	Teaching Assistant
TIMMS	Trends in International Mathematics and Science Study
TTA	Teacher Training Agency
TUC	Trades Union Congress
UCAS	Universities and Colleges Admissions Service
UK	United Kingdom
UKRP	The UK Resilience Programme
UNESCO	United Nations Educational, Scientific and Cultural Organization
VA	voluntary aided (schools)
VC	voluntary controlled (schools)
VLE	virtual learning environment
VR	virtual reality
WEC	Women and Equalities Committee
WHO	World Health Organization

Introduction

Education for a better world

It is through education that we can build a better world. Human flourishing has been created through the worldwide spread of reason, knowledge and ideas. Enormous challenges still face us in the forms of continuing world poverty, climate change, potential ecological disaster and political extremism. The way to overcome them is by building on the ingenuity of people through education. Of course, this is optimistic, but education depends on a belief in progress through the global spread of learning. As students of education, we have the privilege of engaging with humanity's greatest achievements in fostering knowledge of truth and understanding. Education Studies as a free-standing subject began in a few universities in the late 1990s. It is now a highly popular developing subject in some eighty universities in the UK. This is not surprising as Education Studies is an ideal subject as preparation for teaching and other educational careers. But it is also an exciting subject in its breadth of study, from the technical details of children's learning, to the politics and economics of education policy and society, and the wider issues of international education, globalisation and climate change. This book introduces the range of topics with original chapters from experts in the fields.

The origins of Education Studies

Education Studies began as the theory for teacher training in the Bachelor of Education (BEd) degrees in the 1960s. The Robbins Report (Committee on Higher Education, 1963) recommended the expansion of higher education in Britain and that all teachers should be university graduates. This meant that the colleges training teachers on certificate courses were required to provide BEd degrees validated and awarded by their local university. Not surprisingly, the universities insisted that the BEd degrees should include substantial theoretical material. Crook (2002) explains how subject disciplines were drawn in to form the academic basis. R.S. Peters, philosopher of the London Institute of Education, met with C.J. Gill, HMI for teacher training, in a closed seminar at the DES to agree the subjects to be included in the new degrees. The proposal was for Psychology, Sociology, Philosophy and Economics to be the theoretical basis. Economics was subsequently dropped in favour of the History of Education. This was a remarkably autocratic event with little open discussion and agreement of those involved. There was at the time a very limited research base for the disciplines in education in the universities and little academic competence in the subjects in the training colleges. Pedagogy was excluded and Crook details the historical problems which Education Studies encountered alongside demands for practical teacher training:

> … the absence of pedagogy as a core component of Educational Studies in the under-graduate degrees established during 1965–68 was indicative of the general difficulties of educationists making a decisive theoretical contribution to practical problems in education.
>
> (ibid.: 23)

With complaints of teacher training being 'over-theorised' and giving insufficient practical guidance for teachers, the 1980s and 1990s saw teacher training taken over by government controls. The Teacher Training Agency (TTA) was set up and it published *Standards for Teaching*, a long list of criteria which removed much of the theoretical dimension from teacher training. It was government controls and 'de-theorising' that moved academics in universities to begin Education Studies as a degree subject in its own right. It has grown rapidly during the last twenty years with large numbers of students taking it as a precursor either to teacher training or to other graduate careers in education.

The first edition of this book (Ward, 2004) was one of the texts which contributed to the development of the subject, introducing the politics of education, international perspectives and ecological issues. Since that time the curriculum for Education Studies has grown both wider and deeper. This fourth edition continues both to keep up to date and to lead developments with new chapters. Its contributors are experts in their educational fields, and all share the belief that education is an exciting subject which covers a vast range of topics.

Content and structure of the book

This is just one book, which cannot cover the full range of the new Education Studies curriculum. We have selected a range of topics which reflect current and future thinking. Each chapter offers recommended reading to take your knowledge further, as well as questions for discussion which will help you to reflect on your learning. While being an introductory text, the book is much more than 'the basics'. It includes original material which engages in debates around the topics, some of which are controversial. The overriding academic aim of Education Studies is *critical analysis*, and each chapter is designed to help you to understand different ideas and perspectives. You may not agree with the author: good, as long as you can explain why!

Education Studies has grown in breadth, but also in academic 'depth'. In its early days undergraduate courses in education tended to avoid explicit reference to the contributory disciplines of Psychology, Sociology, Philosophy and History of Education, perhaps because of the complaints of 'over-theorised' teacher training mentioned above. However, in recent years Education Studies course leaders have tended to turn back to the disciplines in order to ensure a strong academic framework. Several chapters give explicit insights into the methods and forms of knowledge given by each of the disciplines: Chapter 13 'The sociology of knowledge', Chapter 14 'The social psychology of learning', Chapter 15 'Philosophy and education'. Many chapters begin with a historical survey of the topic, for example Chapter 3 'Race, ethnnicity and education' and Chapter 10 on religious education. The discipline of economics, rejected by Peters and Gill in 1964, is now essential in understanding government neoliberal education policy and is explored in Chapter 1 'Education policy and the marketisation of education', Chapter 5 'Social mobility and education', and Chapter 9 on education and populism.

The book is structured in five sections. The first, 'Policy and politics', recognises the fact that in education politics is inescapable and essential to an understanding of educational structures and decision-making. In the first two chapters, 'Education policy and the marketisation of education' and 'Education and social justice', Stephen Ward and Catherine Simon analyse the underlying political and economic theories which have driven the development of education policy. The long-standing controversies around policies on race, gender and class in education are discussed in the next chapters. Charlotte Chadderton in Chapter 3 'Race, ethnicity and education in England' outlines the development of policies to combat racism in schools but finds that the current political developments in Britain are seeing its return. In 'Gender and work' (Chapter 4) Christine Eden explains that, despite efforts to counter sexism, and while girls succeed at schools, women still suffer discrimination in the workplace. Richard Riddell in Chapter 5 explores issues of class and achievement in 'Social mobility and education'. In Chapter 6 on intersectionality Christine Eden uses a range of research data to show how race, gender and class cross – or intersect – in the subject of educational achievement. In Chapter 7 on 'The inclusion agenda' Zeta Brown and Jo Winwood review the recent political concern and controversy around school inclusion and exclusion.

Section 2 'Global and environmental education' explores the wide-ranging content of education, with some of the most exciting and distinctive features of the Education Studies palette. In Chapter 8 Brendan Bartram discusses the benefits of looking comparatively at other education systems. There is a tendency to think of the education system in which we are brought up as the only one, but reviewing other systems can bring surprises and things to learn about ways to improve education. However, simply importing educational practices from other cultures can be a mistake. Globalisation has been in place for many years and David Coulby in Chapter 9 shows how it has led to the current phenomenon of political 'populism' across the world with the election of Donald Trump in the United States and the 2016 referendum to take the United Kingdom out of the European Union. Much has been written about this in the political press, but here David explains its implications for education. Chapter 10 on religion belongs in this section because, while it is a curriculum item in schools, it has a strong international dimension which Denise Cush discusses in 'Religion and worldviews in education'. Despite Donald Trump's ignorant criticisms, climate change and education for sustainability have become leading political priorities across the world. David Hicks has contributed to the previous editions of this book. In his two chapters, 11 and 12, he brings us up to date with the latest thinking on these matters and shows the role which education must play to rescue the future of the planet.

While the first two sections of the book are concerned with the broad political and global dimensions of education, it is self-evident that knowledge and learning are its central concerns. Again, Education Studies is not about 'how to teach', but it is about the ways in which people learn and 'what to teach', what knowledge is selected to be in a curriculum for children and young people, and how such decisions are made. The third section of the book explores these questions. The first three chapters employ three of the academic disciplines. Rita Chawla-Duggan in Chapter 13 examines the ways in which knowledge is selected for the curriculum in 'The sociology of knowledge'. The psychology of learning has always played a strong role in understanding the ways in which people learn. Cathal Ó Siochrú extends this to an understanding of the social psychology of learning: how the membership of groups in schools and classrooms affects the learning of children and young people. In Chapter 15 Tom Feldges introduces the discipline of Philosophy and the ways in which it can help us to analyse educational topics, and he discusses further the role of the subject disciplines in education. It is impossible to examine every curriculum area, but the two final chapters in the section select two for attention. The first, Art Education, is chosen because of its relative neglect in the current political climate and in Chapter 16 June Bianchi makes the case for the importance of 'Creative pedagogy'. The second subject, Information Technology, is selected because of its growing importance. In Chapter 17 Kyriaki Anagnostopoulou points to the future of learning with the growth of artificial intelligence, and warns critically of some of its dangers.

Child development is both an element of Education Studies and a subject which sits alongside it in many undergraduate programmes. Section 4 introduces some of the current issues in the study of 'Childhood and youth'. In Chapter 18 Ioanna Palaiologou and Zenna Kingdon discuss the latest thinking in early years education. There is a cultural tendency in the West to think of children as helpless and vulnerable. In many ways, of course, they are. But in Chapter 19 Zeta Brown and Jayne Daly introduce the notion of the 'resilient' child: that young people can be strong and resourceful in overcoming difficult life contexts. On the other hand, recent years have seen the emergence of mental health issues among young people. Another new topic for Education Studies and a priority for schools is health education; in Chapter 20 Bethan Mitchell explores the latest theoretical models and policies for supporting health in education.

As we noted above, Education Studies was a breakaway from teacher training and for some years there has been a tendency in undergraduate courses to play down the issue of future employment for students. Now course leaders are recognising the importance of graduates being equipped for employment in education-related careers, including postgraduate teacher education. The book, therefore, concludes with a new short section of two chapters on 'Professionalism and employment'. In order to prepare students for future employment, and to see educational principles working in practice, most Education Studies courses now include placements in educational settings. Catherine Simon in Chapter 21 discusses how students are able to learn from placements in schools and other locations.

In the final chapter Jim Hordern and Kendra McMahon discuss the theoretical issues of professionalism, both globally and in teacher education in England.

Questions for discussion

1. Why did you choose Education Studies?
2. What are your career plans?
3. Does Education Studies benefit from the foundation disciplines of Psychology, Sociology, Philosophy, Economics and History?
4. What do you think about the new perspectives: global, international, ecological and economic?

The Routledge Education Studies Series

This fourth edition is linked to the Routledge Education Studies Series, a sequence of books written by some of the contributors which expand on some of the topics included in the book. The books available to date in the series are:

Zeta Brown (Ed.) (2016) *Inclusive Education: Perspectives on Pedagogy, Policy and Practice*. Abingdon: Routledge.

Christine Eden (2017) *Gender: Education and Work: Inequalities and Intersectionality*. Abingdon: Routledge.

Brendan Bartram (Ed.) (2017) *International and Comparative Education: Contemporary Issues and Debates*. Abingdon: Routledge.

Zeta Brown and Stephen Ward (Eds) (2018) *Contemporary Issues in Childhood: A Bio-Ecological Approach*. Abingdon: Routledge.

Cathal Ó Siochrú (Ed.) (2018) *Psychology and the Study of Education: Critical Perspectives on Developing Theories*. Abingdon: Routledge.

Tom Feldges (Ed.) (2019) *Philosophy and the Study of Education: New Perspectives on a Complex Relationship*. Abingdon: Routledge.

Catherine Simon and Graham Downes (Eds) (2020) *Sociology for Education Studies*. Abingdon: Routledge.

Jessie Bustillos Morales and Sandra Abegglen (Eds) (2020) *The Study of Education and Economics: Debates and Critical Theoretical Perspectives*. Abingdon: Routledge.

Titles forthcoming

Brendan Bartram (Ed.) *Contemporary Issues in Higher Education: Contradictions, Complexities and Challenges*. Abingdon: Routledge.

Nicholas Joseph (Ed.) *History of Education*. Abingdon: Routledge.

The British Education Studies Association (BESA)

Many of the editors and contributors to Education Studies book series are members of BESA. Formed in 2005, BESA is an academic association providing a network for tutors and students in Education Studies. It holds an annual conference with research papers from staff and students; there are bursaries for students on Education Studies programmes.

The website offers information and news about Education Studies and two journals: *Educationalfutures* and *Transformations*, a journal for student publications. Both are available without charge on the website: https://educationstudies.org.uk/

References

Committee on Higher Education (Robbins) (1963) *Report*. London: HMSO.

Crook, D. (2002) Education Studies and Teacher Education. *British Journal of Education Studies* **50**(1), pp. 55–75.

Ward, S. (Ed.) (2004) *Education Studies: A Student's Guide*. Abingdon: Routledge.

Section 1

Policy and politics

Chapter 1

Education policy and the marketisation of education

Stephen Ward

Introduction

This chapter explains the political and economic influences on education in England. While there have been similar developments in Scotland, Wales and Northern Ireland, and across many industrial nations, it is England which has experienced the extreme effects of educational politics. For over a century, education policy has swung between benign indifference, micro-management and free-market economics. The chapter introduces: trends in government policy in England since 1870, political theories and their effects on education policy, and the development of market forces in education.

The beginnings of education policy

We are now so used to government education policy dictating the nature of schooling and education that we tend to take it for granted. But political control varies in different countries and it has changed over time in England. In the 1830s and 1840s schooling for some factory and workhouse children was provided by church foundations (see Chapter 10), but education was mainly for the wealthy in independent fee-paying schools. Only in 1870, later than in other countries in Europe, did the Forster Education Act introduce compulsory state elementary schooling for all. The early influence of the church continues to the present day when there are still large numbers of Church of England (CofE) schools and academies.

In the nineteenth century the industrial revolution and its colonial powers made the British economy the envy of the world. The secret of its success was what economists call 'liberal economics': no state interference in production, with employers free to charge as much as possible for their products and pay as little as they need to their workers. Providers compete with each other, become more efficient, and the economy grows. However, liberal economics creates wide differentials between rich and poor and by 1870, after years of unfettered free markets, British society was close to breakdown. It was time for government to intervene, and the 1870 Education Act was one of a series of reforms to protect the welfare of the poor.

When a government provides education, it wants to make the service 'accountable' to ensure that the tax-payer is getting 'value for money'. The first attempt at education policy was simple: children were taught a basic curriculum of reading, writing and arithmetic and given moral and religious instruction, reflecting the beliefs and values of the day. To ensure that children were taught the curriculum Her Majesty's Inspectors (HMIs) tested them to determine the level of teachers' pay: the so-called 'payment-by-results scheme'.

The political consensus on education

The 1902 Balfour Education Act saw the abolition of payment-by-results, handing control of schooling and the curriculum to the teaching profession. It was an implicit statement of faith in teachers and, for the greater part of the twentieth century, left England with no national curriculum and no structure for monitoring what was going on in its schools. Midway through the century the 1944 Butler Education Act introduced compulsory secondary education, but again did not stipulate a curriculum, except for compulsory religious education and a daily act of corporate Christian worship. In setting up compulsory secondary education, a tripartite system of selective and non-selective schools was constructed: grammar schools for the 'academically able', technical schools for the 'technologically able' and secondary modern schools for those destined for a non-academic and non-technical future. The system was based upon the psychological theory that intelligence testing at age 10 – the 11 plus – could sort the child population into these categories. In reality, few technical schools were built and, in many areas of the country, children were destined for either the grammar school or secondary modern as the country turned its attention to post-war economic needs.

The two main political rivals in the UK are the Conservative and Labour parties. The *right-wing* Conservative Party has been committed to 'freedom' and the protection of property rights in the liberal economic tradition, whereas the *left-wing* Labour Party has been inclined to state intervention with publicly-funded services – schools, hospitals, social workers – to protect the welfare of all. Traditionally, the Labour Party would have higher taxation to fund welfare services, whereas the Conservative Party would charge lower taxes to leave people with personal wealth to spend on services as they wish. Conservatives have criticised Labour for intervening in people's lives.

After World War II the economic theories of John Maynard Keynes became dominant. Keynes argued that the state should be an employer, and that the economy would be successful in a more equal society in which the population was supported by social services, health and education. This became the direction of social policy in Britain with the creation of the National Health Service, social services and free primary and secondary education for all. Political interest in education lay mainly in debates about types of schools, social class and access to schooling. Conservatives argued for selective grammar schools to preserve high standards for an elite, usually middle-class, group. Labour campaigned for equal access for all, regardless of social class, and from 1965 tried to introduce secondary comprehensive schools open to all pupils regardless of income or ability. However, schools were controlled by local education authorities (LEAs) and some Conservative authorities chose to retain selective grammar schools. The left wing of the Labour Party wanted to get rid of independent fee-paying schools as bastions of privilege, but of course they continued.

During this long debate about access and social class, central government took little or no interest in the curriculum, in teaching or in the running of schools. The administration and monitoring of education was left to the local authorities and a small number of HMIs. The tacit agreement not to interfere with schools Lawton (1992) calls a 'political consensus' on education. Economics, again, are important in understanding this 'hands-off' approach. During the twentieth century the British economy continued to be strong, and so, for politicians, there was no need to worry about the education system: it could be left to the local authorities and teachers.

Education and the global economy

The oil crisis of the 1970s brought indifference to an end. Conflict in the Middle East and the loss of Britain's colonial control led to increasing oil prices which hit production in all the European economies. At the same time, there were concerns about rising crime, lower moral standards and the breakdown of traditional moral codes. Politicians looked for culprits, and in 1976 Jim Callaghan (1976), Labour Prime Minister, accused schools of failing to equip young people for industry: falling school standards were the cause of the nation's economic and social ills.

By the 1980s the effects of the global economy were being realised with the Asian 'tiger' economies of Japan, South Korea and Taiwan producing better industrial goods more cheaply and sucking away customers from Britain. Their education systems appeared to benefit from teaching basic skills through traditional methods. Making the curriculum suited to industrial production was seen as one of the means of enabling Britain to compete, and the government began to treat education as the principal means of training industry for competition in the world by becoming more vocationally oriented.

The New Right: neoliberal economics and the marketisation of education

The 1979 general election brought a Conservative government under Margaret Thatcher. She criticised Keynesian economics and social policy for creating a 'nanny state' in which people cease to be independent, functioning human beings. Her plan was to reduce taxation, 'roll back the state' and allow people greater personal control over their lives. This was the so-called 'New Right' politics, derived from nineteenth-century liberalism and so known as 'neo[new]liberalism'. Its ideas are based on the social philosopher Friedrich von Hayek (1899–1992) who argued in his book *The Road to Serfdom* (1991) that the welfare state disables creative energy and that individual freedom, while appearing self-serving and greedy, actually brings public good. For education, neoliberal economics means introducing the competition which made commerce successful. Neoliberals want a 'free market' in education: education becomes a commodity which is bought and sold; schools are the providers and parents and children the consumers, or 'customers'.

It was only after Thatcher's third election win, and twelve years after Callaghan's warning speech, that neoliberal politics arrived with the Education 'Reform' Act of 1988. The act is well known for introducing a national curriculum and standardised testing, but it also introduced 'local management of schools' (LMS). This took financial control away from the local authorities by delegating the spending budget to schools. Schools were to use the money as they wished: to appoint teaching staff or non-teaching assistants, purchase more computers or repair the roof. Such decisions were now to be taken by the headteacher and the governing body of the school, not by local authority officials. LMS made schools into business corporations competing for pupils. The role of school governors was strengthened to get rid of 'provider capture': education was to be determined by the 'customers', not the providers, the education professionals.

The principle was consumer choice with education accountable to its 'customers'. But schools are not open with their goods on display like shops in the high street. So the machinery of a national curriculum, testing, league tables and Ofsted inspection was needed to bring education into the market. It was intended to change education from a public 'good' – a service provided by professionals to everyone for the benefit of everyone – to education as a commodity which can be purchased. Sometimes referred to as 'Thatcherism', it is part of a broader political movement taking place in many parts of the world. (See Chapter 8.)

LMS seems contradictory. On the one hand, the government had taken central control of the curriculum and national testing, but it had de-centralised spending and management. While the 1988 Act appears to devolve power from government to schools, it actually increased the power of central government by disempowering the local authorities. Legislation in 1992 introduced the Office for Standards in Education (Ofsted) with powers to inspect every school in the state system every four years. The Ofsted Frameworks for Inspection give the most detailed list of every possible dimension of a school's work and can be seen as part of a general trend in society towards increased accountability and surveillance. It is difficult to convey the magnitude and complexity of the systems which were put in place for education by the legislation of the late 1980s and early 1990s. They generated prodigious amounts of consultative documents and a variety of government agencies. Another apparent contradiction is that Thatcher, a neoliberal politician who talked of 'rolling back government', introduced this welter of legislation which was designed to control and regulate education. Gray (1998:17) explains that free-market economics cannot happen without government intervention. The idea of neoliberals that free markets do everything and no government is needed is just too simple:

> … encumbered markets are the norm in every society, whereas free markets are a product of artifice, design and political coercion. *Laissez-faire* must be centrally planned: regulated markets just happen. The free market is not, as New Right thinkers have imagined or claimed, a gift of social evolution. It is an end-product of social engineering and unyielding political will.

So there was no contradiction: the free market needed customers to be able to choose between schools, and government controls were to create the conditions for a free market.

New Labour and the 'modernisers'

The Labour Party under Tony Blair won the 1997 general election. But this did not mean a return to Keynesian economics because this was 'New Labour' with a strong commitment to market forces. The politics of New Labour were not identical with the Conservative New Right. Blair did not see market forces as a philosophical doctrine like the neoliberal Conservatives, but simply the way to make the system work through competition. Blair's 'modernisation' meant that commitment to equality of opportunity through comprehensive education ended, with the refusal to abolish independent schools and grammar schools, and with a plan to get rid of 'bog-standard' comprehensive schools. The 2002 Education Act encouraged diversity, with specialist schools allowed to select pupils. Blair claimed this makes sense 'because it works': increasing quality and standards to create an education system which provides the educated workforce for industry in globally competitive markets. Blair's modernising meant 'intervention' and the political will to take on big issues such as child poverty, inequality and underachievement through a mixture of legislation, funding and persuasion. Assessment and school league tables were strengthened with the setting of targets at all levels: national government targets for literacy and numeracy, as well as targets for LEAs, for schools and for individual pupils. Failing local education authorities were taken over by private companies and school building was financed by profit-making organisations in the Private Finance Initiative (PFI). The 'outsourcing' to private companies of school meals, cleaning and other services begun by the Conservatives continued. All were designed to bring capital and private enterprise into the system.

Education for the economy and the standards agenda

Old Labour policy had been to reduce inequalities by providing high levels of resources to schools. But Labour governments in the past had not succeeded in actually producing the finances. Blair's policy was to ensure that the economy was successful by maintaining neoliberal economics. New Labour abandoned its commitment to the egalitarian comprehensive school movement. Priorities were to be 'standards' of achievement, not the 'structures' of schools. New Labour's enthusiasm for privatisation and the market produced the policy for academies: state-funded schools run by private individuals or organisations. Academies set their own curriculum and were free from other constraints of state schools. Like privatising the railways, the assumption was that a school run by a private enterprise will be more efficient and effective than one run by a state body. The theory of markets is that diversity provides customer choice and so it was government policy to increase the diversity of schools. The 2005 Education Act encouraged the expansion of faith schools to add to diversification. (See Chapter 10.)

In ten years Blair had shifted Labour policy onto the centre ground and away from the old Labour socialist 'tax-and-spend' image. The New Labour governments enjoyed a period of economic growth with one of the most efficient economies in Europe. The years saw increases in teachers' salaries and in numbers of teaching assistants, better provision for early years, improved resources, and a commitment to rebuilding all secondary schools by 2015 with the Building Schools for the Future (BSF) programme. In 2007 the new Labour Prime Minister, Gordon Brown (2007), argued for an end to the conflict between education as a market and as a social service: 'We need both strong public services and we need a dynamic market economy to have a fair and prosperous society.'

Brown's other legacy to education was the Education and Skills Act (2008) which recognised that the school leaving age of 16 was too low, given that industry no longer needed 16-year-olds with low qualifications. The act specified a new 'Participation Age' where young people in England and Wales were obliged to attend education or training for at least one day per week until the age of 18. The local authority was to ensure that places were available.

The Coalition and the age of austerity

But 2008 brought world economies to the brink of disaster with the banking crisis sparked by the collapse of Lehman Brothers Bank in the United States. Stiglitz (2010) explains that bankers across the world had made unsecured loans to make short-term profits and bonuses. The culture of reckless lending meant that British banks had to be 'recapitalised' by government loans, bringing government debt in 2010 to a total of some £160bn. The British Prime Minister, Gordon Brown, had led the world in the global policy to support the banks with government funding to prevent the collapse of international capitalism. However, when it came to the general election of May 2010 his global success was not enough to save the Labour government from defeat.

The Conservative Party did not win sufficient parliamentary seats to form a government and was forced to join the Liberal Democrats in the first coalition government in Britain since World War II. A principle of the coalition agreement was that the government would pay off government debt by the end of the parliament in 2015. This meant a period of 'austerity': massive cuts in government spending on social services, health and education. It allowed the new government to legitimate the Conservative political ideology of reducing the role of the state in society and the economy. While this was essentially a return to Thatcher's mission to 'roll back the state', the Prime Minister, David Cameron, depicted it as 'the Big Society': instead of the government bureaucracy managing and funding everything, control is handed to private enterprise and voluntary bodies, and decisions are taken locally by the people whose interests are served.

In education policy economic principles were translated into immediate action by the new Secretary of State, Michael Gove. BSF was scrapped as part of the spending reductions, and the schools promised new buildings under the scheme were disappointed. The Labour government's academies programme had been to revitalise education for working-class pupils in failing inner-city schools. Gove's concept of academies was to free *all* schools from the control of local authorities. The hurried Academies Act (DfE, 2010) permitted any school, including primary schools, to apply for academy status and to be self-governed. Known as 'converted' academies, such schools had to demonstrate that they were of sufficiently high quality to gain the status, as against Labour's 'sponsored' academies, which were formerly 'failing' schools. Gove also forced failing schools to become academies.

The Gove academy, free of bureaucratic control, was a contribution to Cameron's Big Society vision. Part of this agenda was the introduction of 'free schools' which could be set up by any interested community of parents or teachers, like an independent school, but receiving state funding. Free schools were intended to enable the provision of schooling suitable to the local clients, and where special interest groups wish to provide a particular form of education not offered in an existing school. In marketising its education system, Sweden had set up free schools, and Gove was impressed with a concept that fitted neatly into his ideology. However, the evidence from Sweden was that free schools did not raise standards and that they increased inequality (Mulready-Jones, 2011). Another concern about free schools and academies more generally was that they were given the freedom not to follow the national curriculum. Some commentators were concerned about the introduction of fundamentalist religious beliefs in state schools. Further criticism of the free-school policy was that, while a local authority had the responsibility of providing sufficient schooling for the population across the geographical area, free schools were out-side local authority control and could be started up in an area which did not need more school places.

The Coalition's academies programme was intended to remove the control of local authorities in the education system. As schools move out of local authority administra-tion to become academies, the funding and power of the authority are reduced and their role becomes diffuse. During 2012 many secondary schools were rushing to academy status, while primary schools, often sympathetic to the remains of their local authorities, wondered what to do. This made a context of indecision and uncertainty, which might be seen as government policy failure. Really, though, the intended outcome of Conservative policy is a volatile and fluid situation in which a market can operate and commercial and voluntary organisations can thrive. A debate, also originating in Sweden, is whether state schools should be allowed to operate on a for-profit basis, with shareholders taking part of the profits from financially successful schools. Again, if private for-profit com-panies do so well at manufacturing motor cars, why shouldn't for-profit companies run successful schools? However, the excessive funding required for the conversion of schools to academies was criticised in a report by the House of Commons Committee of Public Accounts (2018).

In 2007 Gordon Brown had changed the government Department for Education and Skills (DfES) to the Department for Children, Schools and Families (DCSF), indi-cating a broadening of state concerns beyond the school to the welfare of the whole child and its family with the *Every Child Matters* agenda. (See Chapter 2.) Michael Gove, on taking office, changed its title back to the Department for Education (DfE), as a sign of removing state interference in the family. The *Every Child Matters* material was dropped from the DfE website and the Children's Plan was scrapped. As a sign of a return to traditionalism, the bright multi-coloured décor of the department building was re-painted in magnolia. The first White Paper, *The Importance of Teaching* (DfE, 2010), signalled further 'traditional' Conservative Party policies: because highly knowledgeable people make good teachers, get the best graduates into teaching; because teaching is a 'craft', move teacher training from universities into schools; set up teaching schools to be responsible for initial teacher training and the professional development of teachers; improve behaviour in schools with 'troops to teaching', recruiting retired or redundant members of the armed forces to teaching as cuts to the military budget necessitated a much smaller, leaner defence force.

Gove's Conservative politics led him to a traditional version of the curriculum, teaching and assessment. Another early decision was to scrap the Labour government's review of the primary curriculum which had recommended a more combined subject approach (Rose, 2009). A traditional subject curriculum is what he sought to return to with the introduction of the English Baccalaureate (EBacc) requiring the study of English, Mathematics, Science, a Modern Language and History or Geography. Other subjects, such as Art and Citizenship, are left out of the list and therefore given lower priority by schools. (See Chapter 16.) That Religious Education was left out was criticised by the Church of England. Also discarded were the Labour government's newly-introduced Diplomas which were intended to provide a high-status qualification for vocational subjects such as 'Hair and Beauty' and 'Construction'. The Wolf Report (2011), accepted by Gove, criticised existing vocational education for failing to provide young people with the skills and knowledge required for employment. The direct linking of education to the world of business and work was continued in 2015 with the implementation of 'degree apprenticeships': university degree courses in partnership with employers and businesses.

Another curriculum change again recognised the changing needs of industry in the twenty-first century. Information Technology had restricted knowledge to the 'application' of computer skills: knowing how to use various programs. This had left industry short of employees who could actually create new software. The Computer Science curriculum for England introduced in 2013 provided a growing knowledge of 'computational thinking' through the four key stages. (See Chapter 17.)

Michael Gove's policies had a high impact on education and schools in England. By 2018 some 72 per cent of secondary schools and 27 per cent of primary schools had been turned into academies, many of which were under the auspices of 'multi-academy trusts' (MATs) which were to be inspected by Regional School Commissioners (RSCs). MATs evolved organically in the first instance as schools developed their existing federations and partnerships or created new ones. RSCs were introduced later to manage the responsibilities for schools accrued to the Secretary of State under Gove, particularly failing schools. The DfE (2016: 5) guidance for MATs lists the requirements.

> First, a board that contains a wide range of professional experiences that can deliver the dual responsibility of building strategy to deliver great outcomes for children alongside the culture of accountability that is necessary across the organisation. Second, the appointment of an executive leader, typically an executive head or chief executive officer, who is held to account for standards across the schools. Third, the creation and execution of a school improvement strategy that develops and improves the workforce, builds succession and enables the strongest teachers and leaders to influence outcomes for more children.

The emphasis here is on management with a strong role for the 'executive leader' with a forward-looking strategy; it strengthens the involvement of non-teaching managers. After four years, in 2014 David Cameron reshuffled Gove out of Education, probably because he alienated himself from education professionals, whom he referred to as a 'left-wing blob', and through his controversial policies which were intended to give them that treasure of Conservative Party policy: freedom!

The May-Johnson years and Brexit

When the public voted to leave the European Union (EU) in the referendum of 23 June 2016 David Cameron resigned as Prime Minister to be succeeded by Theresa May. Failing in her attempts to agree a deal with the European Union she was ousted from office in July 2019 to be replaced by Boris Johnson who proposed to end the years of austerity and to increase funding for schools.

The main direction in Conservative education policy in this period was to continue Gove's 'traditionalist' reforms with final examinations replacing coursework in GCSEs and the introduction of T-level qualifications in 2020. These were to be two-year courses to be equivalent to three A-levels but to include work-based learning and to prepare students for the needs of industry.

The policy of marketisation of schools had been repeated in higher education by the introduction of student fees started by the Blair government in 1998. It meant that universities were forced to compete with each other to gain applicants who would pay the fees. Conservative policy in 2010 had been to raise the maximum limit of fees to £9,000, and this had been lucrative for universities during the austerity years. However, government policy then became to pressurise universities to reduce fees and to increase scrutiny of universities through the Office for Students (Ward, 2020). The Brexit debate, taking place at the time of writing (2019), overshadowed all other political dimensions.

Conclusion

Government policies have been to employ market forces to introduce efficiency in education and to equip the labour market for a global economy. The assumption is that a vocationally-educated workforce will improve the economy and the economy will provide a good education system in a virtuous circle. New Labour policy was to equip the population for work in a global economy: to reduce child poverty and to promote social cohesion through 'joined-up' government with co-ordinated health, welfare and education policies. The SureStart Scheme was introduced to co-ordinate the physical, intellectual and social development of young children. 'Every Child Matters' (ECM) was the Labour government's attempt to do this. However, the Inquiry into Primary Education (Alexander, 2010) showed the limited impact on children's learning of government policy on teaching strategies and revealed anxieties among parents about over-assessment in schools. From 2010 the Coalition government strengthened marketisation and reduced the role of local authorities by encouraging (and forcing) schools to become academies and turning attention away from the ECM agenda (although the 2004 Children Act is still on the statute book), reducing spending to cut the national deficit, and returning to Conservative Party models of education with a traditional subject curriculum.

With all the changes noted here, one constant feature is the way that the education of children is dictated by political whim, currently the economic theory that free markets and customer choice are the key to success in all human activity. Writing about government policy is always difficult because it can change so quickly, and it soon becomes out of date. In April 2019 the leader of the opposition Labour Party was promising the teachers at their National Education Union Conference that if Labour came to power it would scrap all SATs, leaving assessment to teachers. As we have seen, SATs are one of the management mechanisms needed for the neoliberal project. The future might see it dismantled!

Summary

- After three-quarters of a century of political consensus and little state control of education, 1988 legislation brought stronger controls than in any other country in the world.
- Market forces were introduced to make education more efficient. Legislation was needed to enable customer choice.
- New Labour policies continued the neoliberal marketisation process and extended it to the privatisation of education services and privately-owned academies.
- The Labour government under Gordon Brown tried to use educational reform as a part of overall social policy with the Every Child Matters agenda.
- The 2010 Liberal–Democrat Coalition government pushed the privatisation of education further with more academies, free schools, and the return to a traditional subject curriculum.
- The Brexit referendum and debate in 2016–19 overshadowed all political discourse and policy-making.

Questions for discussion

- How far should governments be involved in education?
- Is the principal role of education to help people to get jobs and to serve the economy?
- Should education be a public service, or be left to market forces?
- Should state schools be allowed to operate on a 'for-profit' basis?
- Do free schools offer better opportunities for the education of socially disadvantaged children and young people?

Recommended reading

Ball, S.J. (2008) *The Education Debate*. Bristol: The Policy Press.
Benn, M. (2011) *School Wars: The Battle for Britain's Education*. London: Verso.
Simon, C.A. (2017) *Beyond Every Child Matters: Neoliberal Education and Social Policy in the New Era*. Abingdon: Routledge.
Ward, S. and Eden, C. (2009) *Key Issues in Education Policy*. London: Sage.

References

Alexander, R. (2010) *Primary Review: Children, Their World, Their Education*. Cambridge: Esmee Fairburn Foundation, University of Cambridge.
Brown, G. (2007) Speech on education policy at the University of Greenwich, 31October 2007.
Callaghan, J. (1976) Towards a National Debate. Speech at a foundation stone-laying ceremony at Ruskin College, Oxford, 18 October 1976.
DfE (2010) *Academies Act 2010*. London: HMSO.
DfE (2016) *Multi-Academy Trusts: Good Practice Guidance and Expectations for Growth*. London: DfE.
Gray, J. (1998) *False Dawn: The Delusions of Global Capitalism*. London: Granta.
Hayek, F. (1991) *The Road to Serfdom*. London: Routledge.
House of Commons Committee of Public Accounts (2018) *Converting Schools to Academies*. London: House of Commons.
Lawton, D. (1992) *Education and Politics in the 1990s: Conflict or Consensus*. Lewes: Falmer Press.
Mulready-Jones, M. (2011) There is no such thing as a 'free school' for Hackney. London: Hackney Citizen. Online. Available at: http://hackneycitizen.co.uk/2011/03/14/there-is-no-such-thing-as-a-free-school-for-hackney/ (accessed 3 March 2012).
Rose, J. (2009) *Independent Review of the Primary Curriculum*. London: DCSF.
Stiglitz, J. (2010) *Freefall: Free Markets and the Sinking of the Global Economy*. London: Allen Lane.
Ward, S. (2020) The Economics of the University: Knowledge, the Market and the State. In J. Bustillos Morales and S. Abegglen (Eds), *The Study of Education and Economics: Debates and Critical Theoretical Perspectives*. Abingdon: Routledge.
Wolf, A. (2011) *Review of Vocational Education: The Wolf Report*. London: DfE.

Chapter 2

Education and social justice

Catherine A. Simon

It's easy to do justice. Very hard to do right.

(Rattigan, *The Winslow Boy*, 1946)

Introduction

In recent years, social and political thought in Western societies has been dominated by the discourse of social justice. Different political ideologies have generated diverse notions of how the state should promote social justice, for example through education and schooling. Parties on the political left and right see education as a key means of reducing social inequalities, promoting social mobility and enacting a vision of a fair and equal society. But what this means in reality is open to interpretation, such that social justice becomes a slippery term in the hands of policy-writers, academic commentators, theorists and social activists. Social justice is a highly contested term and there are significant differences in the ways in which it is conceptualised. This chapter critiques the complex notion of social justice over time. From its origins as a term in Roman Catholic Christian thinking during the 1840s, to its current adoption by progressive secular social and political thinkers and contemporary opponents of neoliberalism, the chapter argues that, cut off from its Judeo-Christian roots, social justice is unlikely to counter the social injustices it purports to resolve. Drawing on the work of the economist Friedrich Hayek and authors such as Michael Novak and John Rawls, the chapter considers the claims made for social justice in the context of Education Studies and calls for a return to the collective universal understanding and moral responsibilities that attended its original construct.

Understanding social justice

The term 'social justice' has been traced back to Roman Catholic thinkers of the 1840s, although as a concept it is apparent in early Greek philosophy (Plato and Aristotle) and in world religions such as Judaism, Christianity and Islam. The term appeared in the work of the Sicilian priest, Luigi Taparelli d'Azeglio, and was given exposure by Antonio Rosmini-Serbati (1848) in *La Costitutione Civile Secondo la Giustizia Sociale* (Zedja *et al.*, 2006; Novak, 2000). Over a decade later, John Stuart Mill embedded the concept in his work *Utilitarianism* (1861). Taking an anthropomorphic stance, Mill argued that societies can be virtuous in the same way that human beings can.

> Society should treat all equally well who have deserved equally well of it, that is, who have deserved equally well absolutely. This is the highest abstract standard of social and distributive justice, towards which all institutions, and the efforts of all virtuous citizens, should be made in the utmost degree to converge.
>
> (Warnock, 1979: 318)

The original notion of social justice was group-specific rather than referring to the individual. It was applied to a particular people group or nation with the intention of redressing the effects of hierarchical inequalities, particularly those inherited by birth (Reisch, 2002). For example, a Year of Jubilee is provided for every fiftieth year in the early Jewish scriptures (Torah) when slaves were freed, property and land returned to original owners and people were released from their debts and obligations. Yet, as Reisch points out, the application of social justice found in these early texts is not regarded as universal. Rather, it focuses on economic redistribution amongst individuals. It is accepted that people are unequal in terms of material possessions, health or status. It is the responsibility of *all* to care for the needs of the poor, the widow, the orphan, the sojourner and slave.

Universal notions of justice, however, are long-standing, and in Western thought derive from monotheistic religions. The idea of a single, all-powerful God became associated with the pursuit of a divine vision for humankind where universal justice was attained. 'But let justice roll on like a river, righteousness like a never-failing stream!' (Amos 5:24 (Holy Bible New International Version, 2003)). 'He has shown you, O mortal, what is good. And what does the LORD require of you? To act justly and to love mercy and to walk humbly with your God' (Micah 6:8 (Holy Bible New International Version, 2003)). Significantly 'justice' and 'righteousness' (doing right) go hand in hand. There was a moral dimension to justice that moved it beyond the legalistic. However, as religions developed and religiously-sanctioned hierarchies and institutions evolved, this early notion of universal justice was undermined and this was further compounded by rivalry and competition between religions as they became linked with particular nation states (Reisch, 2002) and subject to secular political agendas.

Modern interpretations of social justice have coincided with two shifts in human consciousness: the ascendancy of reason over faith and the development of a command economy. The Enlightenment of the eighteenth century, which signalled for some the 'death of God', reasoned that some external authority, other than a deity, is an essential component of a just society. In the previous century, Thomas Hobbes had argued that humans were naturally unjust and anti-social. The Leviathan, or state, was needed to protect individuals from themselves and each other by enforcing the rule of law. In other words, to live peaceably, citizens entered into a contractual relationship with one another whereby they would give up their natural rights to a sovereign power in exchange for security. Building on this early notion, most social-contract theories, from Rousseau and Mill onwards, have stressed the importance of the state, rather than the individual, in promoting social welfare and protecting the basic inalienable rights of its citizens. Conceptualisations of social justice following this line of argument were based on principles of egalitarianism, solidarity and human rights, insofar as they recognised and upheld the dignity of every human being. It is these principles that underpinned the post-war welfare state in the UK, providing universal access to education, social welfare, and a National Health Service free at the point of delivery.

Thus, according to Harris (2012), there are essentially three key traditions about society in evidence in the West. It is these traditions that have influenced notions of social or distributive justice: the Roman law tradition, the entitlement tradition and the Utopian view. First, in the Roman law tradition (later revived during the medieval period) a 'societas' was conceived as a contractual or partnership arrangement between private individuals. Individuals entered or exited the arrangement at will, with little reference to wider public life (Harris, 2012). Harris points out that this view of society is clearly linked to the idea of property. Those who owned property, be it land, professional services or skills, could enter into a *contract*, whilst those who had nothing to sell (serfs, bondsmen and women) could not fully participate in society. A different tradition to evolve in Europe after the withdrawal of Roman law was that of a person's *entitlement* to support from the local parish. This 'settlement' was derived from levies on private property and distributed to the common people in times of need, a principle publicly recognised in the charitable provision of the Elizabethan Poor Law Act of 1601. The principle of entitlement thus assumed that actions must be linked to moral considerations. Finally, the classical Athenian view of society considered the 'civic' and 'social' spheres to be one and the same. It is this view that found credence particularly amongst Utopian writers such as Plato.

Over time these three ways of conceptualising society merged, but by the mid-seventeenth century the idea of 'society' (both as property ownership and a political unit) had reached its zenith. Hence authors such as Hobbes and Locke argued that membership of a 'civil society' involved the contractual assent of property-owning individuals as subjects of the state. Writing in the eighteenth century, Adam Smith coined the notion of a 'Great Society': a worldwide command economy based on the contractual exchange of goods and services where even the poor could engage in a free market. The old-style communal production regulated by local markets was thereby considered outmoded. Such views were to influence understandings about the role of the state in supporting the poor and for providing education and public health in subsequent decades. The growing tension between state intervention and personal responsibility came to the fore during the industrial revolution as society became more urbanised and required greater infrastructure. 'The market where possible, the state where necessary' (Crouch, 2013: 26) represents the *leitmotif* of conservative and liberal political thought from the late nineteenth century onwards. Philanthropists, mutual societies and activist organisations filled the gap for the growing minority of the poor at the bottom of English society for whom self-help was beyond their reach. By the end of the nineteenth century, social reformers appealed to the ruling classes to attend to the needs of newly-uprooted peasants who had become urban workers or were dispossessed.

What was to emerge was a consensus about 'working in a fair way, where individuals are allowed as much freedom as possible given the role they have within the society'

(Zedja *et al.*, 2006: 10). Social justice, therefore, included a duty to organise social and economic institutions to permit people to fully participate in society in ways that respect their freedom. Thus it was that the key principles of egalitarianism, solidarity and human rights emerged as the underpinnings of a good society. These principles were later encapsulated in the three values and symbols of the French Revolution (1789–1799) – liberty, equality, fraternity – and in the Declaration of Human Rights (1948) drawn up in the aftermath of the Second World War (Zedja *et al.*, 2006). The most famous of declarations, of course, is the US Declaration of Independence:

> We hold these Truths to be self-evident, that all Men are created equal, that they are endowed by their Creator with certain unalienable Rights, that among these are Life, Liberty, and the Pursuit of Happiness – That to secure these Rights, Governments are instituted among Men, deriving their just Powers from the Consent of the Governed, that whenever any Form of Government becomes destructive of these Ends it is the Right of the People to alter or to abolish it, and to institute new Government, laying its Foundation on such Principles, and organizing its Powers in such Form, as to them shall seem most likely to effect their Safety and Happiness.
>
> (United States Declaration of Independence, 1776)

Codifying social justice in this way, however, was to mark a shift in social responsibility. The 'social' no longer referred to the product of the virtuous actions of many individuals, but rather the Utopian goal to which all institutions and individuals are made to converge through coercion (Zedja *et al.*, 2006). In other words, the social in social justice emerges from an abstract ideal imposed from above rather than organically and spontaneously from the rule-abiding behaviour of the free individual (Zedja *et al.*, 2006; Novak, 2000). If the perception is that the Utopian goal has not been reached, it is because of the failings of government and the institutions of civil society. This is the perception that has dominated more recent social justice discourse.

It is against this backdrop that ideas of distributive (or social) justice can be traced. The political left argues for a key role for the state in providing a safety net of benefits and support for the most vulnerable in society. In England, the Beveridge Report of 1942 argued for ways of tackling the 'five giants' of Want, Disease, Ignorance, Squalor and Idleness. Government should ensure citizens had access to adequate income, healthcare, education, housing and employment. Adopted by all parties, the Beveridge Report formed the basis of the post-war welfare state, underpinned by the National Insurance, National Assistance and National Health Care Acts of 1948.

British Prime Minister Margaret Thatcher (in)famously declared there was 'no such thing as society' (*Woman's Own*, 1987). Her statement formed part of an interview with journalist Douglas Keay entitled 'Aids, education and the year 2000'.

> … and who is society? There is no such thing! There are individual men and women and there are families and no government can do anything except through people and people look to themselves first. It is our duty to look after ourselves and then also to

help look after our neighbour and life is a reciprocal business and people have got the entitlements too much in mind without the obligations …

Nine months later an explanatory statement was issued to the *Sunday Times* in July 1988:

All too often the ills of this country are passed off as those of society. Similarly, when action is required, society is called upon to act. But society as such does not exist except as a concept. Society is made up of people. It is people who have duties and beliefs and resolve. It is people who get things done. She prefers to think in terms of the acts of individuals and families as the real sinews of society rather than of society as an abstract concept. Her approach to society reflects her fundamental belief in personal responsibility and choice. To leave things to 'society' is to run away from the real decisions, practical responsibility and effective action.

(Thatcher, 1988)

Perceived inequalities across the social classes have structured debates about distributive or social justice, so too the tensions between mutual rights and obligations, i.e. between contributive and distributive views of justice. Both arguments have implications for the allocation of social rights and responsibilities in the attempt to produce a fair distribution of social goods. For Miller (1976) just distribution is not dependent on the nature of goods allocated or the policy domain but on modes of human relationship. There is little consensus, however, in a social justice framework about the balance between individual and group entitlements and social obligations. Reisch (2002: 345), for example, identifies six different ways in which distributive justice has been described:

1.   Equal rights
2.   Equal distribution to those of equal merit
3.   Equal distribution to those of equal productivity
4.   Unequal distribution based on an individual's needs or requirements
5.   Unequal distribution based on an individual's status or position
6.   Unequal distribution based on 'contractual' agreement

The most popular approach to social justice of the twentieth century was based on notions of utilitarianism. Rawls (1971, 1999), however, has argued that social justice can be used to rationalise a concentration of goods benefiting the privileged classes. Rawls, therefore, bases his conception of distributive or social justice on the premise that all social values are distributed equally unless an unequal distribution is to the advantage of all. This 'maximum theory' is underpinned by two basic principles:

1.   That each person has equal rights to the most extensive system of personal liberty compatible with a system of total liberty for all;
2.   That social and economic inequality is to be arranged such that a) both are to the greatest benefit of the least advantaged and b) both are attached to positions open to all via conditions of fair and equal opportunity.

The principle of redress is derived from such a conceptualisation where social policies are directed to a more just distribution of social goods.

Freidrich Hayek

Economist Freidrich Hayek argued that the major defect of twentieth-century theories of social justice is authors' assertion that they use the term to designate a virtue, yet the descriptions they ascribe to social justice refer to more impersonal states of affairs such as unemployment, income inequality or the lack of a living wage (Zedja *et al.*, 2006). Either social justice is a virtue or it is not. If it is a virtue then is should only be ascribed to the reflective and deliberate acts of individual persons rather than to social systems. It should not, therefore, be used to denote a regulative principle. To this end, Hayek argued that the vagueness of the term became a useful tool in the hands of those seeking justice for their own cause rather than for the greater good. In other words, social justice became an instrument of ideological intimidation for gaining power by legal coercion. A case in point may be the Ashers Bakery case of 2015–2018 where the human rights of the Christian bakery owners were set against gay rights, or the case to extend civil partnerships legalised in 2004 for same sex couples, to heterosexual partners.

However, for Hayek, it is not wrong to perceive that the effects of individual choices and open processes of a free society are not distributed according to a recognisable principle. The meritorious sometimes are tragically unlucky and the evil prosper (Novak, 2000). A system that values trial and error and free choice cannot guarantee outcomes in advance; no party or individual could design rules that would treat each individual according to his merit or even his need (ibid.). Hayek is therefore able to make a distinction between the failures of justice that involve breaking agreed rules of fairness, and those that consist in results that no one designed, foresaw or commended.

For Novak (2000), one characteristic of social justice 'rightly understood' is that it aims at the good of the city, not at the good of one agent. This approach to justice is indeed social; its object, as well as its form, primarily involves the good of others. Such a definition of the virtue of social justice is ideologically neutral, allowing people of good will to reach different, even opposing, practical judgements about the material context of the common good (ends) and how to get there (means). What must be ruled out is any use of social justice that does not attach to the habits or virtues of individuals. Here there is a link to Tocqueville's principle of association which is considered the first law of democracy. If that is the case, then social justice should be the first virtue of democracy. It is the habit of putting the principle of association into daily practice. Neglect of it has the consequences that Hayek had warned of.

Social justice and education

So far, this chapter has outlined the development of some of the key notions of social justice and the tensions and issues they present for current structural reform and practice. Education represents the socio-political space in which the problematic relationship between society and the state is worked out. The notion of social justice attempts to address the desire for a more just, respectful and equitable society for all. However, for Zedja *et al*. (2006) this presents three conceptual and methodological issues.

1. Social justice is assumed to have a monocultural and linear definition when in reality it is a muti-layered, ideal construct.
2. As for many taken-for-granted assumptions, it is assumed that social justice is attainable in any society, even capitalist or meritocratic ones.
3. There are often contradictory connections between the state, social stratification and social justice. The greater the social inequality the less one finds social justice.

In this way, privatisation, decentralisation and marketisation in education and society more widely have had a direct impact on the implementation of social justice principles in schools. The unequal distribution of economic, social and political capital makes it difficult to address differences and oppression in schools and society globally. Diane Reay (2012) has explored in some depth what a socially-just education system might look like. With a focus on social inequality she argues that social injustices in education have increasingly been regarded by the political right as the responsibility of the individuals facing them. 'Social justice', 'choice' and 'diversity' have been used discursively to sanction and exacerbate inequalities. The issue with choice is that it comes with resources that are unevenly distributed. Reay, therefore, argues for a new way of envisioning education which should include a revaluing of vocational and working-class knowledges, and reframing what constitutes educational success. This also has implications for what is taught in schools and classrooms.

In this way Reay makes a two-pronged attack on education in the name of social justice. First in line are the organisational structures of schools and schooling where social inequalities in terms of social, economic and cultural capital favour the middle classes. Through the exercise of parental choice, the middle classes are able to make use of education as a positional good, giving their children certain perceived advantages in a competitive, meritocratic social system. Rather, drawing on the work of R.H. Tawney, Reay argues that a socially-just education system is one where education is seen as an end in itself, a space that 'people seek out not in order that they may become something else but because they are what they are' (Tawney, 1964: 78). In other words, the very antithesis of getting ahead of others, or stealing a competitive edge.

Second, what happens in schools must also change such that children will be taught through 'disruptive pedagogies' to be 'caring, respectful, cooperative, knowledgeable about their own and others' histories, and well informed about contemporary global issues' (Reay 2012: 7). Those disruptive pedagogies include emphasising collectivist rather than individualistic approaches to learning. Social justice thus conceived positions education as both the problem and the solution to social inequalities. Reay's argument highlights the earlier issues described by Zedja *et al*. It is society itself that is at fault for social inequality, evidenced through the system of education and schooling. The main way to have a more socially-just education system is to have a more equal society. More basic systemic interventions are called for at the level of the economy. The argument is circular and points to Hayek's concern about whether social justice is a virtue or not. Perhaps the starting point should be the use of those disruptive pedagogies that promote the bonds of association and valorise the common good, and doing right as an antidote to neoliberal individualism.

Conclusion

This chapter has considered the notion of social justice. Taking a historical perspective it has traced the development of the concept over time from early Jewish and Christian writings to the present day. Discussion has focused on the tensions between the individual, the community and the state. Central to the discussion have been tensions between various ideological standpoints: for example, whether social justice is a virtue, evidenced through the many individual acts of people of good will, or an instrument of ideological intimidation that shuts down open and honest debate in the name of political correctness. Students of Education Studies are encouraged to make a careful critique of the claims made in the name of social justice and decide for themselves which side of the Utopian/virtue divide holds most promise for an 'unjust' world.

Activity

1. Having read this chapter how would you summarise the notion of 'social justice'?
2. Consider the Ashers Bakery case: how might decisions about 'justice' hold a moral dimension?
3. What are the key considerations for educators in promoting a just and equitable education system in a meritocratic society?
4. How do you reconcile 'Justice' and 'doing what is Right'?

Recommended reading

Gorard, S. (2000) *Education and Social Justice: The Changing Composition of Schools and Its Implications.* Cardiff: University of Wales Press.
Novak, M. (2000) *Defining Social Justice.* First Things. Online. Available at: www.firstthings.com/article/2000/12/defining-social-justice (accessed 20 May 2019).
Reay, D. (2012) What Would a Socially Just Education System Look Like? Saving the Minnows from the Pike. *Journal of Education Policy* **27**(5), pp. 587–599.

References

Crouch, C. (2013) *Making Capitalism Fit for Society.* Cambridge: Polity Press.
Harris, J. (2012) Servile State or Discredited State: Some Historical Antecedents of Current 'Big Society' Debates. In J. Edwards (Ed.), *Retrieving the Big Society.* Chichester: Wiley Blackwell.

Hayek, F. (1991) *The Road to Serfdom*. London: Routledge.

Holy Bible (2003) *Quest Study Bible: New International Version*. Michigan: Zondervan.

Miller, D. (1976) *Social Justice*. Oxford: Clarendon Press.

Novak, M. (2000) *Defining Social Justice*. First Things. Available at: www.firstthings.com/article/2000/12/defining-social-justice (accessed 20 May 2019).

Rawls, J. (1971, 1999). *A Theory of Justice*. Cambridge, MA: Harvard University Press.

Reay, D. (2012) What Would a Socially Just Education System Look Like? Saving the Minnows from the Pike. *Journal of Education Policy* **27**(5), pp. 587–599.

Reisch, M. (2002) Defining Social Justice in a Socially Unjust World. *Families in Society* **83**(4), pp. 343–354.

Tawney, R.H. (1964) *The Radical Tradition*. Harmondsworth: Penguin.

Thatcher, M. (1987) No Such Thing as Society. *Woman's Own Interview*, 23 September 1987. Available at: www.margaretthatcher.org/document/106689 (accessed 14 June 2019).

Thatcher, M. (1988) Explanation on Views of Society. *Sunday Times*, 26 April 1988. Available at: www.margaretthatcher.org/document/106689 (accessed 14 June 2019).

United States Declaration of Independence (1776). Available at: www.ushistory.org/declaration/document/ (accessed 20 May 2019).

Warnock, M. (1979) *Utilitarianism, On Liberty, Essay on Bentham*. Glasgow: Collins, Fount Paperbacks.

Zedja, J., Majhanovich, S. and Rust, V. (2006) Introduction: Education and Social Justice. *Review of Education* **52**, pp. 9–22.

Chapter 3

Race, ethnicity and education in England

Charlotte Chadderton

Introduction

The chapter examines how issues of race and ethnicity play out in education. It considers both how notions of race have shaped education policies and how education policy reproduces race inequalities. The chapter begins by considering definitions and understandings of race. It then explores the history of race in education since 1945, briefly looking at some of the key issues, debates, educational approaches and related policies. These include assimilation, integration, multicultural education, antiracism, institutional racism, de-racialisation, and neoliberalism. The chapter argues that education policy, in the main, despite some resistance, has been characterised by racial 'othering' of minority ethnic people and white privilege.

What is race?

Until the mid-twentieth century, race was mostly viewed as a biological notion, a legitimate scientific categorisation of humans based on phenotype. It was thought to describe separate groups of humans who shared common characteristics. Individuals were seen in terms of essential characteristics believed to be natural properties of certain bodies. Such notions have now been scientifically disproved (Solomos, 1993; Winant, 2000). However, these notions still carry some currency and sometimes arise in education. For example, psychologist Herrnstein and political scientist Murray (1994) and geneticist James Watson claimed in 2007 that people of African descent were naturally less intelligent than whites (Herrnstein and Murray, 1994; McKie and Harris, 2007). This work has been widely discredited as unscientific.

Race is alternatively understood as a social construction, 'an arbitrary sign used to divide up the human population' (Nayak, 2006: 415), rather than a biological difference. This understanding is based on the pioneering work of people such as sociologist W.E.B. Du Bois, who saw race, not as biological fact, but as an artificially constructed notion through social and historical conditions, without inherent or essential meaning, historically and geographically contingent and changing over time. Work which takes a social constructionist approach includes various different theorisations of race, such as the Marxist theory-informed racialisation (e.g. Miles, 1993; Cole, 2009), which argues that all social relations are historically specific and reflect the economic system of the time. It also includes critical race theory, which argues that race is socially constructed (e.g. Haney Lopez, 1995) and that social and political arrangements are racially structured. Some scholars argue that race is less to do with skin colour, and more to do with power and social position: '[R]ace is best understood as power relations that define dominant and subjugated positions in society' (Duncan, 2002: 85).

Trends in race and education in England since 1945

Different notions of race in society have shaped education policies and, equally, educa-tion policy has reproduced race inequalities in England. Since 1945 political and social discourses around race have pulled in two different directions. These are 'pluralist, anti-racist, equitable' versus 'anti-pluralist, racist, anti-immigrant' (Figueroa, 2004). These two opposing discourses characterise debates and approaches to education policy to the present day. However, education policy, in the main, despite some resistance, has been characterised by racial 'othering' of minority ethnic people, and white privilege.

Racial 'othering'

The process of 'othering' refers to the dividing of the world into entities which are believed to be separated along the lines of alleged radical difference (Said, 2003). 'Othering' works through stereotyping (Hall, 1997). This involves the marking of 'difference' which is then interpreted in several ways in representations of people who are different from the dom-inant groups. These differences are not fixed, natural facts. There is no essence of 'other-ness'; we only 'know' what the term means because we contrast it with its opposite, i.e. sameness (Hall, 1997). Thus 'othering' refers to a binary form of representation, 'good/bad, civilised/primitive' (Hall, 1997), in which one of the poles in the binary is always superior to the 'other'. This knowledge about the 'other' is held to be neutral and objective (Said, 2003) and an essential, fixed characteristic. Individuals are seen as representative of the group they belong to, or are perceived to belong to. This worldview becomes so deeply embedded that it appears to be natural (Hall, 1997). There is an enormous investment in these 'othering' discourses, which underpin an entire system of institutions and policies. These alleged differences are used to justify the oppression of those who do not belong to the dominant groups in society. Racial 'othering' disadvantages ethnic minorities and upholds the privileges of white people.

White privilege

The notion of white privilege (sometimes referred to as white supremacy or domin-ance, or simply 'whiteness') has been employed by some scholars to describe a deeply engrained system of race inequality present in institutional arrangements, social inter-action, values and attitudes, which ensures disadvantage for racial minorities, and privileges for those politically designated white (e.g. Gillborn, 2005; Ladson-Billings, 1998). It is, in effect, the obvious but frequently invisible flipside to race inequality and racism. 'The term "Whiteness" signals the production and reproduction of dominance rather than sub-ordination, normativity rather than marginality, and privilege rather than disadvantage' (Frankenberg, 1993: 526).

It describes the taken-for-grantedness of privilege for white people, or those categorised as white, an 'unremarked normality' (Rollock, 2016). It can be understood as a racial system of power and privilege so deeply engrained in society it frequently goes unnoticed, unacknowledged or denied by those privileged by it (those oppressed by it tend to be more aware), and yet it pervades all social and economic relations. Fuelling white privilege can be unwitting as well as deliberate. The notion of white privilege challenges more common and traditional notions of racism as an aberration, individual, deliberate or violent act. It is important to understand that white privilege does not (necessarily) refer to a skin colour, rather to a system of structural discrimination which shapes identities and interaction. Not all people classified as white are equally privileged, as whiteness is always gendered and classed (Ladson-Billings, 1998).

Policy phases in education

Education policy can be understood as a series of policy phases and trends (Gillborn, 2008) where these different approaches to race and education policy can be observed.

Assimilation and integration

The period from 1945 to the late 1950s was characterised by ignorance and neglect as regards race in education. Racism was overt and common, including in public services and education. Issues around race inequality and ethnic diversity were however largely ignored by policy.

In 1958, reportedly following white men's attacks on a racially mixed couple, but also in the context of economic decline and endemic racism, violence broke out against minority ethnic people, including attacks co-ordinated by Fascist groups, in Nottingham and London. Although the perpetrators were white, the unrest was defined as 'the colour problem' and there was a widespread view in politics and the media that there were 'too many' minority ethnic people. The policy response from the late 1950s to the late 1960s was one of assimilation. It involved

- the eradication or reduction of signs of racial or cultural difference;
- major immigration controls, e.g. the Commonwealth Immigrants Act which placed restrictions on entry.

In education this was characterised by the viewing of black and minority ethnic children as a 'problem' and as a threat to white children's education. Policy focused on practices which were 'remedial, compensatory or coercive' (Carby, 1994: 183), for example limiting minority ethnic children in classes because their numbers were perceived as too high, which in some areas involved the bussing of minority ethnic children to other schools further from their homes.

Largely due to calls for action, and as a way of reducing tensions and social unrest, some efforts were made from the mid-1960s to change the rhetoric and the approach to addressing race inequality and diversity. Rather than 'assimilation', there were calls for 'integration', generally understood as the incorporation of different populations into society as equals, without requiring them to relinquish all signs of cultural difference. The Race Relations Act 1976 established the Commission for Racial Equality to work towards better race relations and advise on changes to the law. However, in practice, 'integration' as an approach was little different from 'assimilation'. Underpinned by the assumption that minorities were the problem, it involved demands that minorities should adapt to indigenous lifestyles, while no such demand was made of white people. Education policy involved a focus on minority groups' perceived lifestyles and 'cultures', in which they were 'othered': stereotyped and portrayed as exotic, alien and sometimes primitive. The book *How the West Indian Child Is Made Educationally Sub-normal in the British School System* by Bernard Coard appeared in 1971 and drew attention to the way in which the education system stereotyped minority ethnic children as less intelligent than their white counterparts.

Multiculturalism and antiracism

In the early 1980s there was further social unrest, with disturbances and protests in Brixton, Toxteth and Chapeltown, Leeds in 1981. Root causes included high unemployment and sus laws (a stop and search law which permitted the police to potentially arrest anyone they suspected of being in breach of the Vagrancy Act), which were disproportionately used on black men. The disturbances put pressure on the government to address racial issues. A government inquiry was launched into racial issues in education, and what the government referred to as 'the educational failure of West Indian children'. The Rampton Report (DES, 1981) provided the first official acknowledgement that racism both in society and in schools was a factor in black children's achievement. The inquiry found:

- evidence of cultural biases in IQ testing;
- the negative racial stereotyping of minority ethnic students by teachers;
- inadequacy of teacher training in preparing teachers for multicultural classrooms.

The teaching unions were outraged and the chairman of the inquiry, Anthony Rampton, was replaced by Michael Swann.

At this time, there was a move towards an approach referred to as 'multicultural education'. The focus of multicultural education was 'a celebration of difference' and valuing of cultural pluralism. However, critics argued first that the 'celebration of difference' involved little more than cultural stereotyping, and referred to it as 'the 3 s's: saris, samosas and steel bands', and secondly that there was still no mention of the reality of racial inequalities (Modood and May, 2001).

An alternative to multicultural approaches in education was antiracist approaches. These approaches focus on power inequalities as well as cultural understanding. However, they 'mostly remained a radical outsider perspective' (Gillborn 2008: 74) and also received criticisms:

- They focused on biological racism and did not address cultural racism (see below for a discussion of cultural racism).
- They fed into a perceived dichotomy between black and white (thus also ignoring the experiences of other ethnic groups).

Antiracism as an educational approach was discredited after the report on the murder at Burnage High School in Manchester in 1986 in which a white pupil killed an Asian pupil, Ahmed Iqbal Ullah. It was misrepresented by the press, which blamed antiracist practice for exacerbating racial tensions.

A further inquiry into education resulted in the Swann Report in 1985, which reported on the impact of both individual racism and a 'more pervasive climate of racism'. It also reported that IQ is not a significant factor in the underachievement of minority children. However, in the end the report shifted its recommendations away from overt antiracist strategies toward a form of 'inclusive multiculturalism', and recommended 'education for all'. While this may initially sound equitable, the report was criticised for shifting the focus away from racial inequality. Furthermore, the short guide to the report made no reference to racism. The Education Secretary rejected the report on the day of publication and ethnic diversity was effectively removed from the national policy agenda.

Thatcherism: cultural racism and colour-blind policy

The nature of racism shifted from the 1980s, from 'biological racism', to 'cultural racism'. Cultural racism often doesn't actually mention race (it is 'de-racialised'), rather it focuses on the 'incompatibility' of cultures, an alleged 'natural' fear of 'outsiders' and 'innate' differences between ethnic or religious groups. It seems to break with biological notions, but is actually similar because it involves the 'othering' of groups considered to be essentially and inescapably different, and still fuels white privilege.

The Conservative governments of Margaret Thatcher and John Major were characterised by 'imperial views of traditional British identity which rejected debate over cultural diversity and racial equality' (Tomlinson, 2005: 166). In 1988 the Education Reform Act introduced a national curriculum for England and Wales with no meaningful acknowledgement of ethnic diversity. It involved the imposition of a notion of national identity and unity on all pupils. Education policy was de-racialised or 'colour-blind'. Colour-blind approaches are those where race and racism are not explicitly addressed. They are believed to be fair and apply equally to all and race is believed not to matter. However, policy which claims to be colour-blind in theory, functions to maintain existing racial inequalities and white privilege in practice (Williams, 1997; Ladson-Billings, 1998). Under the Conservative government, issues of race became invisible in political discourse and multicultural and antiracist educational approaches were excluded. Issues of social equality in general were marginalised. Instead, policy began to focus on standards and targets, performance, and the needs of the individual.

New Labour: multiculturalism and equal opportunities

When new Labour was elected to government in 1997, there was a renewed focus on multiculturalism and equal opportunities for all. The White Paper *Excellence in Schools* (DfEE, 1997) showed a commitment to equality of opportunity and an open acknowledgement of race inequalities. Moreover, the outcome of the MacPherson Report (1999), in response to the 1993 racist murder of African-Caribbean Stephen Lawrence by a gang of white men in Eltham, London, gave for the first time official legitimacy to the notion of 'institutional racism', which it defined as:

> The collective failure of an organisation to provide an appropriate and professional service to people because of their colour, culture or ethnic origin. It can be seen or detected in processes, attitudes and behaviour which amount to discrimination through unwitting prejudice, ignorance, thoughtlessness and racist stereotyping which disadvantage minority ethnic people. It persists because of the failure of the organisation openly and adequately to recognise and address its existence and causes by policy, example and leadership.
>
> (Macpherson, 1999: 28)

The inquiry found that the police had failed to investigate the incident properly, and their handling of the case was corrupt and affected by racial perceptions. The notion of 'institutional racism' is significant because it challenges the widespread, more usual understanding of racism only as individual, aggressive or violent acts, and introduces the notion that a whole organisation, including an educational institution, can discriminate against a certain group structurally, regardless of conscious intentions.

The Race Relations Amendment Act (2000) also came into force in this period. This extended the act of 1976 and, importantly, stipulated that public bodies, including educational institutions, should actively promote race equality. However, some have argued this progress fuelled a backlash from Conservatives (Warmington *et al.*, 2017).

In education, the government's approach to equal opportunity and multiculturalism in fact remained mostly superficial. Their most significant action in support of equal opportunities in education was to grant state funding to a small number of Islamic schools for the first time, although some accused them of fuelling separatism.

New Labour: multiculturalism, Muslims and citizenship (2001–2010)

In 2001, the mood changed. In the summer there were protests in the northern towns of Oldham, Bradford and Burnley; some called them 'race riots'. Indeed, the root causes included industrial decline, poverty and racism, in particular against British Asians. In

September, the attacks of 9/11 fuelled the notion that multiculturalism had failed. Indeed the media and politicians blamed these acts and events on 'multiculturalism', arguing again that minorities were not integrated. The 2005 London bombings fuelled a debate around 'Britishness': how could a British person have perpetrated such terrorism? Again, there was a suggestion that the British Asian perpetrators could not have been properly integrated into British society. After the protests and terrorist attacks, there was an increase in racist attacks on Muslims, or people assumed to be Muslims.

In 2004 Trevor Phillips, Head of the Commission for Racial Equality, and one of the country's leading black political and social commentators, also argued that multiculturalism fuelled separatism. The solution to this alleged failure of multiculturalism was touted as 'community cohesion', the solution also suggested in the report on the protests in northern England in 2001. However, in that report, 'community cohesion' was understood as an expectation that British Asians should adapt and assimilate better to modern British life, with no expectation at all that the white population adapt in any way. Indeed the report blamed the unrest on unquestioned, alleged cultural differences between Asian and white people in that area, and the inability of British Asians to assimilate and adapt which in turn was seen to have led to racial segregation and social tensions. This masked the historical context of structural inequalities, de-industrialisation, racist attacks and police harassment (Home Office, 2001; Alexander, 2004).

In education at this time, attention was given to the citizenship agenda. Citizenship Education was introduced as a discrete subject in secondary schools in 2001. The subject was linked to ideas around building 'community cohesion', and also to the MacPherson Report, and some supporters hoped it would focus on cultural pluralism, equity and antiracism. In fact, Citizenship Education policy and practice actually 'othered' minority ethnic groups, and portrayed Britishness as white and monocultural (Gillborn, 2006; Chadderton, 2009). There was also an increase in verbal attacks on what were referred to as 'monocultural' schools, suggesting these were separatist and non-British. These never included white schools and always targeted schools with large numbers of minority ethnic pupils (Gillborn, 2008). The Labour government did succeed in reducing the very high levels of exclusions among black pupils at this time. Black pupils had always been excluded from school at a much higher rate than their white counterparts, and academics, activists and families had argued that this was a systemic issue related to perceptions of black children as challenging and underachievers (Carby, 1994). As the government review stated, 'Many argue that the disparity in exclusion rates for Black pupils (the "exclusions gap") is a modern manifestation of the same process that saw so many Black pupils classified as "Educationally Sub-Normal" in the past' (DfES, 2006). The review also acknowledged low teacher expectations as an issue contributing to black pupils' schooling experience.

'Post-racial' neoliberalism

Since 2010, Britain has had a coalition government led by the Conservatives with the Liberal Democrats, followed by a majority Conservative government (2015–2017), and at the time of writing, the Conservatives have formed a coalition government with the Northern Irish Democratic Unionist Party. The neoliberal discourse that Western liberal democracies are meritocracies and race no longer matters has fuelled the popular narrative that we are living in a post-racial era. This narrative suggests that, under current conditions, every individual can succeed, they just need to work hard and aspire high. However, narratives of meritocracy and individualism mask structural racism and render race inequality an individual choice or personal flaw (Robbins, 2009). A glance at the wider political and social context suggests that race matters as much as ever. Some have argued that neoliberal regimes in fact further marginalise minority ethnic populations and polarise racial identities. Racial profiling is increasing and anti-immigration sentiment is stoked. The most recent figures show that unemployment for minority ethnic groups stands at 9.9 per cent in comparison with 5.4 per cent for the overall population despite a recent improvement (DWP, 2016). In line with the neoliberal focus on containment and policing, incarceration rates are also increasing, and proportionately far more black individuals are serving a prison sentence than whites. The outcome of the 2016 Brexit referendum was in part based on the appeal of narratives of perceived threats to (white) natives by refugees, migrant workers from Eastern Europe, and workers in countries such as India and China who work for lower wages. These narratives, even those around Eastern Europeans, who are generally pale-skinned, are racialised, and contain messages about ethnic threat.

Equally the education context is shaped by these discourses. The notion that we are now post-racial and living in a meritocracy where equal opportunities have been attained carries much weight. In fact, studies show that neoliberal initiatives are increasing existing inequalities, including race inequality in education.

First, evidence suggests that the academisation process in England – the removal of schools from local authority control allegedly to increase school autonomy – is fuelling race inequality (Gillborn, 2013; Kulz, 2017). Second, and related to the first point, there has been a renewed focus on improving behaviour in schools since the Education Act 2011, including giving school staff greater powers in the use of force, involving increased freedom on exclusions and detentions and increased search powers. These increased powers for staff appear to be impacting more harshly on young people from minority ethnic groups by sharpening existing issues, particularly in academies: black pupils are treated more punitively than white pupils when engaging in similar behaviour (Kulz, 2017). Third, both fixed-term and permanent school exclusions have been rising since 2010 and, once again, black males are significantly more likely to be excluded than other groups. This is a particular issue in sponsored academies, where exclusions are especially high (DfE, 2017). Equally the introduction of the English Baccalaureate, a school performance measure which prioritises pupil success in five core areas – English, Maths, Science, History or Geography and Languages – is in fact disadvantaging black students, who are disproportionately more likely to be entered for Arts subjects (Gillborn, 2013). In addition programmes such as the government-run 'Prevent', which aim to tackle extremism in young people, focus disproportionately on Muslims (Sian, 2015; Miah, 2017). This fuels existing 'othering' discourses and neglects other types of extremism such as right-wing extremism.

Conclusion

This chapter has argued that race is a social construction, rather than a fixed, natural or scientific biological and cultural difference. It has considered the way in which socially constructed ideas about race have influenced education policies, and education policy has fuelled the social construction of beliefs and attitudes to race, cultural and religious groups and reproduced race inequality. Efforts have been made to create a more equitable society and education system, by activists, parents, some academics and policy-makers. However, mostly, education policy since 1945 has been characterised by racial 'othering' of minority ethnic people, the perception of ethnic or cultural diversity as threatening and destabilising, and the protection of white privilege.

Questions for discussion

- Consider how people talk about race in educational settings. Is it viewed as a fixed, innate, biological or cultural difference, or a social construction?
- How do assumptions made in education and schooling around ethnicity, race, culture and migration reflect those made by the media or by politicians?
- Can you think of political policies, or institutional policies, which impact differently on different ethnic, cultural or religious groups?

Summary points

- Race is socially constructed, including by the education system.
- The education system has generally reproduced racial inequality and racial 'othering' and has systematically disadvantaged minority ethnic people.
- The continued disadvantaging of minority ethnic people fuels white privilege.
- Racism should not only be understood as individual, deliberate, overt or violent acts; racism is also institutional, systemic, covert and unwitting.

Recommended reading

Carby, H.V. (1994) Schooling in Babylon. In Centre for Contemporary Cultural Studies, The Empire Strikes Back: Race and Racism in 70s Britain. London and New York: Routledge.

Gillborn, D. (2008) *Racism and Education: Coincidence or Conspiracy?* London and New York: Routledge.

Tomlinson, S. (2005) Race, Ethnicity and Education under New Labour. *Oxford Review of Education* **31**(1), pp. 153–171.

Warmington, P., Gillborn, D., Rollock, N. and Demack, S. (2017) They Can't Handle the Race Agenda: Stakeholders' Reflections on Race and Education Policy, 1993–2013. *Educational Review* **70**(4), pp. 409–426.

References

Alexander, C. (2004) Writing Race: Ethnography and the Imagination of 'The Asian Gang'. In M. Bulmer and J. Solomos (Eds), *Researching Race and Racism,* 134–149. Abingdon and New York: Routledge.

Carby, H.V. (1994) Schooling in Babylon. In Centre for Contemporary Cultural Studies, *The Empire Strikes Back: Race and Racism in 70s Britain*. London and New York: Routledge.

Chadderton, C. (2009) Discourses of Britishness, Race and Difference: Minority Ethnic Students' Shifting Perceptions of Their School Experience. Unpublished PhD dissertation, Manchester Metropolitan University, Manchester.

Coard, B. (1971) *How the West Indian Child Is Made Educationally Sub-normal in the British School System*. London: New Beacon Books.

Cole, M. (2009) *Critical Race Theory and Education: A Marxist Response*. New York and London: Palgrave Macmillan.

DES (1981) *West Indian Children in Our Schools: Interim Report of the Committee of Inquiry into the Education of Children from Ethnic Minority Groups (The Rampton Report)*. London: HMSO.

DfE (2017) *Permanent and Fixed-Period Exclusions in England: 2015 to 2016*. Online. Available at: www.gov.uk/government/statistics/permanent-and-fixed-period-exclusions-in-england-2015-to-2016 (accessed 2 May 2019).

DfEE (1997) *White Paper: Excellence in Schools*. London: HMSO.

DfES (2006) *Exclusion of Black Pupils: Getting It. Getting It Right*. London: DfES.

Duncan, G.A. (2002) Critical Race Theory and Method: Rendering Race in Urban Ethnographic Research. *Qualitative Inquiry* **8**(1), pp. 85–104.

DWP (2016) *Labour Market Status by Ethnic Group*. Online. Available at: www.gov.uk/government/uploads/system/uploads/attachment_data/file/515622/labour-market-status-by-ethnic-group-april-2016.pdf (accessed 2 May 2019).

Figueroa, P. (2004) Multicultural Education in the United Kingdom. In J.A. Banks and C.A.M. Banks (Eds), *Handbook of Research on Multicultural Education* (2nd edn). San Francisco, CA: Jossey-Bass.

Frankenberg, R. (1993) *White Women, Race Matters: The Social Construction of Whiteness*. Minneapolis: University of Minnesota Press.

Gillborn, D. (2005) Education Policy as an Act of White Supremacy: Whiteness, Critical Race Theory and Education Reform. *Journal of Education Policy* **20**(4), pp. 485–505.

Gillborn, D. (2006) Citizenship Education as Placebo. *Education, Citizenship and Social Justice* **1**(1), pp. 83–104.

Gillborn, D. (2008) *Racism and Education: Coincidence or Conspiracy?* London and New York: Routledge.

Gillborn, D. (2013) Interest-Divergence and the Colour of Cutbacks: Race, Recession and the Undeclared War on Black Children. *Discourse: Studies in the Cultural Politics of Education* **34**(4), pp. 477–491.

Hall, S. (1997) The Spectacle of the 'Other'. In S. Hall (Ed.), *Representations: Cultural Representations and Signifying Practices*. London: Sage/Open University Press.

Haney Lopez, I.F. (1995) The Social Construction of Race. In R. Delgado (Ed.), *Critical Race Theory: The Cutting Edge*. Philadelphia: Temple University Press.

Herrnstein, R.J. and Murray, C. (1994) *The Bell Curve*. New York: Free Press.

Home Office (2001) *Community Cohesion: A Report of the Independent Review Team Chaired by Ted Cantle*. Online. Available at: http://tedcantle.co.uk/pdf/communitycohesion%20cantlereport.pdf (accessed 2 May 2019).

Kulz, C. (2017) *Factories for Learning: Making Race, Class and Inequality in the Neoliberal Academy*. Manchester: Manchester University Press.

Ladson–Billings, G. (1998) Just What Is Critical Race Theory and What's It Doing in a Nice Field Like Education? *International Journal of Qualitative Studies in Education* **11**(1), pp. 7–24.

MacPherson, W. (1999) *Report on the Stephen Lawrence Inquiry*. London: Cm 4262.

McKie R. and Harris, P. (2007) Disgrace: How a Giant of Science Was Brought Low. *The Guardian*. Online. Available at: www.guardian.co.uk/uk/2007/oct/21/race.research (accessed 2 May 2019).

Miah, S. (2017) *Muslims, Schooling and Security: Trojan Horse, Prevent and Racial Politics*. London: Palgrave Macmillan

Miles, R. (1993) *Racism after 'Race Relations'*. New York and London: Routledge.

Modood, T. and May, S. (2001) Multiculturalism and Education in Britain: An Internally Contested Debate. *International Journal of Educational Research* **35**, pp. 305–317.

Nayak, A. (2006) After Race: Ethnography, Race and Post-Race Theory. *Ethnic and Racial Studies* **29**(3), pp. 411–430.

Robbins, C.G. (2009) Racism and the Authority of Neoliberalism: A Review of Three New Books on the Persistence of Racial Inequality in a Color–Blind Era. *Journal of Critical Education Policy Studies* **2**(2), pp. 244–275.

Rollock, N. (2016) Editorial. *Whiteness and Education* **1**(1), pp. 1–2.

Said, E.W. (2003) *Orientalism*. London: Penguin.

Sian, K.P. (2015) Spies, Surveillance and Stakeouts: Monitoring Muslim Moves in British State Schools. *Race Ethnicity and Education* **18**(2), pp. 183–201.

Solomos, J. (1993) *Race and Racism in Britain* (2nd edn). New York: St Martin's Press, Inc.

Tomlinson, S. (2005) Race, Ethnicity and Education under New Labour. *Oxford Review of Education* **31**(1), pp. 153–171.

Warmington, P., Gillborn, D., Rollock, N. and Demack, S. (2017) They Can't Handle the Race Agenda: Stakeholders' Reflections on Race and Education Policy, 1993–2013. *Educational Review* **70**(4), pp. 409–426.

Williams, P.J. (1997) *Seeing a Colour-Blind Future: The Paradox of Race. The 1997 Reith Lectures*. London: Virago.

Winant, H. (2000) The Theoretical Status of the Concept of Race. In L. Back and J. Solomos (Eds), *Theories of Race and Racism: A Reader*. London and New York: Routledge.

Chapter 4

Gender and work

From school to the labour market

Christine Eden

Introduction

Any analysis of patterns of educational attainment will at some point focus on the fact that females have higher levels of attainment than males across social class, ethnicity and gender categories. It is therefore initially surprising to find that entry into the labour market reverses this pattern: men earn more than women and are much more represented in positions of power and influence. This becomes less of a shock when it is recognised that both the school and work environments are saturated with values and attitudes still rooted in stereotypes and essentialist understandings of masculinity and femininity which embody assumptions about women's responsibility for childcare and who has access to what type of work (Eden, 2017). This chapter explores the impact of these attitudes and how they contribute to an understanding of the contradiction between women's educational achievements and their experiences of the workplace.

During the nineteenth century and much of the twentieth century in the UK, the idea that men and women act differently and have different futures led to a curriculum that for girls focused on homemaking and child-rearing skills, while boys were educated to take their place in the economy. The women's movements of the latter half of the twentieth century, plus changes in the economy, led to a new perspective on girls' education and a significant increase in women's employment. But these considerable changes have not eradicated the patriarchal power relations and associated models of masculinity and femininity that allocate responsibility for domestic labour and childcare predominantly to women, and underpin legislation, workplace practices and gender relations in the family. This ensures that women do not enter the labour market on the same terms as men and perpetuates their economic dependency on men (Walby, 2013). Changes are occurring but these unequal power relations remain the backdrop against which both young men and women, particularly those from working-class backgrounds, experience their schooling and the workplace. This chapter spells out how these power relations translate into discrimination and unequal access to work opportunities.

Girls' experience of schooling and women's experience of the workplace are both located in the overall context of gender relations that permeate wider society. In both cases gender relations are characterised by unequal power and steeped in discrimination and misogyny, in spite of significant changes in women's positions in society and a greater recognition of diverse sexual orientations. Being male or female remains rooted in a powerful heteronormative model which has major implications for:

- how care responsibilities are valued and shared;
- participation in the labour market;
- how equalities legislation is interpreted by employers.

Assumptions about appropriate gendered modes of behaviour and the associated policing of sexual behaviour remain consistently powerful in the culture of society, the school and the workplace. For minority ethnic girls and women these pressures are compounded by rising and increasingly overt racism in Britain (see Chapter 3). Work experiences are located in these cultures.

Frequently the experiences of mainly white British women are generalised to be representative of all women. The available data often does not break down the category of gender to show the diverse experiences of women from a wide range of groups (Fawcett Society, 2019). A black woman's experience of the workplace will differ from that of a white woman. A middle-class woman may face inequality and sexism but it will differ from that of a working-class woman. Within this chapter we will draw largely on overall patterns and use available data for different ethnic groups to indicate the considerable diversity of experience hidden within the overall category of 'female'.

Since the middle of the twentieth century women's participation in the labour market has changed dramatically, with a strong economic incentive for women to work associated with declining wages, anti-discrimination legislation and changes in the occupational structure. More women are in paid employment than ever before: 71 per cent of women aged 16–64 are in paid work, the highest employment rate since records began (ONS, 2018a). There are, though, major differences in the experiences of women from different ethnic groups:

1. Seventy-three per cent of white British women are employed.
2. Seventy-one per cent of Pakistani/Bangladeshi men are in employment compared to 38 per cent of women.
3. Black Caribbean women's unemployment is twice that of white British women (DWP, 2019).

Women's disadvantage in the job market contrasts with their educational achievements. While women are now just under half of the total labour force, they still predominantly have responsibility for childcare, have limited opportunities to secure the most high-paying and high-status jobs, are still subject to gender pay gaps, are employed in work below their levels of qualification, and dominate in part-time, insecure and low-paid work. These disadvantages are not the inevitable result of biological factors but are socially constructed and rooted in models of hegemonic masculinity and femininity intersecting with social class and institutional racism to create inequalities. Power is exercised by men over women, by white ethnic groups over minority ethnic groups, and by those occupying positions of class privilege and its associated entitlement. This results in women's labour being viewed as separate from that of men, with childbirth and maternity leave seen as women's 'problems' rather than fundamental to the organisation of the workplace.

These issues are explored under four sections:

- gendered participation and segregation in the labour market;
- gendered experiences within the labour market;
- men and women's roles and the extent to which these remain embedded within a heteronormative model;
- policies and their effectiveness.

The gendered labour market

Occupational segregation

There is a vast amount of data on gender and the workplace published by the government as well as research from a number of organisations such as Business in the Community (BITC), the Fawcett Society, the Resolution Society, the TUC, and the Joseph Rowntree Foundation (JRF). These data are frequently presented under the broad heading of gender rather than being broken down into the experiences of women from varied backgrounds, although the development of the Race Disparity Audit has led to considerable data on employment patterns being available on the Ethnicity Facts and Figures website (DWP, 2019).

A significant feature of the labour market is its segregation into different sectors, some of which employ predominantly male or female workers. This has encouraged, and often hidden, differential pay levels and disadvantages. Such segregation follows from a number of factors, one of which is the gendered subject choices made at A-level and subsequently at university. Although the national curriculum would claim to have countered traditional stereotypes, A-level choices continue to be firmly gendered (DfE, 2019a). Such choices are rooted in the hidden curriculum, including teachers' and pupils' attitudes, that reinforce behaviour likely to win approval and fit with a heteronormative model of gender and sexuality (Eden, 2017). These attitudes carry forward into degree options and the labour market and contribute to a segregated occupational structure and its associated inequalities.

The majority of women are clustered in three main occupational groups: administrative and secretarial, personal service, and sales and customer service occupations. The most common sectors of employment for women are health and social work (accounting for 21 per cent of all jobs held by women at September 2018), wholesale and retail (14 per cent) and education (12 per cent). Seventy-nine per cent of jobs in the health and social work sector and 70 per cent of jobs in the education sector are held by women. In some sectors only a small proportion of jobs are held by women, such as construction (14 per cent) and manufacturing (25 per cent) (House of Commons, 2019).

The sectors in which women predominate are characterised by work which does not reflect their educational attainment:

- relatively low hourly pay and minimum-wage jobs: 47 per cent of women work in jobs classified as low-skilled, compared to 18 per cent of men, leading to 25 per cent of employed women having low pay compared to 15 per cent of employed men;
- disproportionate participation in the part-time insecure job market: 41 per cent of women compared to 13 per cent of men;
- women with low or no qualifications have much lower employment levels than men with equivalent backgrounds;
- other than for Indian and Chinese ethnic groups, there is significant disadvantage for most ethnic groups, who have a lower average hourly pay level than those from the white ethnic group and higher risks of unemployment (DWP, 2019; Weekes-Bernard, 2017).

A significant feature of the UK industrial economy is the number of low-paid part-time jobs, and these are largely undertaken by women: 41 per cent of women in employment work part-time compared to 13 per cent of men (Fawcett Society, 2019). Care responsibilities also limit the opportunities for progression and acquisition of new skills. This leads to many women in part-time jobs working below their skills and qualification level and in increasingly casualised areas of work (Joseph Rowntree Foundation, 2018). This is illustrated by the domiciliary care sector where zero-hours contracts are the predominant work arrangement and 84 per cent of the workers are female, with 20 per cent born outside the UK.

Gendered experiences within paid work

The gender pay gap

Equal pay for equal work has been legally binding since 1970. But since 2015, there has been a requirement on all employers with more than 250 employees to submit details of their gender pay gap, which is the difference in the average hourly wage of men and women. The headline message is that in 2019 the national average gender pay gap for full- and part-time workers stood at 17.9 per cent, and was 8.6 per cent among full-time employees (House of Commons, 2019). This highlights differences in working patterns and raises questions about how women get stuck in low-paid, low-skill work with little opportunity for career development (EHRC, 2018). The government has tried to tackle women's low pay by introducing additional free childcare, raising the national minimum wage, extending the right to request flexible working to all employees and introducing shared parental leave. In spite of these developments, the gender pay gap remains.

The pay gap widens as workers grow older as the expectation and reality of women's responsibility for childcare restricts employment opportunities (House of Commons, 2019; Grimshaw and Rubery, 2015). The gender pay gap exists across all class groupings, from those in graduate careers, where female graduates still earn about 22 per cent less per hour than male graduates, down to unskilled part-time work (Social Mobility Commission, 2019). Even before they have children, women earn about 10 per cent less than men. But that gap then increases rapidly for many women after they have children and look for flexible work arrangements (Costa Dias et al., 2018: Joyce and Xu, 2019).

Most minority ethnic groups are at an additional disadvantage in relation to pay, although the gender pay gaps faced by minority ethnic women vary significantly. For example, there is a considerable pay gap between black African women and Chinese women, who earn more than the median for women. There are also significant variations in pay by religion or belief (Fawcett Society, 2019). In an attempt to tackle this issue a consultation was launched in 2018 by the Prime Minister in association with BITC. This aimed to expose the significant disparities in the pay and progression of minority ethnic employees compared with their white counterparts (BITC, 2018a). One significant explanation of the gender pay gap relevant to all women is recognising how the power relations rooted in a heteronormative model of men and women give greater value to men's skills while undervaluing women's. The closer women's work skills are to the skills they use in the family, the more likely they are to be undervalued in the workplace, and the segregation of occupations facilitates this process (Grimshaw and Rubery, 2015).

Access to well-paid and senior positions – horizontal segregation

A higher percentage of women graduates (78 per cent in 2017/18) achieve a first or upper second degree compared to men (72 per cent) (HESA, 2019), but this does not lead to success in terms of accessing influential and highly paid jobs:

- Within the working-age population in 2018, males across all qualification groups have higher median salaries than their female counterparts. The difference is most pronounced for graduates, and the gap increases over time, where ten years after graduation males earn £9,500 more than females.
- At the top of the job hierarchy ladder, women with postgraduate degrees earn well below men with only undergraduate degrees (DfE, 2019b, 2019c).
- More men than women work in senior posts with 13 per cent of men in these roles compared to 8 per cent of women (House of Commons, 2019).
- Women are less likely to be rated as having 'high potential', which reduces their access to training programmes and opportunities that lead to leadership roles (BITC, 2014).
- The pay penalty experienced by black graduate women relative to white women sits at 9 per cent, equating to a full-time equivalent of over £3,000 a year (Henehan and Rose, 2018).

The Fawcett Society produces a yearly report on *Sex and Power* (Jewell and Bazeley, 2018). Their reports show that women are still systematically excluded from public positions of power and from the most powerful positions in private sector corporations. In 2018 there were just six women at the top of FTSE 100 organisations, none of whom were from a BAME background. In June 2018, 29 per cent of FTSE 100 directorships were occupied by women, and 24 per cent of FTSE 250 directorships were held by women (House of Commons, 2019).

Motherhood penalty

While many of the penalties that women have to deal with affect all women, there are particular issues associated with pregnancy, returning to work and career opportunities. In one study, three in four mothers reported a negative experience during pregnancy, maternity leave, or on return from maternity leave, with minority ethnic mothers more likely to report financial loss or a negative experince (EHRC, 2016; TUC, 2016a). Pay penalties are greater for those women who return to part-time work, but women at the very top of the income pyramid are likely to receive no motherhood penalty. Women see children having a negative impact on their career and do not believe employers are supportive in helping them balance their responsibilities for work and home. These barriers are not recognised by men who hold the majority of senior leadership positions (BITC, 2014).

Bullying and harassment

The UK has a culture awash with sexualised images of women, which is reflected both in the culture of schools and in the workplace. While many schools try to support gender and sexual diversity, the classroom and playground are spaces where 'normal and natural' heterosexual identities are policed, with pupils trying to maintain their status within a hegemonic masculinity framework. Gender binary choices are frequently inevitable, and sexual harassment is the normal everyday experience of girls and those with diverse sexual orientation (Eden, 2017). LGBT identities are seen as deviant and to be attacked as challenging masculine hegemony. These attitudes and behaviour carry through into the workplace where females are required to possess an idealised body image and any challenges to heterosexual normality lead to harassment and sexual abuse, cross-cut by racism, class cultures and homophobia. Within both schools and the workplace, sexist jokes and comments are everyday experiences, which contributes to a culture that views it as acceptable to treat women this way and helps normalise sexual violence (Women and Equalities Committee (WEC), 2016, 2018a).

Within the work environment bullying and harassment are experienced by both men and women, but to a greater degree by women. Data on bullying indicate that black British African Caribbean women with disabilities and bisexual and lesbian gay women are particularly vulnerable, with high incidences of bullying rooted in racism, homophobia and disability prejudice from both managers and colleagues (BITC, 2014, 2018a; TUC, 2016b).

Sexual harassment and abuse

The scale of sexual harassment and abuse within the workplace is masked by the fact that four out of five women and most LGBT workers do not report sexual harassment to their employer, and when they do, only a small number see a positive outcome (TUC, 2016b; WEC, 2018a). This ensures that workplace cultures continue to reproduce sexual harassment with little fear of punishment.

Various reports suggest that over 50 per cent of women have experienced some sexual harrassment, and for young women the figure is greater (TUC, 2016b). One in ten of the women who had been harrassed said they had been sexually assaulted (WEC, 2018a). The

TUC (2016b) points out that specific groups are disproportionately affected or suscep-tible to sexual harassment at work, such as young women between the ages of 18 and 24, employees with a disability or long-term illness, ethnic minorities and members of sexual minority groups. Workers with irregular employment contracts, common in the services sector, are more likely to experience sexual harassment. For black women, harassment is often accompanied by racism and the power relations of the workplace make this very dif-ficult to confront and address. LGBT workers face significant discrimination which leads to high levels of abuse: around seven out of ten LGBT workers experienced at least one type of sexual harassment at work (68 per cent) and almost one in eight LGBT women (12 per cent) reported being seriously sexually assaulted or raped at work (TUC, 2016b).

Changing gender relations in the family and labour market

Attitudes towards care responsibilities

For women to access the labour market without discrimination, change needs to occur in cultural attitudes and practices within the family as well as in the workplace. The British Social Attitudes Survey (Phillips et al., 2018) found traditional attitudes in decline across society, reflecting the reality of more mothers in work and increased use of childcare. Of particular interest for the issues discussed in this chapter is the continuing move away from the heteronormative model of men as breadwinners and women as homemakers:

- Seventy-two per cent disagree with the view that a man's job is to earn money, a woman's job is to look after the home and family, up from 58 per cent in 2008.
- There had been a decline in those who thought a mother should stay at home if they have a child under school age, from almost two-thirds in 1989, to a third in 2018 (Phillips et al., 2018).

These changes in attitudes do not however challenge the reality that it is usually women who do more childcare than men, with a recent study finding this the case for more than half of mothers (55 per cent) compared to 18 per cent of fathers (Working Families, 2019). Twenty-nine per cent of couples said they shared the childcare equally. It is women there-fore who adjust their labour-market participation in the light of childcare responsibilities. The ONS (2018b) reports that almost six in ten mothers worked less than thirty hours a week when their youngest dependent child was aged 3 to 4 years. When the age of the youngest dependent child was between 11 and 18 years, both parents were more likely to be in full-time employment. Women put in more than double the proportion of unpaid work when it comes to cooking, childcare and housework (ONS, 2018b). Change has occurred but not to a degree that fundamentally shifts the reality of men and women's behaviour.

Attitudes to fathering

There is, though, evidence of a shift in attitudes. Younger fathers, aged 16 to 35, are more likely to express a wish to spend more time caring for their children and are more likely to be considering reducing their hours or taking pay cuts to obtain a better balance between work and family life (BITC, 2018c; Gatrell *et al.*, 2015). The 2018 Modern Family Index (MFI) (Working Families, 2019) found that young fathers felt resentful about their work and family balance in contrast to men aged 36 to 45. A BITC (2018c) survey also reported that men saw expectations and organisational practices as standing in the way of greater family involvement. The WEC (2018b) also received evidence that younger couples are searching for equality at home and at work but are not finding a work culture that facilitates this.

It is not, though, just employer practices which prevent men taking more responsibility for childcare: traditional gender attitudes towards work and care remain powerful influences on decisions by both men and women. The 2018 MFI (Working Families, 2019) shows men and women differentially adjusting their working lives on becoming a parent:

- Seventeen per cent of women had taken a pay cut to work fewer hours compared to 7 per cent of men.
- Twenty-four per cent of women had reduced their hours compared to 15 per cent of men.

However, the wish to be more involved is changing practices: working fathers aged 16 to 35 admitted faking being sick to meet family obligations, and 68 per cent regularly dropped their children off at school. Women though are still burdened with a responsibility for the moral status of the family and the expectation that they are the first contact if there is a childcare issue. This attitude permeates the family and workplace practices (Working Families, 2019).

Policies for change

Government legislation is a key factor in establishing conditions which can facilitate and encourage women's access to the labour market. Such legislation, though, operates in a context where:

- the male breadwinner power model is still entrenched within households and occupational cultures and practices;
- legislation has not caught up with the current economic structure where self-employed fathers or those in casualised jobs are not eligible for parental benefits.

Two examples illustrate the impact of such concerns on attempts to facilitate women's participation.

Flexible working

This policy was introduced in 2002 to enable employees to balance their personal and working lives and employers to benefit in terms of workforce recruitment, motivation and retention. In 2019 the MFI survey asked parents whether they thought flexible working was a genuine option for men and women in the workplace, and both mothers and fathers saw a gap between policy and practice with this being a more genuine option for women than men (Working Families, 2019). The WEC (2018b) also argues that fathers in employment feel marginalised from access to flexible working opportunities, due to their managers' assumption that they are the breadwinner. They also comment on the difficulties of less well-off fathers who want to take advantage of such opportunities. This gap between aspirations and reality was also found in BITC (2018c) research which identified cultural values and organisational barriers of job design and management strategies that influence employees' conceptions about the costs associated with flexible working and who it is for.

Shared parental leave

In 2015 the Conservative government introduced shared parental leave (SPL), which aimed to promote gender equality following childbirth. This legislation has failed to acknowledge current labour market employment patterns in that fathers in insecure work and self-employed are not eligible for it and it is low-paid. Actual take-up has been very poor (TUC, 2019). These problems have led to calls for statutory paternity pay and that shared parental leave pay be increased to 90 per cent of the father's pay (WEC, 2018b). The TUC also argues these benefits should be available for the self-employed, agency workers and those on zero-hours contracts. These changes are essential, but again there is evidence that underlying assumptions amongst mothers and fathers also need to change. The MFI reports (Working Families, 2017, 2019) and the BSA report (Phillips *et al.*, 2018) consistently show that fathers and mothers believe that mothers make the best carers and time-off for mothers is more important than time-off for fathers. Such assumptions underlie gender pay gaps and patterns of participation in the labour market. Tackling gendered assumptions remains crucial to broadening parental choice.

Conclusion

The dominance of the patriarchal and heteronormative model of gender relations with its view of appropriate male and female behaviour runs through gendered choices in education and into the workplace, in spite of women's high levels of educational attainment. The fundamental values underpinning the maintenance of hegemonic masculinity and the power relations between men and women impact on access to the school curriculum, and women's options in the labour market. They affect the organisation of work and employers' approaches and deny women access to paid work on the same terms as men. The segregated labour market places women in less well paid and less powerful positions, exposing the unequal value given to men's and women's work. The assumption that women should carry the main responsibility for childcare, leaving men to pursue careers in higher-paid positions in the labour market, is entrenched in the family and in the workplace.

But the economic realities of women's participation in the labour market have led to attitude changes and there is evidence that younger men are looking to take a greater share of care responsibilities. Legislation and how that is enacted by employers is critical in supporting such shifting assumptions and eroding traditional gender relations. Currently many organisational cultures and styles of management do not support a good work/life balance. Governments need to promote, monitor and enforce equalities legislation, leading to a re-evaluation of work design and organisational culture and enhancing opportunities for women. This would promote change in men's and women's assumptions and opportunities within the family and challenge the culture of male entitlement, power and privilege that currently dominates organisations. Changes also in areas such as childcare, statutory paternity leave for all male workers, enforcement of plans to address the gender pay gap, economic policies on minimum wage levels and the casualisation of work could all undermine traditional patriarchal perspectives and promote greater equality for men and women in the family and workplace.

Questions for discussion

Do you agree that women's work is undervalued compared to men's?
How could the entrenched attitudes that support the male breadwinner/female carer model be encouraged to change?
Do you think racism and sexism permeate the workplace?

Summary

- In spite of women's high educational achievements they do not have equal access to the workplace and suffer a number of disadvantages.
- The segregated structures of the labour market, women's participation in low-paid, part-time work and the value given to women's work contribute to the gender pay gap.
- More data are needed to help understand the diversity of experiences amongst women, but many women confront racism and sexism.
- Traditional views of gender roles are shifting and becoming more fluid, particularly amongst younger fathers, but gender equality in the home and workplace is embedded in a male-dominated culture that continues to perpetuate traditional models of breadwinner/carer.
- Promoting and enforcing equalities legislation is crucial in changing household and employer attitudes and could encourage a more balanced family/work lifestyle for men and women.

Recommended reading

Eden, C. (2017) *Gender, Education and Work*. (Chapters. 8, 9 and 10.) Abingdon: Routledge.
Fawcett Society (2018) *Invisible Women*. The Fawcett Society and Young Women's Trust.
Social Mobility Commission (2019) *State of the Nation 2018–2019*. London: Social Mobility Commission.

References

BITC (2014) *Opportunity Now: Project 28–40, the Report*. London: BITC.

BITC (2018a) *Race at Work; the Scorecard Report: 2018*. London: BITC.

BITC (2018b) *Gender Pay Gap and Public Reporting*. London: BITC.

BITC (2018c) *Equal Lives: Parenthood and Caring in the Workplace*. London: BITC.

Costa Dias, M., Joyce, R. and Parodi, F. (2018) *Mothers Suffer Big Long-Term Pay Penalty from Part-Time Working*. London: Institute of Fiscal Studies.

DfE (2019a) *National Tables: A Level and Other 16 to 18 Results 2017 to 2018* (revised). London: DfE.

DfE (2019b) *Graduate Labour Market Statistics: 2018*. London: DfE.

DfE (2019c) *Graduate Outcomes*. London: DfE.

DWP (2019) *Ethnicity Facts and Figures: Work, Pay and Benefits*. London: DWP.

Eden, C. (2017) *Gender, Education and Work*. Abingdon: Routledge.

EHRC (2016) *Pregnancy and Maternity-Related Discrimination and Disadvantage*. London: EHRC.

EHRC (2018) *Closing the Gender Pay Gap*. London: EHRC.

Fawcett Society (2019) *Gender Pay Gap Reporting Briefing April 2019*. London: Fawcett Society.

Gatrell, C.J., Burnett, S.B., Cooper, C.L. and Sparrow, P. (2015) The Price of Love: The Prioritisation of Childcare and Income Earning among UK Fathers. *Families, Relationships and Societies* **4**(2), pp. 225–238.

Grimshaw, D. and Rubery, J. (2015) *The Motherhood Pay Gap: A Review of the Issues, Theory and International Evidence*. Geneva: International Labour Office.

Henehan, K. and Rose, H. (2018) *Opportunities Knocked? Exploring Pay Penalties among the UK's Ethnic Minorities*. London: Resolution Foundation.

HESA (2019) *Higher Education Student Statistics: UK, 2017/18*. London: HESA.

House of Commons (2019) *Women and the Economy*. London: House of Commons.

Jewell, H. and Bazeley, A. (2018) *Sex and Power*. London: Fawcett Society.

Joseph Rowntree Foundation (2018) *Budget 2018: Tackling the Rising Tide of in-Work Poverty*. York: JRF.

Joyce, R. and Xu, X. (2019) *The Gender Pay Gap: Women Work for Lower-Paying Firms Than Men*. London: Institute for Fiscal Studies.

ONS (2018a) *Employment and Labour Market 2018*. London: ONS.

ONS (2018b) *Families and the Labour Market, England: 2018*. London: ONS.

Phillips, D., Curtice, J., Phillips, M. and Perry, J. (Eds) (2018) *British Social Attitudes: The 35th Report*. London: The National Centre for Social Research.

Social Mobility Commission (2019) *State of the Nation 2018–2019*. London: Social Mobility Commission.

TUC (2016a) *The Motherhood Pay Penalty: Key Findings from TUC/IPPR Research March 2016*. London: TUC.

TUC (2016b) *Still Just a Bit of Banter? Sexual Harassment in the Workplace in 2016*. London: TUC.

TUC (2019) *Shared Parental Leave Isn't Working: New Parents Need Stronger Rights*. London: TUC.

Walby, S. (2013) *Patriarchy at Work: Patriarchal and Capitalist Relations in Employment, 1800–1984*. London: John Wiley & Sons

WEC (2016) *Sexual Harassment and Sexual Violence in Schools*. London: House of Commons.

WEC (2018a) *Sexual Harassment in the Workplace*. London: House of Commons.

WEC (2018b) *Fathers and the Workplace*. London: House of Commons.

WEC (2018c) *Race Disparity Audit*. London: House of Commons.

Weekes-Bernard, D. (2017) *Poverty and Ethnicity in the Labour Market*. York: Joseph Rowntree Foundation.

Working Families (2017) *Modern Families Index*. London: Working Families and Bright Horizons.

Working Families (2019) *Modern Families Index 2019*. London: Working Families and Bright Horizons.

Chapter 5

Social mobility and education

Richard Riddell

> I share a vision for a country where we raise our ambitions for every child, whatever their background. Education is at the heart of this, giving everyone the chance to fulfil the spark of potential that exists in them.
>
> Damian Hinds, Secretary of State for Education, announcing the appointment of new Social Mobility Commissioners (Hinds, 2018)

Introduction

Damian Hinds is the most recent Secretary of State for Education in the UK to characterise inadequate ambition for children, or aspiration, and failure to realise 'potential', as national weaknesses that need to be addressed through education, primarily through schools. This idea that while 'talent is spread evenly across the country, opportunity is not' (DfE, 2017: 5) has found expression in national policies since the early 2000s intended to increase *social mobility*. This chapter explores what is meant by social mobility and the role that schools may or may not play in promoting it. In doing so, the chapter briefly introduces aspects of the policies of the Labour, Coalition and Conservative UK governments within the context of the UK's arguably relatively poorer recent record in encouraging social mobility. It considers the wider social and other mechanisms whereby advantage (or privilege) and disadvantage are transmitted from generation to generation and questions some of the assumptions on which social mobility policies rest, against the background of the 'social congestion' identified by Philip Brown (2013).

Social mobility and opportunity

Perhaps the easiest way to consider social *mobility* is that it represents *movement* within our society, usually from one occupational group or background to another of differing status and, in the eyes of some, worth. One way of thinking about the society in which we live is as a *structure* – of differing incomes, wealth, power, influence – of these occupations. Many analyses of society and how it works begin with occupation, and in the UK this is measured by the National Statistics Socio-Economic Classification Analytic Classes (or NS–SEC for short). See Table 5.1.

Table 5.1 National Statistics Socio-Economic Classification Analytic Classes (ONS, 2010)

1	Higher managerial and professional occupations
	1.1 Larger employer and higher managerial and professional occupations
	1.2 Higher professional occupations
2	Lower managerial and professional occupations
3	Intermediate occupations
4	Small employers and own account workers
5	Lower supervisory and technical occupations
6	Semi-routine occupations
7	Routine occupations
8	Never worked and long-term unemployment

The Office for National Statistics places all jobs in the UK within one of these categories – these can be explored on the ONS website. Other bodies, such as UCAS, also use them to analyse the social background of students entering UK universities and make comparisons over time. Policy documents such as the Coalition government's (Cabinet Office, 2011) Social Mobility Strategy represent *increasing opportunity* as moving upwards in this structure – hence *mobility*. This is seen as the most desirable state of affairs, either in comparison to one's peers (often termed *relative* social mobility) or one's parents' generation (*intergenerational* or *absolute*).

In other words, if society is analysed using this occupational structure, or *opportunities structure* as some sociologists term it (for example, Wendy Bottero, 2005), then promoting movement upwards becomes the focus of policies: what governments wish to achieve for the people they serve. Sometimes this is expressed as the *social ladder* (Cabinet Office, 2011), so that *climbing* the ladder is then seen as desirable for individuals and something that aspirational and ambitious young people should attempt to do.

So, measures of social mobility represent the aggregate changes over time in social and economic positions for individuals in comparison with their peers, or the rest of society. This can be measured in terms of *income mobility*, or alternatively by *social class mobility*, by comparing relative position in the NS–SEC framework. Very often, but not always, income levels are more or less reflected by socio-economic position.

Activity 1

Is 'ascending' the social ladder the most desirable goal we can offer to young people? When might it not be? And for whom?

How has the UK done?

The public policy narrative – the story reflected in government statements such as that above of the Secretary of State and web and broadcast media – is that the UK has a *poor* record in intergenerational social mobility, especially recently, though that may not be reflected in the individual stories told about many who may have 'succeeded against the odds'. Such stories make good reading.

The conventional view is that social mobility in the UK steadily increased from a low base during the 1940s until the 1970s, whether measured by income or social class (Boston Consulting, 2017; Goldthorpe, 2016). From the 1980s, however, social mobility appears to have stalled or deteriorated on both measures (Bukodi and Goldthorpe, 2019). And comparatively, the UK (along with the United States) is one of the poorest-performing affluent or developed countries (ibid.).

There have been a number of graphical representations of this – see for example Figure 5.1 (Resolution Foundation, 2016, quoted in Boston Consulting, 2017: 7).

Figure 5.1 shows the pattern in social class and income, with class mobility largely plateauing currently and income mobility falling. This pattern in the UK also reflects the narrowing of income inequality from the end of the Second World War until the 1970s and its widening from then until now. The *Gini coefficient* is one measure designed to assess income inequality. It does so across the whole of society, not just between the richest and the poorest. If just one person received all the income in a society and everyone else received nothing, then the coefficient would be 1. If everyone received exactly the same income, then the coefficient would be 0. So the lower the coefficient, the more equal the society. There are lots of explanations of how this works, but see Wilkinson and Picket (2009: 17–18) for an extremely clear one. Current measures, using the Gini coefficient, show UK income inequality to be higher than in any other European country except Lithuania (Dorling and Tomlinson, 2019: 94). In one sense, this makes perfect sense for falling social mobility: the steeper the ladder, the harder it must be to ascend.

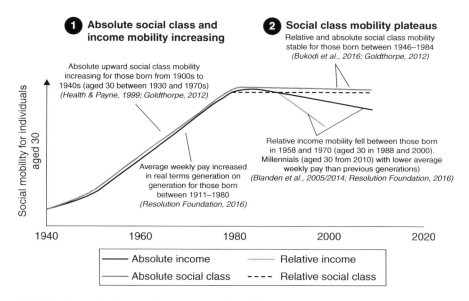

Figure 5.1 Trends in absolute and relative social mobility

This relative decline first came to public attention in the UK with the publication of the Milburn Report (2009). This, properly termed the 'Panel on Fair Access to the Professions', was commissioned by the Labour government in 2009. It made great play of the comparison between the cohort born in 1958 (that is, everyone born that year) and that born in 1970 – people currently in their late forties. It found a decline in income social mobility. In 1958, 31 per cent of the men born into families in the lowest income quartile (that is, the bottom 25 per cent of incomes in the country) had fathers in the same quartile. Thirty-five per cent of men in the highest quintile did so. For the 1970 cohort, the figures had become 35 per cent and 42 per cent respectively. It was 'becoming harder for young men from working class backgrounds to elevate their positions and less likely in the professional classes ("top" of the NS-SEC) that they would reduce theirs' (Riddell, 2010: 148).

Milburn was appointed to chair the Social Mobility Commission (originally the Social Mobility and Child Poverty Commission) that was set up by the Coalition government following the publication of their Social Mobility Strategy (Cabinet Office, 2011). This is still government policy at the time of writing (June 2019). Milburn and his fellow Commissioners collectively resigned at the end of 2017, however, as they did not consider social mobility had sufficient priority in government action, partly due to preparations for leaving the European Union, or 'Brexit'. His successor published their own 'State of the Nation' report (the sixth overall of the Commission) which stated categorically that they wished to 'lay bare the stark fact that social mobility had stagnated over the last four years at virtually all stages form birth to work' (Social Mobility Commission, 2019: v).

With this sort of statement, supported by data, it is easy to see how a picture can be painted of declining opportunity over time: that it is harder for young people to 'better' or 'improve' themselves than it has been; that the UK has become less full of promise. In one sense, this might well be true *factually*. Bear in mind that social mobility (or 'promotion') has to take place within the structure of our society, which can be expressed in the relative balance between the NS-SEC categories shown above. But John Goldthorpe (see Goldthorpe, 2016, for example), the chief architect of the NS-SEC framework, and his colleagues have documented that this structure had also been changing since the end of the Second World War. As he expressed it, the 'salariat' or 'white collar' jobs had been expanding as a proportion of the workforce at the expense of working-class ones, in particular the falling demands for manual labour. In other words, this 'golden age' as he called it of opportunity and mobility did of course exist, but that was because the occupational structure of society, the economy, was rapidly becoming more middle-class. In these circumstances, of course, a greater proportion of younger people would be able to benefit from more opportunity, without harm to anyone else. No one would have to be 'demoted'. He also observes as a footnote that none of this change resulted from better education or qualifications, which had not changed, but just the changing structure of the British economy and the jobs it creates.

By contrast, he argues, a generation later (Milburn's later cohort) more people *began* at a more advantaged social position than before and, unless the economic structure of the country changes again, there would be less possibility of change unless more people were socially *demoted*. In light of the 'stickiness' of class position that he refers to, there is now greater likelihood of remaining in the same class as one's parents, as Milburn argued. This is the situation that Brown (2013) refers to as social 'congestion': the economic (and hence social) structure has changed but is not currently changing significantly now. In this situation, unless there is a regular compiling and recompiling of pecking orders based on 'ability' or 'worth' – some would regard this as a 'meritocracy' *based on educational performance* – whereby the 'best' performing people were promoted socially and economically, and the 'worst' demoted, the chances of upward mobility remain diminished. The notion of promoting just such a meritocracy is arguably the often unstated but underlying assumption behind social mobility policy for the past twenty years.

Two footnotes before we examine this notion further. First, it is possible to have increasing absolute income mobility at the same time as static relative mobility – in times of increasing overall incomes but an unchanging social and economic structure. Watch for this assumption in political announcements. Second, it was Milburn's argument that there would be more professional (Goldthorpe's 'white collar') jobs from 2020 onwards, for which he argued more UK citizens should be helped to qualify through educational improvements. In the event, Brown argues that the assumptions on which this was based were flawed, but we shall see!

Maintaining and transmitting advantage and disadvantage

Against the background of a static social and economic structure, therefore, the policy argument returns to whether the 'right' people (i.e. deserving it because of their educational or other merit) continue to occupy the higher occupational groups and are replaced by similar people as they age and retire and leave the labour market. There are certainly many who argue that this is the case, often from positions of relative privilege socially, educationally and professionally (see Riddell, 2010, 2016, and more recently Friedman and Laurison, 2019): by this they mean that the 'very best people' do in fact get into the most selective universities and then enter the highest-earning professions and occupations.

In one obvious way, this assumption is certainly true. Elsewhere in this volume (Chapter 6), the close, continuing and historical deep and long-lasting association between social background, advantage and disadvantage and educational attainment is explored. This is not the place to consider the reasons for this, but obviously the better the qualifications, the easier it is to progress to the higher echelons of society, including, as some people refer to it, the 'elite', the people who really run things. And the opposite is also true. Indeed, the National Audit Office (2015) identify low academic attainment at the age of 16 as a key mechanism for transmitting poverty, because it can halt the path to basic qualifications as entry to more education, training and better-paid jobs. So in this sense the recruitment to, say, Russell Group universities – who argue they are the elite institutions – just reflects the wider inequalities of society, no more.

But there appear to be some deeper social mechanisms at work here. First, it has long been known and often argued that private schools in the UK – usually referred to as independent schools, or some as 'public' schools – are the most effective at enabling students to

Table 5.2 Percentage of 'top' professionals from independent and state schools (Kirby, 2016: 4)

	Profession	School	
		Independent	State
	(UK population)	7%	93%
Today	Law (Judiciary)	72%	28%
	Law (Barristers)	71%	29%
	Military	71%	29%
	Medicine	61%	39%
	Journalism	51%	49%
	Law (Scholars)	51%	49%
	Politics (Cabinet)	50%	50%
	Civil Service	48%	52%
All time	Film (Oscars)	67%	33%
	Nobel Prizes	63%	37%
	Film (BAFTAs)	42%	58%
	Pop music (Brits)	19%	81%

gain access to elite universities and professions. The Sutton Trust, for example, have regularly analysed the relationship between attendance at private school and membership of top professions. Below are their most recent figures – see Table 5.2 (Kirby, 2016: 4). They compare the percentage of each 'top' profession with the percentage of the population that actually attends independent schools (7 per cent, and more post-16).

If you haven't seen such figures before, you may not be surprised by the figures for the higher echelons of the legal profession, for example (Judiciary and Barristers), or the Cabinet (the central committee of the UK government), but you might find those for top journalists more surprising. But also note that winners of Oscars, BAFTAs and Brit awards are also disproportionately from private schools. Further, we know also from the Sutton Trust that 32 per cent of Team GB's 130 medallists at Rio went to fee-paying schools, though this was down from 36 per cent at the London Olympics.

Bear in mind that these schools are fee-paying – only 1 per cent of pupils at private schools have full assistance with fees, though 32 per cent receive some (ISC, 2017) – and are academically selective, so they are not open to all. To reinforce this point, research published in 2017 (Reeves *et al.*) found young people attending the 'top' nine public schools (they include Eton, Harrow, St Paul's, Charterhouse and Winchester among others) were, in the period from 1897 onwards, ninety-four times more likely to enter elite positions in society (the very top of the NS-SEC table) than *all other schools combined*. These are very successful institutions.

Finally on this point, Friedman and Laurison (2019) examined some of the other barriers to getting on in, particularly, elite professions (for example, medicine, law and finance) – the focus of the original Milburn Report and, of course, continuing Sutton Trust work. The conundrum on which they founded their work was that, even when 'upwardly mobile' young people, say from working-class backgrounds, did achieve the highest educational credentials, including from 'top' universities, they failed to convert this into the sort of premium income enjoyed by their peers from more elite social backgrounds (parents with occupations at the higher end of the NS-SEC framework). Their research is interesting because they wanted to move beyond just the characteristics of individuals trying to 'better themselves' – often referred to popularly as the sorts of 'confidence' that result from elite education of various sorts – which they regard as an inadequate explanation. They wished to explore some of the 'lived experience' inside some of the well-paid top professions and how it suggested the wider system worked. Friedman and Laurison found that the above confidence is 'situational' and an adjunct of where the individuals feel they 'fit' and 'belong'. This often included, for example, shared humour, cultural affinity, shared tastes and interests that enabled a 'better fit'. Besides the advantage of being able to draw on the 'Bank of Mum and Dad' (particularly in London), they point out that many of the individuals doing the actual selecting for elite professional posts are themselves from elite backgrounds, and take advice from similar people. There are some memorable interview data, including analyses of these 'best fit' decisions, and they argue that much of what is classified as 'merit' in the elite workplaces they were analysing was in fact 'impossible to separate from the "following wind" of privilege' (Friedman and Laurison, 2019: 27).

Activity 2

Why do private schools appear to work so well as social mechanisms? Do you think we have the 'brightest and the best' individuals running society?

Policies intended to improve social mobility

When an issue is identified in society – socially, economically, culturally – if it is defined and considered a problem, or unjust, say, then *changing policy* can be considered by the government of the day. To make effective policy, the causes of the problem need to be identified and who or what is responsible for it. The varying educational outcomes by social and ethnic background and gender, and how these relate to each other – intersect – has historically been identified for some forty years as one of the causes of poor mobility. (See Chapter 6.) The best people are not making it. Policy to improve schools in particular – as part of the Global Education Reform Movement (GERM – e.g. Sahlberg, 2015) is considered elsewhere in this volume (for example Chapters 1 and 2).

One of the important early policy narratives in social mobility policy was the notion of 'ambition' referred to by Damian Hinds. It became intertwined very early on with the notion of 'aspiration'. It is difficult to identify quite when this became a focus, but one of Hinds' predecessors was already talking about the 'poverty of aspiration' in some (working-class) communities (Blunkett, 2000) at the turn of the century, and about the role of schools and others, such as careers services, in raising the sights of many students. Within the context of a 50 per cent participation target for higher education (HE), this became focused on encouraging participation in HE, especially from certain areas, or postcodes, with higher levels of social disadvantage, for which universities used to be financially rewarded (Riddell, 2010). This work survives in continuing 'Widening Participation' work at many universities, employing a variety of policy technologies such as 'Student Ambassadors'.

There are several issues to consider here. Most of us who teach at new universities will know students who are the first from their families to attend university, and many anecdotally put this down to comments made to them at certain times in their educational careers, for example, by teachers. The research into 'raising aspirations' work is not positive, however: Gorard *et al.* (2012), in a meta-review, could find no measurable impact on attainment and participation of attitudes and aspirations and hence interventions to 'improve' them. But again there are deeper issues here. Archer *at al.* (2003) were among earlier researchers to question the legitimacy of challenging the career aspirations of young people for working-class occupations (hairdressing seems to be taken as a common example) and seeming to recommend higher education as preferable. More recently, Hoskins and Barker (2015) have done so too. In any case, whereas 'aspiration' has commonly been seen to be the prerogative of middle-class families, we know now that this is just not the case (Riddell, 2010); what seems to be more problematic is knowing (Kintrea *at al.*, 2011), or even 'owning', the roadmap of how to actually get there (Gale, 2015). This is about what might be termed 'knowing the market' better.

So although this research has limited the scope for effective action on social mobility – considered to be not good enough by bodies such as the Social Mobility Commission – national strategies have been developed in the UK, including various strands already touched on. Widening access to the *professions*, including the 'top' ones, as identified by the original Milburn Report (Panel of Fair Access, 2009), is one strategy, and (presumably) why he was asked to be Chair of the then new Commission. This was included in the Coalition government's Social Mobility Strategy published in 2011 – *Opening Doors, Breaking Barriers* – already referred to several times (Cabinet Office, 2011).

This strategy was a significant document with all-party support – the ossifying of social and economic structures was one of the policy problems recognised at the time. The strategy takes a 'life cycle approach' to improving mobility. This includes the 'Foundation Years' (0 to 5 years old), School Years, Transition Years (largely what happens post-16 including access to higher education) and then Adulthood, where career entry, including to the professions, became a key focus, but less so retention and progression once there (Riddell, 2013). Much of the development work identified in the strategy was not new, but had been developed and sometimes publicised elsewhere, but this is not a criticism of such a wide-ranging strategy.

For example, the reform of the Early Years and Foundation Stage featured in 'Foundation Years', including fifteen hours of free nursery provision for disadvantaged children. The school reforms included a focus on the poorer attainment outcomes of disadvantaged children, and raising their aspirations via the new Pupil Premium (a cash allocation to schools for every child who had ever claimed a free school meal in the past six years – 'Ever6FSM'), but also a new task force to get employers into schools talking about 'the jobs they do' (Cabinet Office, 2011: 6). This had started with members of the then Cabinet. 'Transition Years' included the plans to get more young people into education, training or employment with training and reform of the vocational awards system. 'Adulthood' included changes to the welfare system, encouraging more people into work, and the development of paid internships in major professions.

This was a wide-ranging and ambitious programme, as might be expected from a recently elected government. Besides the continuing school reforms, however, to which we will return shortly, the government no longer professed to be responsible for some of the changes. These included access to the professions and the university reforms being agreed at the same time, conceived, it was argued, to influence largely autonomous institutions that would remain so. The strategy launch took place at the Accountants' Hall in the City of London (Riddell, 2013) where an 'invitation to business' (one of a number of 'invitations' at the time) was issued by the government to recruit employees from much wider social backgrounds – their own version of 'widening participation'. Some of the major professional associations, including rightly enough the Institute of Chartered Accountants, and large companies developed entry recruitment schemes accompanied by student mentoring from their own staff. This will have benefited some young people, of course, but it is not possible to gauge what sort of wider strategic impact this might have on the sorts of problems identified by Friedman and Laurison. It could be argued to be the case for most policy changes of course.

It is worth dwelling on the School Years section, however, as this has remained a feature of government policy until the present. The reform strands in the Social Mobility Strategy unsurprisingly reflected the White Paper (DfE, 2010) published the previous year – action to raise standards through the 'ratchets' of higher Ofsted expectations, a national expectation that every school would be good or outstanding, specific recommended strategies for disadvantaged students (supported by the Pupil Premium), raised floor (minimum) targets for attainment, academisation (greater school autonomy) and a more 'knowledge-based' national curriculum to be introduced from 2014, with tougher assessments, including a complete revamp of GCSE (Riddell, 2016). This change in itself makes it difficult to make comparisons between years, and indeed this is what has happened as they have been dropped from intervention plans and, arguably, the new Ofsted Inspection Framework introduced in 2019.

There has been some evidence of successful policy of narrowing 'the attainment gap' between more- and less-advantaged students: for example, through the London Challenge (Whitty and Anders, 2013). Because of the importance of attainment at transition to later career and life prospects for these students (National Audit Office, 2015), this must be welcomed, whatever view is taken generally. And greater progression to higher education seems also desirable. Whatever view is taken, the statistical evidence shows that attending a good school does make a difference, especially to students from disadvantaged backgrounds (Rasbash *et al.*, 2010). But the issue has always been, as schools improve, do they improve for all students in the same way, maintaining an overall attainment gap, but achieving higher levels overall?

Six years after the Social Mobility Strategy, however, the by now Conservative government issued its 'Social Mobility Action Plan' (DfE, 2017), just before Christmas, 2017, with little publicity. Under the strapline 'No Community Left Behind' (ibid.: 7), this plan, which was to be read, it argued, alongside the government's Industrial Strategy, outlined five key strands named as 'ambitions'. They were closing the 'word gap' in the early years (that is, closing development gaps, especially early language and literacy skills), more on closing the attainment gap, providing 'better post-16 education choices' which now included better technical qualifications (so-called 'T-levels' being developed), greater access (again) to higher education, and finally better careers advice. The significant change was the identification of a number of 'Opportunity Areas' for extra funding where the social mobility 'challenge' was identified as greatest. These began with West Somerset, Fenland and East Cambridgeshire, Norwich and Ipswich, Blackpool, Hastings and the North Yorkshire Coast, and Derby, Doncaster, Bradford, Oldham and Stoke-on-Trent. Each of these areas was to be allocated funding and staff appointed to develop an Opportunity Plan, overseen by partnerships with representation from employers, colleges and schools. The first tranche of funding for these plans does not run out until 2020 and their evaluation will then follow.

Activity 3

Will the Social Mobility Strategy and Action Plan work? How? Does it matter? Are schools the key to improving social mobility?

Conclusion and suggested further reading

All these policies intended to increase social mobility represent work in progress, so it is difficult to provide a final word on these matters and whether any of it will be effective. But one such word could be that the whole project could be seen to be counterproductive. Diane Reay (2017), for example, writing as a professor at Cambridge University from a working-class background, presents the social mobility efforts in policy as an illusion. Whereas opportunities may come to some working-class students, she says, the idea itself of social mobility is based on the assumption that our current, unequal social and economic structure will remain. What do you think?

If you wish to read more on this subject, you may find the Sutton Trust website a very helpful place to start (look at their manifesto for the 2017 election for example). You can find a good overall guide to social mobility in *Social Mobility and Its Enemies* (Elliot Major and Machin, 2018), but the Coalition government's Social Mobility Strategy itself, though a bit old now, is clear, drawing on many academic authors.

References

Archer, L., Hutchens, M. and Ross, A. (Eds) (2003) *Higher Education and Social Class: Issues of Exclusion and Inclusion*. London: Routledge.

Blunkett, D. (2000) *Raising Aspirations in the 21st Century – a Speech Given to the North of England Conference*. London: DfEE.

Boston Consulting Group/Sutton Trust (2017) *Social Mobility in the UK*. London: Sutton Trust. Available at: www.suttontrust.com (accessed 26 May 2019).

Bottero, W. (2005) *Stratification: Social Division and Inequality*. Abingdon: Routledge.

Brown, P. (2013) Education, Opportunity and the Prospects for Social Mobility. *British Journal of Sociology of Education* **34**(5–6), pp. 678–700.

Bukodi, E. and Goldthorpe, J. (2019) *Social Mobility and Education: Research, Politics and Policy*. Cambridge: Cambridge University Press.

Cabinet Office (2011) *Opening Doors, Breaking Barriers: A Strategy for Social Mobility*. London: Cabinet Office.

DfE (2010) *The Importance of Teaching – Schools White Paper 2010*. London: DfE.

DfE (2017) *Unlocking Talent, Fulfilling Potential: A Plan for Improving Social Mobility through Education*. London: DfE.

Dorling, D. and Tomlinson, S. (2019) *Rule Britannia: Brexit and the End of Empire*. London: Biteback Publishing.

Elliot Major, L. and Machin, S. (2018) *Social Mobility and Its Enemies*. London: Penguin Books.

Friedman, S. and Laurison, D. (2019) *The Class Ceiling: Why It Pays to Be Privileged*. Bristol: Policy Press.

Gale, T. (2015) To Aspire: A Systematic Reflection on Understanding Aspirations in Higher Education. *Journal of Education Policy* **42**, pp. 139–153.

Goldthorpe, J. (2016) Social Class Mobility in Modern Britain: Changing Structure, Constant Process. *Journal of the British Academy* **4**, pp. 89–111.

Gorard, S., See, B.H. and Davies, P. (2012) *The Impact of Attitudes and Aspirations on Educational Attainment and Participation*. York: Joseph Rowntree Foundation.

Hinds, D. (2018) Education Secretary Appoints New Social Mobility Commissioners. Available at: www.gov.uk/government/news/education-secretary-appoints-new-social-mobility-commissioners (accessed 24 May 2019).

Hoskins, K. and Barker, B. (2015) *Education and Social Mobility*. London: IoE Press.

Independent Schools Council (2017) *2016/17 Key Figures*. Available at: www.isc.co.uk (accessed 31 May 2019).

Kintrea, K., St Clair, R. and Houston, M. (2011) *The Influence of Parents, Places and Poverty on Educational Attitudes and Aspirations*. York: Joseph Rowntree Foundation.

Kirby, P. (2016) *Leading People 2016: The Educational Backgrounds of the UK Professional Elite*. London: Sutton Trust.

National Audit Office (2015) *Funding for Disadvantaged Pupils*. London: The Stationery Office.

ONS (2010) *National Statistics Socio-Economic Classification Analytic Classes*. London: ONS. Available at: www.ons.gov.uk/methodology/classificationsandstandards/otherclassifications/thenationalstatisticssocioeconomicclassificationnssecrebasedonsoc2010 (accessed 10 August 2019).

Panel of Fair Access to the Professions (2009) *Unleashing Aspiration: The Final Report of the Panel on Fair Access to the Professions*. London: The Cabinet Office.

Rasbash, J., Leckie, G., Pillinger, R. and Jenkins, J. (2010) Children's Educational Progress: Partitioning Family, School and Area Effects. *Statistics in Society* **173**(3), pp. 657–682.

Reay, D. (2017) *Miseducation: Inequality, Education and the Working Classes*. Bristol: Policy Press.

Reeves, A., Friedman, S., Rahal, C. and Flemmen, M. (2017) The Decline and Persistence of the Old Boy: Private Schools and Elite Recruitment 1897 to 2016. *American Sociological Review* **82**(6), pp. 1139–1167.

Resolution Foundation (2016) *Stagnation Generation*. London: The Resolution Foundation.

Riddell, R. (2010) *Aspiration, Identity and Self-Belief: Snapshots of Social Structure at Work*. Stoke-on-Trent: Trentham Books.

Riddell, R. (2013) Changing Policy Levers under the Neoliberal State: Realising Coalition Policy on Education and Social Mobility. *Journal of Education Policy* **28**(6), pp. 847–863.

Riddell, R. (2016) *Equity Trust and the Self-Improving Schools System*. London: Trentham Books at UCL IOE Press.

Sahlberg, P. (2015) *Finnish Lessons 2.0: What Can the World Learn from Educational Change in Finland?* New York: Teachers College Press.

Social Mobility Commission (2019) *State of the Nation 2018–19: Social Mobility in Great Britain*. London: Social Mobility Commission.

Whitty, G. and Anders, J. (2013) *(How) Did New Labour Narrow the Achievement and Participation Gap*. London: Institute of Education, Centre for Learning and Life Chances in Knowledge Economies and Societies.

Wilkinson, R. and Pickett, K. (2009) *The Spirit Level: Why More Equal Societies Almost Always Do Better*. London: Penguin Books. [Please note there are later editions of this book.]

Chapter 6

Class, gender and ethnicity
Educational attainment and intersectionality

Christine Eden

Introduction

There is a vast amount of data available to show that pupils with diverse characteristics and backgrounds have different patterns of educational attainment. One explanation of such data is to argue that issues such as biological inferiority, lack of family commitment to education or individual laziness are the cause. A different approach, taken here, is to recognise that people's relationship to systems of power plays a major role in who succeeds within the education system and that much of success or failure is socially constructed. We are going to look at these different patterns in terms of the location of individuals within the intersecting structures of social class, gender and ethnicity and consider the effect of education policies introduced to address the attainment gap. Special educational needs and disability also have a major impact on pupil attainment, but within the limits of the chapter the focus is on those overarching structural factors of social class, gender and ethnicity.

The discussion is organised in three sections:

- how intersectionality reveals the complexity of attainment;
- the influence of social class/socio-economic status (SES), gender and ethnicity on patterns of differential attainment;
- the effect of education policies.

Intersectionality

For a considerable number of years in the UK explanations of inequality in educational attainment have been rooted in models of social class, identifying the different advantages and deprivations associated with location within the stratification system. This emphasis on social class was interrupted for a short while by the 1960s women's movement which fairly swiftly was replaced by an outcry about the educational underachievement of boys, particularly white working-class boys. There has also been to a lesser extent a recognition of the difficulties faced by minority ethnic groups and their exposure to particular negative effects of the education system such as school exclusions and institutional racism. (See Chapter 3.)

In this chapter we look beyond a one-dimensional approach to consider the complex way in which social power operates. 'Intersectionality' is to recognise that dimensions of inequality are not discrete but involve reciprocal relations and conflicts. Class, gender and ethnicity intersect through people's daily lives, varying according to time and place and cultural values and attitudes. Attempts to effect change involve recognising people's complex relations to more than one set of power relations and how that influences access to, and experience of, educational opportunities and the impact of policies.

Differential attainment patterns

Social and economic status

Over many years evidence has focused on social class/socio-economic status (SES) as the strongest predictor of attainment, drawing on a wide range of indicators such as home background, occupation, attitudes and aspirations. The writings of Bourdieu (Bourdieu and Passeron, 1977) have been particularly influential in identifying how class systems reproduce and maintain privilege. He has identified how families provide social, economic and cultural capital that ensures some children arrive within the education system already equipped to benefit from its systems of knowledge and attitudes, while for other children school can be an alien environment. The attitudes and values deriving from a family's class position are fundamental to the reproduction of education inequalities (Eden, 2017).

Governments of all political perspectives are concerned to address the link between educational attainment and socio-economic background, whether from a concern for social justice or society's ability to compete in the global marketplace. Political orientation affects judgements about specific policies, but all governments of the last thirty years have intervened actively in what goes on in classrooms, in the nature of the curriculum and in determining the structure of the education system. (See Chapter 1.) The twentieth-century political emphasis on structural inequalities of social class has moved during the twenty-first century to focus on the importance of parental responsibility, theorising a deficit model of the home learning environment for lower SES families. At the same time, since 2010 the Conservative government has been imposing a range of austerity policies intended to reduce the UK economic deficit but which have also added to the number of children in poverty in UK society, without acknowledging that poverty impacts on low SES pupils' attainment (Bradshaw and Keung, 2018).

The government collects a considerable amount of data on attainment and progress of students. A key measure of attainment identifies the gap between those eligible and not eligible for free school meals (FSM), using this as a proxy for social class. Children from lower socio-economic groups are behind on entry to early years settings, and the gap between the performances of children from the most and the least deprived backgrounds grows, rather than narrows, over the school years (Crawford et al., 2017). Children from better-off families who have low cognitive ability at age 2 have almost caught up with high-ability children from poorer families by age 5. The harmful effects of relative poverty on children's cognitive development derive from stress, lack of time for mental stimulation, the quality of the physical environment and a lack of access to the attitudes and experiences that equip pupils to do well within the education system. Parents from high SES groups possess the cultural capital that enables them to navigate the education system, knowing which subjects are needed to get into good universities, providing additional tuition, or buying privilege through access to independent schools (Sammons *et al.*, 2015). In one research report, 14 per cent of professional parents reported moving to an area with good schools, compared to just 4 per cent of the working-class group. Thirty-one per cent of parents from higher socio-economic backgrounds were also five times more likely to report their children had received private tuition compared to working-class parents (Montacute and Culliname, 2018a).

FSM eligibility, ethnicity and gender

The social class/SES/FSM gap is experienced by *all pupils*: children eligible for free school meals consistently perform less well than those who are not eligible across all age phases, gender and ethnicity. A similar pattern for *all pupils* is also found in relation to a gender gap. But when the data are broken down to reveal the intersectionality of socio-economic status with ethnicity and gender these patterns reveal considerable differentiation.

Culliname and Kirby (2016), researching GCSE results for pupils eligible for FSM, found that the academic attainment of disadvantaged pupils at 16 varies dramatically between different ethnic groups and in relation to gender. Some headline data illustrate this:

- Chinese pupils from disadvantaged homes are almost three times as likely as white working-class pupils to get five good GCSEs and have the smallest attainment gap for both genders.
- Bangladeshi, Indian, black African and Pakistani pupils from poorer homes all perform well above the national average for disadvantaged pupils.
- White working-class pupils achieve the lowest grades at GCSE of any main ethnic group, with just a quarter of boys and a third of girls achieving five good GCSEs.
- Working-class girls are the lowest-achieving group among girls, indicating that the concern over the low achievement of white working-class pupils should be as great for girls as for boys.
- When ethnic groups are ranked by the gap between FSM girls and FSM boys, the black Caribbean group shows the largest differential: 16.5 percentage points, in favour of girls, suggesting boys face particular challenges.
- If all pupils are considered, not just FSM, black pupils are the lowest performing major ethnic group.

(Culliname and Kirby, 2016)

Social and cultural capital specific to the Chinese groups may explain their attainment as their strong family and community networks with positive educational aspirations are a good fit with the UK education system. That black African pupils perform better than black Caribbean pupils may be linked to the aspirations associated with first-generation immigrants who have not experienced long-term racism.

Racism

Minority ethnic students experience significant everyday racism in and out of school, as illustrated by the disproportionate application of 'stop and search' police activity. Research found that when asked about 'unconscious bias' ethnic minorities were three times as likely to have been thrown out of, or denied entrance to, a restaurant, while 38 per cent of the black, Asian and minority ethnic (BAME) people said they had been wrongly suspected of shoplifting in the past five years, compared with 14 per cent of white people (Mohdin, 2019). Surveys are reporting an alarming increase in racial discrimination and abuse including amongst young people (Minhas, 2019). Marsh and Mohdin (2018) report a record number of children excluded for racist bullying. The number of such cases is rising at a faster rate than student population growth and could be seen as reflecting the government's 'hostile environment' policy towards immigrants.

Strand (2012) has argued that the low attainment and poor progress of black Caribbean students cannot be accounted for by social class, nor by a wide range of student, family, school or contextual variables, but may be explained by in-school factors such as teacher expectations, which will inevitably embody some of the prevailing racist discourse. There are subtle ways in which teacher behaviour and institutional racism can operate; black Caribbean students are the only ethnic group to be consistently under-represented relative to white students in entry to higher mathematics and science test tiers. Strand (2012) found a tendency for teachers to underestimate black Caribbean academic potential which may be distorted by perceptions of their behaviour as problematic, leading to low expectations.

Critical race theory (see Chapter 3) argues that the pattern of underachievement for minority ethnic groups is a consequence of white supremacy ideology and the primacy of racism. This approach sees the inequalities in educational attainment as actively structured by education policy and systems that emerge from the fundamental racism of UK society. This is often obscured by an emphasis on white working-class pupils which disguises the pervasiveness of racism. The educational attainment of ethnic groups and its intersection with class and gender can only be understood by recognising the 'everyday mundane actions and policies that shape the world in the interests of white people' and how these impact on minority ethnic pupils (Gillborn, 2008: 34).

The effect of such everyday racism is illustrated in a piece of research which shows how the power of cultural capital is undermined through the power of racism which limits black parents' ability to use their class cultural capital to the advantage of their children, as is the case for white pupils. Rollock *et al.* (2014) found that teachers' underlying attitudes and behaviour, rooted in racist models, interact with social class in a way that disadvantages black pupils. Teachers tended to have systematically lower academic expectations of black children, male and female, alongside a regime of heightened disciplinary scrutiny and criticism, regardless of students' social class background. Their conclusions illustrate how the cultural and social capital of those with high SES can be 'trumped' by racism, with the high aspirations of black parents thwarted by racist stereotyping and exclusion.

Gender and sexism

The gender attainment gap favours girls so it can easily be assumed that gender relations work to the advantage of girls within the education system. This assumption hides the reality of experiences and choices which are not advantageous to girls. Schools reflect traditional heteronormative gender stereotypes of male entitlement which lead to teachers having lower expectations of girls' academic success compared to boys, girls receiving less time from teachers than their male peers and teachers differentially rewarding boys' and girls' behaviour.

For both boys and girls traditional gender stereotypes have considerable bearing on subject choices. The Fawcett Society (2019) published a report which showed that seven in ten younger women (18–34) affected by stereotypes say their career choices were restricted. This is reflected in gendered A-level choices. In 2017, only 22 per cent of students starting physics degrees were women, while for computing the figure was 8 per cent, and for boys taking English literature the figure was 23 per cent (DfE, 2019a).

As with racism, gender relations in the school are located within the ideologies of sexuality and misogyny that characterise UK society. This affects not only subject choices but the behaviour necessary to secure approval from both peer groups and teachers. The way in which pupils act out their sexual identities will also be affected by their ethnicity and class. While men and boys also experience sexual violence, young women and girls at school are much more likely to be the targets of sexual harassment and sexual violence, much of it emotional, and are also overwhelmingly the target of sexual violence and harassment online. The Women and Equalities Committee (2016) found that children in both primary and secondary schools experience widespread sexual harassment and abuse. In many cases schools appeared to fail girls, who are effectively told to put up with this behaviour, in spite of surveys consistently reporting high levels of sexual harassment and sexual violence in schools:

- Fifty-nine per cent of girls and young women aged 13–21 said in 2014 that they had faced some form of sexual harassment at school or college in the past year.
- Nearly three-quarters (71 per cent) of all 16–18-year-olds (boys and girls) say they hear sexual name-calling with terms such as 'slut' or 'slag' used towards girls at school on a daily basis or a few times a week (WEC, 2016). BAME pupils are likely to be called names that reflect both sexism and racism.
- Groups such as lesbian, gay, bisexual, and transgender (LGBT) pupils are particularly vulnerable, with more than half of gay pupils experiencing verbal homophobic bullying, almost a quarter experiencing cyberbullying and one in six gay pupils experiencing physical abuse (Guasp, 2015).

Gender and class

Guasp (2012) has argued that, while the education system works to affirm positive white upper- and middle-class identities, there is rarely positive affirmation for the working classes, and that affects both males and females. She sees white working-class boys in particular showing the greatest sense of alienation and significantly less likely to continue onto an academic route post-16 than girls. White working-class girls also feared failure and their working-class culture and identity operated as a hindrance to academic achievement. This has particular implications for young working-class girls and women who are considering entering university. Research by Evans (2009) found this involves a process of cultural separation from their class backgrounds that can be extremely difficult. She argues that for working-class girls who access higher education (HE) there is an underlying persistence of class and gender attitudes and family ties, including responsibility for care work. This prevents them considering application to the most prestigious universities, unlike their middle-class peers.

University access and experience

A good illustration of how intersectionality exposes the complexity of educational attainment comes from looking at the patterns of access to, and experiences of, university. Discussions about the expansion of higher education over the last thirty years have largely focused on social class. Significant resources have been expended to try to close the gap in access to universities, but socio-economic differences in HE participation remain substantial. Pupils from the highest socio-economic quintile group are around 40 percentage points more likely to go to university than those in the lowest socio-economic quintile group. The gap in progression to university between independent and state schools has actually widened in recent years (DfE, 2018a).

It is not just access that highlights differential opportunities, but who goes to which university and who benefits most. Girls go to university in higher numbers than men and are around 8 percentage points more likely than boys to go to university at age 18 or 19. But they are over-represented in the new lower-status universities, and in some cases outnumber males by a ratio of three to one. Equally, students from disadvantaged backgrounds are not recruited by elite universities (Office for Students, 2018). Exploring who goes to high-status universities reveals the link between white men, private education, elite universities and high-status positions in the government and the establishment:

- Twenty-one per cent of higher education applications from independent schools in England are for Oxford or Cambridge, compared to 5 per cent from comprehensive schools and 4 per cent from sixth form colleges.
- Independent school pupils are seven times more likely to gain a place at Oxford or Cambridge compared to those in non-selective state schools, and over twice as likely to gain a place at the high-status Russell Group universities.
- While white students have the lowest rate of attendance at university of all ethnic groups, they have better rates of entering elite universities.
- Black African and Pakistani students show the largest differential between high university attendance and low enrolment in Russell Group universities (Montacute and Culliname, 2018b).

- Those from high SES backgrounds have a greater chance of making it into the top 5 per cent of high earners than those from low-income families, although women have roughly half the chance of being top earners compared with men (DfE, 2019b; Sullivan *et al.*, 2018).

The extent to which students benefit from university also varies with socio-economic status. Individuals from higher SES backgrounds are more likely to gain higher grades and complete their degrees. Differences in social and cultural capital such as resilience, motivation or independent study skills play a key role in explaining the socio-economic differences in drop-out, degree completion and degree class (Office for Students, 2018). Research has also shown that students from more disadvantaged social groups and minority ethnic groups are more likely to live at home, thus missing out on wider university activities that improve their networks and life skills. Only 13 per cent of the top social group live at home compared to 45 per cent for the bottom group, while British Pakistani and British Bangladeshi students are over six times more likely than white students to live at home and study locally (Donnelly and Gamsu, 2018).

The motivation to succeed found in minority ethnic groups has led to their participation in HE increasing more rapidly than for white pupils. Indian and Chinese pupils are, on average, more than twice as likely to go to university as their white British counterparts. Strikingly, Chinese pupils in the lowest SES category are 10 per cent more likely to go to university than white British pupils in the highest socio-economic group as well as having extremely high participation rates, with 66 per cent going to university (Crawford and Greaves, 2015). This is in spite of the fact that racism appears to be at work in the process of gaining access to elite universities. More than half of white students achieving three A★s at A-level and applying to Oxford in 2010 and 2011 were awarded a place, compared to one in three Chinese or Asian students, and less than one in four black applicants (Kelly, 2019).

There is also significant variation in degree outcome for students from different ethnic backgrounds, raising questions about how students actually experience and benefit from university. The Office for Students (2018) released figures which showed huge variations in achievement within English universities. They showed especially wide gaps in attainment for black students compared with other ethnicities. The Equality and Human Rights Commission (EHRC) is sufficiently concerned about racial harassment of minority ethnic students and staff to have set up an inquiry into the issue to report during 2019. Such experiences are likely to contribute to the fact that black students receive lower grades and are also more likely to drop out of university than their fellow students.

Policies and attainment gaps

The last thirty years have been littered with education policies claiming to raise standards and address poor attainment levels associated with low SES. The key ideological driver of these policies has been a belief that a quasi-market characterised by diversity, choice and competition, with parents as consumers, would lead to higher standards of attainment, benefiting all pupils and reducing the attainment gap for those eligible for FSM. This has led to a high degree of accountability and diversity and choice in school types, including academies controlled directly by the Secretary of State.

It appears, though, that the beneficiaries of this approach have been the middle class whose social and cultural capital has ensured access to the highest quality schooling and educational opportunities. While standards have risen overall, the attainment gap still demonstrates that pupils from poor economic backgrounds, particularly those considered to be more able, have lost out in the process. The competitive nature of the diversity and choice agenda has led school leaders to prioritise the interests of their school over the interests of particular groups of usually more vulnerable children in the attempt to recruit those students most likely to do well, given they are assessed on the basis of their exam results. This leads to a vicious circle where those schools judged outstanding admit fewer children eligible for free school meals, while schools judged 'requires improvement' and 'inadequate' see on average an increase in pupils with FSM eligibility (Greany and Higham, 2018).

The effect of economic and educational policies together has led to a situation where the inequalities between schools are becoming wider, as parents with high levels of social and cultural capital manage and manipulate access to the best educational provision, while at the same time economic policies are leading to an increase in child poverty. In the three years to 2016/17 the number of people living in poverty in working families rose by over one million (Joseph Rowntree Foundation, 2018) with families with children now living, on average, further below the poverty line than they did ten years ago (Bradshaw and Keung, 2018). The effects of poverty are also particularly experienced by those from black and minority ethnic backgrounds who are twice as likely to experience poverty as someone from a white background in the UK (Weekes–Bernard, 2018).

Research indicates the price of such policies:

- The National Education Union (NEU) and Child Poverty Action Group (2018) found that 97 per cent of respondents in maintained schools, academies, free schools and further education colleges reported that poverty was getting worse and affecting their students' learning.
- Asked to identify the effects of poverty on learning, three out of four respondents said they saw children suffering from fatigue (78 per cent), poor concentration (76 per cent) or poor behaviour (75 per cent); more than half said their students had experienced hunger (57 per cent) or ill health (50 per cent) as a result of poverty; and more than a third (35 per cent) said students had been bullied.
- A Sutton Trust (2019) report identified significant cuts in school staffing with 69 per cent of secondary senior leaders reporting having to make cuts to teaching staff for financial reasons, along with 70 per cent for teaching assistants and 72 per cent for support staff; 72 per cent of primary school heads also report cutting teacher assistant posts.
- Families in the most affluent areas are twice as likely to secure their child a place at their first choice of secondary school on appeal as those in the poorest, and children from some minority ethnic backgrounds were less likely to get into their preferred school using the system of appeals and waiting lists (Hunt, 2019).

- The aim that academies would ensure disadvantaged pupils performed above the mainstream average has not succeeded, with 38 of 58 academies having an average attainment below the mainstream, including eight which were well below average (Hutchings and Francis, 2018).
- There has been a marked increase in exclusions, which have particular consequences for those eligible for FSM and black Caribbean pupils who had a permanent exclusion rate nearly three times higher than the school population as a whole (DfE, 2018b).

Gorard (2018) has argued that funding should be directed to improving the experiences of disadvantaged children rather than to rewarding those schools which are in a position to deliver good examination results. What school tests and exam results reflect is pupil intake. New types of schools and competition do not address, but exacerbate, those factors. Government austerity policies since 2010 have also led to draconian cuts in a wide range of social services, leading to the loss of facilities, such as reductions in mental health facilities, loss of support for care leavers, loss of extra-curricular activities and reduced funding for applied FE provision, all of which are likely to have negative consequences for disadvantaged young people. In London alone, 100 youth centres have been shut, and since 2011 560 youth workers have lost their jobs (Berry, 2019; Culliname and Kirby, 2016).

Policies concerned with the FSM gap are aimed at SES disadvantaged pupils but do not address the disadvantages faced by female and minority ethnic groups. The evidence on subject choices points to the underlying sexism and racism that permeate schools and communities. The Equality Act (Government Equalities Office, 2010) offers some protection against racism and sexism, but whereas schools used to have a duty to monitor racist bullying, the Coalition government of 2010–15 removed this obligation. As the rhetoric of the government's hostile environment policy has legitimated a negative approach to migrants, it is not surprising that racist incidents have increased.

Conclusion

In this chapter we have looked at evidence that shows the complexity of social class, gender and ethnicity all differentially impacting on pupil experiences. Policies aiming to reduce the attainment gap have developed a competitive market-led model of education resulting in a wide diversity of school types. These policies, though, have been to the advantage of parents with higher SES who utilise their social and cultural capital to ensure their children secure access to the best educational opportunities, while the implementation of austerity policies has exacerbated poverty with its significant educational disadvantages. The prevailing racism and sexism of society negatively influence the experiences of women and minority ethnic groups and there needs to be a much higher level of 'zero tolerance' towards racist and sexist behaviour in schools. But dealing with increased racism and sexism in schools is not just a behaviour-management issue. The prevailing discourse in society presents migrants as a burden and a heteronormative, sexualised model of males and females as desirable. Neither can schools deal with the consequences of poverty for people from different class, gender and ethnic backgrounds.

The emphasis on failing schools needs to be re-directed to the failing structures and discriminatory attitudes of society and issues of community cohesion, while recognising the complexity and intersectionality of class, gender and ethnicity.

Summary points

- Experiences that contribute to pupil attainment are affected by class, gender and ethnicity and policies aimed at reducing the attainment gap need to take account of that intersectionality.
- Evidence shows that, in spite of rising standards, the FSM gap remains throughout pupils' educational careers.
- Racism and sexism are powerful influences on children's school experiences and the education system needs to directly confront these within both staff and student groups.
- The effect of poverty on attainment has been exacerbated by austerity policies in reducing resources within schools and increasing children living in poverty.
- Education policies cannot on their own counter the racism and sexism that permeate society, but schools should be required to enact zero-tolerance policies in these areas.

Questions for discussion

- How does social and cultural capital advantage some students within the education system?
- How do sexism and racism manifest themselves in the classroom and playground?
- Have diversity and choice of schools increased inequalities in attainment?

Recommended reading

Eden, C. (2017) *Gender, Education and Work: Inequalities and Intersectionality*, chapters 3, 4 and 5. Abingdon: Routledge.
EHRC (2016) *Healing a Divided Britain: The Need for a Comprehensive Race Equality Strategy*. London: EHRC.
Reay, D. (2014) *Written Evidence Submitted to House of Commons Education Committee, Underachievement of White Working-Class Children*. London: Education Committee.
Strand, S. (2010) Do Some Schools Narrow the Gap? Differential School Effectiveness by Ethnicity, Gender, Poverty and Prior Attainment. *School Effectiveness and School Improvement* **21**(3), pp. 289–314.

References

Berry, S. (2019) *London's Lost Youth Services*. London: City Hall.
Bourdieu, P. and Passeron, J.-C. (1977) *Reproduction in Education, Society, and Culture*. Beverly Hills: Sage.
Bradshaw, J. and Keung, A. (2018) *UK Child Poverty Gaps Still Increasing*. London: Child Poverty Action Group.

Crawford, C. and Greaves, E. (2015) *Socio-Economic, Ethnic and Gender Differences in HE Participation*. London: Department for Business Innovation and Skills.

Crawford, C., Macmillan, L. and Vignoles, A. (2017) When and Why Do Initially High-Achieving Poor Children Fall Behind? *Oxford Review of Education* **43**(1), pp. 88–108.

Culliname, C. and Kirby, P. (2016) *Class Differences: Ethnicity and Disadvantage*. London: Sutton Trust.

DfE (2018a) *Widening Participation in Higher Education, England, 2016/17 Age Cohort*. London: DfE.

DfE (2018b) *Permanent and Fixed Period Exclusions in England: 2016 to 2017*. London: DfE.

DfE (2019a) *National Tables: A Level and Other 16 to 18 Results 2017 to 2018* (revised). London: DfE.

DfE (2019b) *Graduate Labour Market Statistics: 2018*. London: DfE.

Donnelly, M. and Gamsu, S. (2018) *Home and Away*. London: Sutton Trust.

Eden, C. (2017) *Gender, Education and Work*. London: Routledge.

Evans, S. (2009) In a Different Place: Working-Class Girls and Higher Education. *Sociology* **43**, pp. 340–355.

Fawcett Society (2019) *Gender Stereotypes and Child Literature*. London: Fawcett Society.

Gillborn, D. (2008) *Racism and Education: Coincidence or Conspiracy?* Abingdon: Routledge.

Gorard, S. (2018) *Evidence of Equity and Effectiveness*. London: Policy Press.

Government Equalities Office (2010) *Equality Act*. London: Gov.UK.

Greany, T. and Higham, R. (2018) *Hierarchy, Markets and Networks: Analysing the 'Self-Improving School-Led System' Agenda in England and the Implications for Schools*. London: University College, Institute of Education.

Guasp, A. (2012) *The School Report: The Experiences of Gay Young People in Britain's Schools in 2012*. London: Stonewall.

Hunt, E. (2019) *Fair Access to Schools? The Impact of the Appeals and Waiting List System*. York: Joseph Rowntree Foundation.

Hutchings, M. and Francis, B. (2018) *Chain Effects: The Impact of Academy Chains on Low-Income Pupils*. London: Sutton Trust.

Joseph Rowntree Foundatiion (2018) *Budget 2018: Tackling the Rising Tide of in-Work Poverty*. York: Joseph Rowntree Foundation.

Kelly, A. (2019) A New Composite Measure of Ethnic Diversity. *British Educational Research Journal* **45**(1), pp. 41–82.

Marsh, S. and Mohdin, A. (2018) A Record Number of UK Children Excluded for Racist Bullying. *The Guardian*, 30 November 2018.

Minhas, P. (2019) *Racism Rising since Brexit Vote*. London: Opinium.

Mohdin, A. (2019) Racism in Britain: How We Revealed the Shocking Impact of Unconscious Bias. *The Guardian*, 26 January 2019.

Montacute, R. and Culliname, C. (2018a) *Parent Power: How Parents Use Financial and Cultural Resources to Boost Their Children's Chances of Success*. London: Sutton Trust.

Montacute, R. and Culliname, C. (2018b) *Access to Advantage: The Influence of Schools and Place on Admissions to Top Universities*. London: Sutton Trust.

NEU and Child Poverty Action Group (2018) *Child Poverty and Education*. London: NEU and CPAG.

Office for Students (2018) *How Do Student Outcomes Vary by Ethnicity?* London: OfS.

Rollock, N., Gillborn, D., Vincent, C. and Ball, S.J. (2014) *The Colour of Class: The Educational Strategies of the Black Middle Class*. Abingdon: Routledge.

Sammons, P., Toth, K. and Sylva, K. (2015) *Subject to Background: What Promotes Better Achievement for Bright But Disadvantaged Students?* London: Sutton Trust.

Strand, S. (2012) The White British–Black Caribbean Achievement Gap: Tests, Tiers and Teacher Expectations. *British Educational Research Journal* **38**(1), pp. 75–101.

Sullivan, A., Parsons, S., Greene, F., Wiggins, R.D. and Ploubidis, G. (2018) Elite Universities, Fields of Study and Top Salaries: Which Degree Will Make You Rich? *British Educational Research Journal* **44**(4), pp. 663–680.

Sutton Trust (2019) *School Funding and Pupil Premium 2019.* London: Sutton Trust.

Weekes–Bernard, D. (2018) *Integration Strategy Must Focus on Tackling Poverty for BME Families.* London: Sutton Trust.

Women and Equalities Committee (2016) *Sexual Harassment and Sexual Violence in Schools.* London: Women and Equalities Committee.

Chapter 7

The inclusion agenda

Is it practically possible in mainstream primary schools?

Zeta Brown and Jo Winwood

Introduction

This chapter focuses on the practical implementation of the inclusion agenda in mainstream primary schools in England. The chapter does not detail a complete historical account of the development of inclusion, which can be found in separate publications, including Brown (2016) and Williams-Brown and Hodkinson (2020). We focus on current practice and link to relevant historical developments that have influenced the way we practically implement inclusion today.

We begin by detailing the complexity in defining 'inclusion' and how historical changes have influenced the purpose of inclusion over time. In an attempt to explain what inclusion should mean in current practice, we consider the agenda in its broadest sense to mean the inclusion of all mainstream pupils (Brown, 2016). The chapter then outlines how inclusion works in practice, including leadership and management strategies. We detail a need to move away from traditional interpretations of leadership associated with specific posts and instead see leadership as the responsibility of every teacher, with practice transformed by shared ownership, a willingness to try different approaches and valuing diversity. Finally, the chapter details some of the additional barriers to implementing inclusion, including the dominance of the standards agenda. We conclude by critically considering whether inclusion is practically possible in mainstream primary schools.

Various terms have been used in the past; here we use 'children with Special Educational Needs and Disabilities' (SEND) as it is currently used in England to describe children with additional needs.

What is meant by the inclusion agenda?

The inclusion agenda was introduced in England by New Labour in 1997. The party showed a commitment to reform the way children with Special Educational Needs and Disabilities were educated and wanted to reflect the intent internationally to move away from integration and towards inclusion (Hodkinson, 2005). The United Nations *Standard Rules on the Equalization of Opportunities for Persons with Disabilities* (1993) had determined that children with SEND should be considered within all planning and curricular activities, with an assurance that appropriate additional support would be available (Rustemier, 2002). This meant moving away from integration and focusing on the placement of children with SEND into mainstream settings (Thomas and Vaughan, 2004). In 1994, representatives from 92 governments and 25 international organisations met in Salamanca, Spain to affirm a rights-based approach to education, determining that countries should 'concentrate their efforts on the development of inclusive schools' (UNESCO, 1994: 13). The Salamanca statement insisted on education for all children and from that moment onwards the inclusion agenda became part of government rhetoric (Hodkinson, 2011).

Individual/group task

We would advise at this point that you research in more detail the difference between the terms 'inclusion' and 'integration'. You are likely to find differing definitions of what is meant by 'inclusion'.

In England, the New Labour government emphasised a commitment to increasing equity and social justice by enhancing the quality of education for all within the schooling system. This ambition appeared in the White Paper *Excellence in Schools* (1997) which emphasised that the rights of children with SEND should be upheld, and that education should benefit all children in mainstream schools. In the same year, the Green Paper *Excellence for All Children: Meeting Special Educational Needs* (1997) marked a departure from the era of integration by focusing on the principles of inclusion. It included the provisions and support necessary for children with SEND to succeed (Sikes *et al.*, 2007). Inclusion emphasised that schools needed to 'accommodate' the needs of children with SEND and adapt educationally to meet their needs (Hodkinson and Vickerman, 2009).

However, at a theoretical level inclusion aimed to change societal and educational perceptions of disability by encouraging an acceptance of diversity. Avramidis *et al.* (2000: 192) suggest that 'the concept of inclusion becomes part of a broad human-rights agenda that argues that all forms of segregation are morally wrong'. In this context, Nutbrown and Clough (2006) argue that inclusion was, and is, a platform for social justice, dependent not only on structural changes in provision and support, but on educating schools and professionals on inclusive practice in relation to equality, diversity and the rights of all children.

Confusion in defining inclusion

However, despite the cogent argument that inclusion was educationally and socially desirable, the term in its practice application became 'subject to conceptual confusion and terminological ambiguity' (Hodkinson and Devarakonda, 2011: 54). It became a complex ideological construct that lacked clear definition. The question that came to dominate educational discourse during this time was 'what is this inclusion of which we speak?' (Hodkinson, 2011: 179). For instance, words such as 'whenever possible' and 'children should generally take part in' were used in inclusion legislation which suggested the government intended to pursue a 'twin-track system' of SEND where segregation of some children would continue.

New Labour's educational policy promoted inclusion as the teaching of disabled children and their peers in neighbouring schools, and set out targets for meeting the needs of children with SEND in England by 2002. However, inclusion legislation remained focused on the placement of children with SEND into mainstream schools and there was no strong stance on restructuring schools to ensure that every child, regardless of disability, was fully included.

The lack of one clear definition and the multiplicity of its manifestations led Nutbrown and Clough (2006) to consider inclusion as operational instead of conceptual. Historically, legislation focused on disability alongside separate legislation that promoted issues of advantages and marginalisation (Frederickson and Cline, 2002). It can be seen from the titles of the two 1997 government papers: *Excellence for All Children* (1997) and *Excellence for All Children: Meeting Special Educational Needs*. Policies that specifically focus on the education of children with SEND include the Green Paper *Support and Aspiration: A New Approach to Special Educational Needs and Disability* (2011) and the White Paper *Reform and Provision for Children and Young People with Special Educational Needs* (2012). Differing concepts of inclusion focus on acknowledging all children and disputing any form of marginalisation at the same time as continuing to consider children with SEND separately (Frederickson and Cline, 2002).

Individual/group task

Find a selection of definitions of inclusion in books published from 1997. Consider the differing ways inclusion is defined in these publications. In particular, really consider the terms used. Are they stating that inclusion is focused on children with SEND, possibly disadvantaged children or all children? Or are they advocating part or full inclusion in mainstream settings?

Inclusion for all mainstream pupils

The Index for Inclusion (Booth and Ainscow, 2004) viewed inclusion in its broadest sense to consider the needs of all mainstream pupils. This was a significant move away from focusing inclusion on the needs of children with SEND. Its definition focused on equality by highlighting the need to value all pupils by celebrating all children's achievements and viewing difference as a resource to support learning (Booth and Ainscow, 2004). This broad definition of inclusion includes SEND, age, gender, sexual orientation, race, ethnicity, culture and social class. Booth and Ainscow (2004: 118) stated:

> Some continue to want to make inclusion primarily about 'special needs education' or the inclusion in education of children and young people with impairments, but that position seems absurd. If inclusion is about the development of comprehensive

community education and about prioritising community over individualism beyond education, then the history of inclusion is the history of these struggles for an education system which serves the interests of communities and which does not exclude anyone within those communities.

This approach considers the social model of disability by acknowledging disability in the context of the barriers present in the education system. In doing so, it promotes the creation of a non-discriminatory environment in which differences are positively embraced. The *Index* seeks to include all children within the inclusion agenda. However, this development in definition again did not lead to any significant changes in practice in order to 'accommodate' the needs of all learners. It has been nineteen years since the publication of the *Index for Inclusion*, yet inclusion continues to be focused solely on children with SEND. This may be perpetuated by the specific tailored support and provision that focuses on the needs of children with SEND in mainstream settings and the current system. In order to meet the needs of children with SEND the government developed various separated systems, including the p-scale system attached to the national curriculum, a separate statementing process, and specialised resources, and appointed Special Educational Needs and Disabilities Co-ordinators (SENDCO). Brown (2016) found that when teachers in her study were asked about inclusion they automatically referred to these separated systems and the inclusion of children with SEND.

The role of SENDCO and inclusion

The existence of a Special Educational Needs and Disabilities Co-ordinator (SENDCO, also still referred to as SENCO) can be interpreted as supporting this ongoing focus on individual needs mentioned above, rather than how learning and teaching might be adapted to enable all pupils to learn and achieve within an inclusive environment. Adding to the complexities of the SENDCO role is that, within the education system, some settings have interpreted the role as co-ordinator and teacher, so that the SENDCO is the main teacher of pupils with additional needs. Although this is not universally true, the interpretation of the role as going beyond co-ordination to 'doing' has further supported the view of the SENDCO being responsible for children identified with SEND. This is in contrast to almost all other co-ordination roles, and does not reflect the main tasks outlined for the role within the *Code of Practice* (CoP) (DfE, 2015). Subject co-ordinators are likely to be responsible for the development of the subject area across the school, policy development, schemes of work and advising and supporting colleagues in order for the area (and provision generally) to develop and improve, but not all teaching and learning within their subject area. Having a co-ordinator post which is interpreted in the SEND teacher context sustains the deficit view of SEND and does little to support the development of inclusive practices for all children.

Previous versions of the CoP have also supported the notion of SENDCO being part of the senior leadership team, recognising that the role is equivalent in responsibility to that of core subject co-ordinators. But the 2015 version suggests only that the SENDCO is part of the Senior Leadership Team, stating

> The SENDCO has an important role to play with the headteacher and governing body in determining the strategic development of SEN policy and provision in the school. They will be most effective in that role if they are part of the school leadership team.
>
> (DfE, 2015: 108)

Despite this guidance, uncertainty about the focus of the role remains, and whilst the CoP outlines typical tasks, the role has been interpreted differently by each school (Hallett and Hallett, 2017). This can be seen as a benefit, allowing each setting to develop the role to reflect the needs of their school, but Winwood's (2016) research suggests that the vague definitions can mean that the role becomes all-encompassing with class teachers, passing ownership of the needs of the pupil from themselves to the SENDCO, as soon as any SEND has been identified. These insights reflect the views outlined by Dyson in 1990 before the role was formalised in the first code. Dyson (1990: 117) suggested that the role should be an 'Effective Learning Co-ordinator (ELC)' who would focus on the develop-ment of effective learning and teaching for all pupils, moving away from deficit notions of SEND, and enabling all pupils to actively participate in the learning opportunities within class. Other authors have explored how the role might be reconceptualised so that it moves from SEND and instead supports inclusion across the setting. Winwood (2016) suggested the role might become that of a 'knowledgeable guide' with the SENDCO being part of the leadership team with responsibility for developing staff knowledge and confidence when working with diverse needs, and developing pedagogical practices for all pupils. Ekins (2015: 60) proposed a role of 'facilitator; enabler; supporter', again stressing the whole-school aspect of the role, working with staff, rather than one person doing all SEND-related tasks. All of these suggestions recognise that SENDCOs are trying to support inclusion, despite having to work alongside other, sometimes contradictory, legis-lation such as the standards agenda (see below). However, broad interpretations are making the role very challenging to manage and execute in a meaningful way which supports inclusive ideals and practices. One way to move forward would be to strengthen the lead-ership element by using the knowledge SENDCOs have about learning and teaching to support professional development for all learners, which has the potential to increase inclusion and achievement.

Individual/group task

Can schools be fully inclusive for all children and young people? Which children are harder to include and why? Is there a role for alternative provisions alongside main-stream settings within an inclusive education system?

Inclusion: all can achieve?

There is a significant difference between embracing the differences of all learners and including all mainstream learners in an existing education system. One can conclude that inclusion has become locked into focusing on children with SEND because of the priority placed by schools on standards. The standards agenda has dominated educational discourse since the 1980s. It was developed by the Conservative government to instil achievement and accountability in schools (see Chapter 1). The entire education system was moved to a neoliberal marketised basis. Teacher autonomy was reduced and they were depicted as not responding to the needs of parents and children. With the 1988 Education Reform Act the government took over centralised control of many aspects of education, including the curriculum. Standards agenda policies were responsible for the development of the national curriculum, Statutory Assessment Tests (SATs), league tables and Ofsted inspections to ensure that teachers and schools were accountable for their actions. The publication of SATs results in league tables prioritised high-stakes assessment for schools and were used to judge school and teacher success.

Bines (2000) described the limitations of inclusion as being determined by the dominance of the standards agenda. From the beginning of inclusion, emphasis was placed on all children achieving. For instance, inclusion in *Meeting Special Educational Needs: A Programme for Action* meant:

> The participation of all pupils in the curriculum and social life of mainstream schools; the participation of all pupils in learning which leads to the highest possible level of achievement; and the participation of young people in the full range of social experiences and opportunities once they have left school.
>
> (DfEE, 1998: 23)

This definition focused inclusion on the involvement of all pupils in all aspects of the existing education system, including standards agenda objectives. Emphasis was placed on standards being equally important for children with SEND as for their peers. The identification of SEND was seen as integral to reduce educational underachievement. Key principles included the need for early intervention, effective support in the classroom and a commitment to reducing the need for statementing. For children with SEND who did not need a statement (now referred to as an 'Education, Health and Care Plan') this meant that the classroom should change to support the needs of the child, rather than the child needing additional support to fit the existing system. However, the standards agenda did not change with the development of inclusion; in fact, it became more prescriptive over time. Children with SEND, regardless of need, have been considered in the same context as their peers in relation to existing standards objectives, such as the national curriculum and the SAT process which was designed for pupils who can achieve the national average (Bines, 2000). This meant a need for all children to conform within narrow parameters of success (Armstrong, 2005). As a consequence, children with SEND were discussed in relation to improving standards alongside their peers, whilst also having specialised additional provisions in order to be 'included' in mainstream schooling without any negative impact on standards. In effect, this represented a distinctive pedagogy wherein the same teaching and standards were to be considered effective for all children. Gamarnikow and Green (2003: 209) said 'there are, of course, winners and losers … [promoting] belief in the myth, or at least acquiescence to the rhetoric, of excellence for all – everyone's a winner'.

One of the significant difficulties in benchmarking inclusion against the standards agenda objectives is that children who cannot meet these standards can often end up excluded either inside or outside mainstream schooling. Glazzard (2013: 184) states:

> Contemporary discourses of inclusion serve a disciplinary function, rather than promoting equity … and those who threaten the status quo are isolated and contained in special units. Children with behavioural, social and emotional issues are segregated and contained in Pupil Referral Units and consequently marginalised. They are labelled as deviants without any critical interrogation of the 'within schools' factors (inappropriate curriculum or assessment processes that label them as failures) or external factors (inappropriate parenting or lack of cultural capital) that may have contributed to their 'undesirable' behaviours. Other children with special needs are subjected to additional intervention, which further reinforces a sense of failure and highlights their differences …

Barriers to implementing inclusion

Individual/group task

List three barriers that you think may be present in practically implementing the inclusion agenda?

It is impossible to consider the practical implementation of the inclusion agenda without acknowledging the barriers presented by the standards agenda. Brown (2016) investigated teachers' positions on the inclusion and standards agendas and whether they could be implemented simultaneously. Her study included the views of twenty-six teachers from six mainstream primary schools. She found that many of the teachers discussed the standards agenda as a significant barrier to the practical implementation of inclusion. For some of these teachers the implementation of standards completely consumed their practice and meeting their roles in both agendas. Overall, these teachers discussed practical barriers that related to the government's lack of focus on inclusion. Five barriers were identified: funding, support from the local education authority, training, resources and time.

The inclusion and standards agendas have been introduced and regulated in very different ways. Standards agenda objectives were designed with specific instruction for day-to-day classroom implementation and are of great importance for the measurement of both teacher and school success. When the agenda was introduced it completely overhauled the education system, placing significant importance on accountability and achievement and permanently changing schools into a marketable commodity. While the inclusion agenda is thwarted by inconsistencies in definition, purpose and direction, it does provide an ideological plan for the future of education, without clearly stating how it should be practically implemented in current practice. Crucially, the education system did not change when inclusion was introduced in England. Instead, add-on or separate systems were put in place to support children with SEND and there were attempts to limit underachievement in the existing standards-driven system. This led to inclusion remaining focused on children with SEND rather than the broader concept of inclusion being about the education of all children. It also locates the barriers of not fully implementing inclusion within the child, rather than considering the barriers children face in mainstream schools. Justifications are made for children with SEND who cannot participate in standards objectives, or who will not meet the national average, based on the child's needs. It seems fundamentally impossible for inclusion to be 'fully' practically possible in the existing standards-driven system. Winter (2006: 553) argues for:

> … the radical reconceptualisation and reconstitution of schooling to embrace all students through the recognition, legitimisation and celebration of difference, be it 'disability', race, gender, class, sexuality, bilingualism, ethnicity, geographic position … It is the schooling that is understood to be problematical, defective and dysfunctional; it is the school curriculum, pedagogy and assessment that require radical change, rather than students.

The standards agenda would need to change to acknowledge the needs and achievements of all mainstream pupils. In doing so, the assessment process and terms such as *success* and *achievement* would need to be redesigned and redefined to fully consider the educational development of all learners (Lloyd, 2008).

Moving forward: SENDCO or INC-CO?

Transforming the SENDCO role from manager to leader has the potential to impact positively on both the role and the development of inclusion. Inclusion is often seen as an ongoing journey because pupils are individuals and, whilst staff can develop different pedagogic responses, a flexible approach to learning and a willingness to try different things are essential when aiming for inclusion. Winwood's research (2016) recognised that teachers are often very supportive of the principles of inclusion but struggle with how to translate the theory into practical responses in the classroom. Some of the most effective schools have been creative in the way they understand support and how it is utilised to enable students to learn and achieve. This notion of quality teaching for all pupils can be seen in current policy guidance, but at the same time there are debates about the need for specialised teachers and pedagogies for pupils with SEND, such as a specific SEND-specialist teacher training route. However, rather than maintaining this deficit approach to SEND, many authors, including Jordan, Schwartz and McGhie-Richmond (2009), suggest that effective teachers are also inclusive, and it is the teachers' attitudes and beliefs about inclusion which impact on whether they create inclusive environments for the pupils they work with. From this perspective, the SENDCO role could be redefined as Inclusion Co-ordinator (INC-CO), focusing on pedagogy and supporting professional learning with colleagues. This would encourage professional dialogue and reflection about what inclusion means and how to move forward within the context of the setting. From this starting point, inclusion and attainment can be positively influenced while teaching staff are supported in being learners about their own practice.

Conclusion

This chapter has focused on the practical implementation of the inclusion agenda in mainstream primary schools in England. It has detailed the complex barriers we experience in practice in defining and practically implementing the inclusion agenda. The chapter also highlights what we believe could be done to improve current practice and to focus more on the inclusion agenda. Inclusion should be considered in its broadest sense to mean the inclusion of all mainstream pupils; the practical implementation of inclusion should be the responsibility of all teachers; and importantly, inclusion can only be practically possible if it is given the same significance and attention as the standards agenda.

Summary

- The concept of inclusion is part of a broad human rights agenda.
- Inclusion should be focused on its broadest definition in considering the inclusion of all mainstream pupils.
- Inclusion has become locked into focusing on children with SEND because of the significance placed on standards objectives.
- There are significant barriers to practically implementing inclusion due to the importance placed on the standards agenda.
- Inclusion can only be practically possible if it is given the same significance and attention as the standards agenda.
- Schools need to reflect on the development of inclusion and the SENDCO role can offer practical support in enabling inclusion to become a reality for learners in mainstream classrooms.

Recommended reading

Booth, T. and Ainscow, M. (2004) *Index for Inclusion: Developing Learning and Participation in Schools*. Bristol: Centre for Studies on Inclusive Education.
Brown, Z. (2016) *Inclusive Education: Perspectives on Pedagogy, Policy and Practice*. Abingdon: Routledge.
Hodkinson, A. (2012) Inclusion 'All Present and Correct?' A Critical Analysis of New Labour's Inclusive Education Policy in England. *Journal of Critical Education Policy Studies* **11**(4), pp. 242–262.
Hodkinson, A. and Vickerman, P. (2009) *Key Issues in Special Educational Needs and Inclusion*. London: Sage.

References

Armstrong, D. (2005) Reinventing 'Inclusion': New Labour and the Cultural Politics of Special Education. *Oxford Review of Education* **31**(1), pp. 135–151.

Avramidis, E., Bayliss, P. and Burden, R. (2000) A Survey into Mainstream Teachers' Attitudes towards the Inclusion of Children with Special Educational Needs in the Ordinary School in One Local Education Authority. *Educational Psychology* **20**(2), pp. 191–211.

Bines, H. (2000) Inclusive Standards? Current Developments in Policy for Special Educational Needs in England and Wales. *Oxford Review of Education* **26**(1), pp. 21–33.

Booth, T. and Ainscow, M. (2004) *Index for Inclusion: Developing Learning and Participation in Schools*. Bristol: Centre for Studies on Inclusive Education.

Brown, Z. (2016) Primary Teachers' Perspectives on Implementing the Inclusion Agenda. In Z. Brown (Ed.), *Inclusive Education: Perspectives on Pedagogy, Policy and Practice*. Abingdon: Routledge.

DfE (2015) *Special Educational Needs and Disability Code of Practice: 0–25 Years*. London: DfE.

DfEE (1998) *Meeting Special Educational Needs: A Programme for Action*. London: DfEE.

Dyson, A. (1990) Effective Learning Consultant: A Future Role for Special Needs Co-ordinators. *Support for Learning* **5**(3), pp. 116–127.

Ekins, A. (2015) *The Changing Face of Special Educational Needs* (2nd edn). Abingdon: Routledge.

Frederickson, N. and Cline, T. (2002) *Special Educational Needs, Inclusion and Diversity: A Textbook*. Buckingham: Open University Press.

Gamarnikow, E. and Green, A. (2003) Social Justice, Identity Formation and Social Capital. In C. Vincent (Ed.), *Social Justice, Education and Identity*. London: RoutledgeFalmer.

Glazzard, J. (2013) A Critical Interrogation of the Contemporary Discourses Associated with Inclusive Education in England. *Journal of Research in Special Educational Needs* **13**(3), pp. 182–188.

Hallett, G. and Hallett, F. (2017) *Transforming the Role of the SENCO* (2nd edn). Maidenhead: Open University Press.

Hodkinson, A. (2005) Conceptions and Misconceptions of Inclusive Education: A Critical Examination of Final Year Teacher Trainees' Knowledge and Understanding of Inclusion. *Research in Educatio,* **73**(1), pp. 15–29.

Hodkinson, A. (2011) Inclusion: A Defining Definition? *Power and Education* **3**(2), pp. 179–185.

Hodkinson, A. and Devarakonda, C. (2011) Conceptions of Inclusion and Inclusive Education: A Critical Examination of the Perspectives and Practices of Teachers in England. *Educationalfutures* **3**(1), pp. 52–58.

Hodkinson, A. and Vickerman, P. (2009) *Key Issues in Special Educational Needs and Inclusion*. London: Sage.

Jordan, A., Schwartz, E. and McGhie-Richmond, D. (2009) Preparing Teachers for Inclusive Classrooms. *Teaching and Teacher Education* **25**(4), pp. 535–549.

Lloyd, C. (2008) Removing Barriers to Achievement: A Strategy for Inclusion or Exclusion? International Journal of Inclusive Education **12**(2), pp. 221–236.

Nutbrown, C. and Clough, P. (2006) *Inclusion in the Early Years*. London: Sage.

Rustemier, S. (2002) *Social and Educational Justice: The Human Rights Framework for Inclusion*. Bristol: Centre for Studies on Inclusive Education.

Sikes, P., Lawson, H. and Parker, M. (2007) Voices on: Teachers and Teaching Assistants Talk about Inclusion. *International Journal of Inclusive Education* **11**(3), pp. 355–370.

Thomas, G. and Vaughan, M. (2004) *Inclusive Education: Readings and Reflections*. Maidenhead: Open University Press.

UNESCO (1994). *The Salamanca Statement and Framework for Action*. Madrid: UNESCO/Ministry of Education and Science.

Winter, E. (2006) Preparing New Teachers for Inclusive Schools and Classrooms. *Support for Learning* **21**(2), pp. 85–91.

Williams-Brown, Z. and Hodkinson, A. (2020) Development of Inclusive Education in England: Impact on Children with Special Educational Needs and Disabilities. In Papa, R. (Ed.) *Handbook on Promoting Social Justice in Education*. New York: Springer.

Winwood, J. (2016) *Leading and Managing for Inclusion*. In Z. Brown (Ed.), *Inclusive Education*. Abingdon: Routledge.

Global and environmental education

Chapter 8

Exploring international and comparative education

Brendan Bartram

Introduction

This chapter offers an introduction to an area of educational studies often described as 'international and comparative education'. This field of study rests on a long tradition, and the chapter begins by sketching its early origins and examining the ways the discipline has evolved. It moves on to a discussion of its various aims and purposes and considers the reasons why educational comparisons have become of growing global interest. Finally, the chapter looks at a number of important considerations that sometimes call into question the validity of educational comparisons and what they are claimed to show.

What is international and comparative education?

Students of education employ a range of lenses through which to view and understand what education is, means and how it operates. Concepts and analytical tools are often employed from the disciplines of sociology, psychology, history or political science in an attempt to explain educational processes, trends and developments. In a sense, international and comparative education is just an additional lens that can be adopted to sharpen our insights into the nature of schools and schooling. However, given its ability to add contours and textures to the educational landscapes under investigation by bringing together theoretical perspectives in contrasting contexts, international and comparative education is an important field of enquiry in its own right.

Its origins are often linked to a number of nineteenth-century figures such as the Frenchman Victor Cousin, the German Friedrich Thiersch, Mathew Arnold in England and Horace Mann in the USA. These educationists have been described as being 'motivated by a desire to gain useful lessons from abroad' (Noah and Eckstein, 1969: 15), a motivation which led to them being among the first to produce studies examining and comparing aspects of education in other countries. Many of their reports were influential in the authors' home countries – Mathew Arnold (1822–1888), for example, a renowned educational inspector in his day, paid numerous visits to schools across continental Europe as part of a fact-finding mission for the Newcastle Commission (1861) and the Taunton Commission (1868), whose findings had a particular steer on elementary and secondary school reforms in England. Such early political interest in overseas education systems has continued and indeed expanded ever since, with growing numbers of academics, universities and international organisations around the world promoting the development of the discipline.

As a result of this growth, international and comparative education is now a wide-ranging, multidisciplinary field, accommodating many different areas of interest and types of investigation. Trying to categorise the range of studies that fall under this broad umbrella term is not an easy task, though many scholars offer us their views. Alexander (2014) provides a useful categorisation of different types of study within the field. Under type one, he refers to the growing number of large-scale surveys and studies that have come to characterise much of the work done in the field. Examples include many of the projects carried out by the Organisation for Economic Cooperation and Development (OECD), such as the Trends in International Mathematics and Science Study (TIMSS) and the Programme for International Student Assessment (PISA) surveys. Burghes (2018) offers an interesting discussion and analysis of such studies in Bartram (2018).

With regard to the second type of studies, Alexander (2014) refers to reports which often draw on data derived from the kinds of enquiries mentioned above under type one, but use the data collected as a basis for advocating particular policies and approaches that are regarded as central elements in whatever the data are claimed to show – usually high levels of student performance in particular subjects. This kind of policy advocacy is often regarded with a degree of scepticism by educationists, though politicians frequently exercise less caution (as discussed below). Reasons for widespread educational scepticism are discussed in the chapters by Burghes and Field in Bartram (2018), but in essence relate to the ways in which some of these reports claim a causative connection between educational practices and outcomes – often the success of particular policies relies on complex amalgams of social and cultural factors alongside educational approaches that cannot always be easily transferred and replicated. Phillips and Ochs (2004) offer an interesting analysis of the processes of policy borrowing, and the merits and demerits of the research approaches made use of.

The third and final type of studies described by Alexander (2014) concerns the very broad array of academic articles published around the world based on an almost endless number of educational themes, from the organisation and development of school curricula, to contrasting approaches to adult/vocational education, funding and management mechanisms, and myriad aspects of teaching, learning and assessment at different system levels. My own work is a good illustration of this third type, and reflects an equally broad-ranging set of topics, from the construction of learner attitudes to modern foreign language learning in England and Holland, to the factors that motivate students to enrol at university in Germany and Portugal (Bartram, 2012, 2016).

Activity

In groups, select two education systems and use the following as an analytical frame-work for comparing them. Eurydice has an excellent database of all European education systems – go to www.eurydice.org and click on the Eurybase link.

- social and political contexts
- underlying educational ideologies
- broad goals
- overall system structure
- curriculum content
- teaching and learning principles
- main assessment approaches
- current educational developments

The aims of international and comparative education

There are a number of purposes behind educational comparison, and once again, many scholars have set about the task of defining explicitly the nature of these purposes. One rationale, as Phillips describes it, is that 'comparing is a fundamental part of the thought processes which enable us to make sense of the world' (1999: 15). Alexander (1999: 27) has argued that 'comparison is actually essential to educational progress … education by its nature requires hard choices of both a technical and moral kind. To make such choices requires an awareness of options and alternatives, together with the capacity to judge what is most fitting.' These ideas reflect two elements that are fundamental to the discipline – the ideas of extending educational understanding and making improvements. The interest in educational improvement has grown significantly over the past thirty years or so, though a concern simply to develop our understanding and knowledge through comparison was arguably the key motive for much of the discipline's history. Lauwerys and Tayar (1973: xii) highlight this central aim:

> Comparative education is not, in essence, normative: it does not prescribe rules for the good conduct of schools and teaching. It does not aim at laying down what should be done. It does not offer views as to what education ought to be like. It attempts only to understand what is being done and why.

Marshall (2014) provides a useful synopsis of additional reasons for educational comparison:

- to learn about our own education system and that of others;
- to enhance our knowledge of education in general;
- to improve educational institutions; their content, processes and methods;
- to understand the relationship between education and society;
- to promote international understanding;
- to find possible solutions to educational issues.

Understanding the ways in which the nature of different societies affects education systems is an ongoing interest for comparativists, though the challenge it presents is not a simple one. Cowen (2005: 179) nicely articulates the complexities involved in this task:

> How do societies relate to (that is, affect, shape, influence, frame, penetrate or determine) educational systems and their components, such as teacher education provision, types of schools, administrative structures, universities, examination systems and so on? The problem is a tricky one because clearly, history, economics, social stratification patterns, politics and religious belief systems are all potentially forces that define the 'nature' of societies, and in ways that are not crystal clear, extend into the institutional patterns of educational systems … and curriculum practices.

For many years, the notion of educational ideologies has been helpful to comparativists. Though the idea of ideology may have fallen out of favour in some quarters in more recent times as a result of competing post-modern perspectives, they offer us a set of analytical tools for trying to account for the ways in which society influences education. Based on the idea that a particular society may be based on a broadly shared set of beliefs and values (i.e. an ideology) we can then look to see how such values have infused and informed educational developments in that country. Since ancient Greek times, scholars have sought to investigate these ideological linkages. More recently, though still some fifty years ago, Brubacher (1966) outlined the influence of twelve different educational ideologies (from sophism to pragmatism), while Holmes and McLean (1989) refer to a more restricted set of ideologies in order to explore how predominant beliefs in certain parts of the world have influenced educational developments. They compare the overarching ideologies of essentialism, encyclopaedism and pragmatism. Essentialism is described as a non-utilitarian, elitist view of education which sees clear divisions and levels of status between vocational and academic education – and indeed, who these should be geared towards. They link this way of thinking to the classical humanist ideology and discuss the notions of morality, specialisation and individuality which they argue to have been key influences on education in England.

This is contrasted with encyclopaedism, an ideology regarded as especially influential in many continental European countries. Holmes and McLean argue that this ideology is 'based on the premise that the content of education should include all human knowledge' (1989: 11), and that this view gained strong traction in post-revolutionary France, where the principles of rationality, universality and utility that are fundamental to the encyclopaedic perspective were adopted because of democratic desires to equalise society.

Pragmatism, a different ideology altogether, is attributed to the American educationalist John Dewey. These authors describe a more naturalistic vision of education that focuses strongly on the needs of the learner, social development and the relationship between the individual and society. The distinction between education and training that is so marked within the essentialist perspective above is viewed as an artificial and potentially damaging division from this ideological standpoint.

Activity

Search the internet for information on classical humanism, encyclopaedism and prag-matism/naturalism. Birgit Pepin's article 'Curriculum, Cultural Traditions and Pedagogy' is a useful starting point, and is available at: www.leeds.ac.uk/educol.documents/000000872.htm. When you have made notes, consider the following questions:

- How do the ideologies described above influence educational practices in countries you are familiar with? Think about possible linkages between ideologies and the structure of education systems, the nature and content of the curriculum, the rela-tionship between academic and vocational education, approaches to teaching and learning, pupil organisation (mixed ability and setting, streaming, differentiation).
- Research and discuss some of the key differences between education systems that have been strongly influenced by encyclopaedic traditions (e.g. the French and Japanese systems).
- Do you feel ideologies are a useful/adequate tool for explaining cultural differences and priorities in education? In what ways might we critique the use of ideologies as a set of explanatory strategies? List three potential criticisms.

As we can see from Marshall's (2014) list above, one of the main aims of the field is the search for improvements with regard to educational policy and practice. Though this is not always as easy as some may think, learning from elsewhere is clearly an important aim. In one way, looking at other education systems helps us to maintain an open mind by shining a light on alternative ways of doing things. This sometimes leads to a re-assessment of current practices which can provide a useful platform for considering reforms. Phillips (2000), for example, shows us how UK interest in the German system was partly respon-sible for various changes and reforms here, from the foundation of a national system in the nineteenth century, to the ways in which German curricular approaches were utilised to inform discussions that led to the Education Reform Act in 1988.

Growing appetites for educational comparison

Clearly, interests in educational comparisons are far from a recent phenomenon, though these interests have certainly grown over the last thirty years or more. Part of the reason for this has to do with the way in which access to other education systems has changed. The expansion of exchange programmes means that school pupils, university students and staff have first-hand, direct experience of other systems. Bartram (2009) discusses how other developments in travel, media, the advent of the internet, and changes in geo-political relations have added to these impetuses to look beyond borders in all spheres of life, including education. At the same time, demands for transparency and comparability of qualifications by an increasingly mobile 'global' workforce have created further interest in education in other countries. Arguably the most significant reason for this growth in interest, however, is political, as national governments have become increasingly interested in the relationship between education and economic competition and cost-effectiveness since the birth of the knowledge economy (see Budd, 2018). Such sentiments are clearly evident in UK government thinking: 'What really matters is how we're doing compared with our international competitors. That is what will define our economic growth and our country's future' (DfE, 2010: 3).

This politically driven interest has 'for the wider general public its most visible mani-festation in ... the shape of cross-national studies of educational achievement, and the widespread influence of related league tables' (Crossley, 2006: 7). The ubiquity of such international rankings has both promoted appetites for comparison and heightened pol-itical sensitivities, in that political reactions to a perception of poor performance have prompted educational reforms in many countries (e.g. in Germany and Denmark after the 2001 PISA results were published – see Morris, 2012). League tables can of course be informative, but they require careful interpretation and scrutiny.

Activity

Search the internet to see what you can find out about the OECD-led PISA (Programme for International Student Assessment) study and the TIMSS (Trends in International Mathematics and Science Study). Discuss the following issues:

- Which countries appear to perform particularly well?
- What reasons (social and educational) *might* be responsible for such performance?
- How might it be wrong to value an education system on the basis of its ranking?

Challenges and problems

Clearly, then, educational comparisons have much to offer us, but careful interpretation is paramount, as is an understanding of the contextual factors within which an educa-tion system operates. A major question in this respect concerns the extent to which the comparison is valid. The need to compare like with like is one of the central tenets of the discipline (Grant, 1999: 132), and yet it is not always adhered to, or differences might not always be sufficiently recognised. A good example relates to the word 'private' as used in education. In English, the use of this word is very different from how it is used in the Netherlands, where it refers to *state-funded schools that develop their own curricula* based on particular religious or philosophical principles. In the 1980s, the then Prime Minister, Margaret Thatcher, frequently referred to the popularity of Dutch 'private' schools (about 75 per cent of Dutch schools) to support her argument for expanding private provi-sion in England, without acknowledging this very important conceptual distinction. This example illustrates the need for careful consideration of background detail relating to the issues and countries being compared.

Morris (2012) has been particularly critical of the ways in which politicians make selective use of information, often choosing particular elements that they can draw on to substantiate their own policy preferences. He gives the example of the ways in which the UK government, keen on overhauling the teacher training system at home, attributed Finland's success in PISA rankings to that country's highly rigorous and selective teacher recruitment policy. Japan, however, with different national priorities focused more on moving away from traditional teaching methods, cited Finland's strong commitment to progressive teaching methods.

Notwithstanding political selectivity, there are many other reasons for exercising caution when interpreting and making comparisons. Important demographic differences may also call into question the validity of comparison. Countries like Japan and South Korea, for example, are often praised for their performance in literacy league tables. It should be remembered, however, that both these countries have largely indigenous populations, and consequently, the majority of pupils speak Japanese and Korean as their first language. This is very different from the situation in many European countries whose education systems have in recent years accommodated large numbers of migrant pupils who are often – at least initially – less proficient in the language in which they are assessed at school. Once again, ignoring this important contextual difference when judging comparative surveys of literacy would be highly questionable, as would any claims that might be made on this basis about superior teaching methods in the Far East.

Even when such differences have been allowed for, Bartram (2009) argues that further scrutiny may still be called for. Continuing the literacy theme, many international league tables during Tony Blair's time as Prime Minister saw England and Wales performing well – no doubt to some extent as a result of New Labour's key focus on literacy at that time (Alexander, 2001). In one respect, this is unsurprising given the priority of literacy development as a national educational aim. However, not all education systems focus on the same priorities. Murray Thomas (1990) illustrates how very different goals may be identified in different countries – some nations may focus on the development of self-fulfilment, vocational skills, social cohesion and identity formation in the wake of political unrest and upheaval, etc. Comparisons can therefore sometimes simply reflect differences in government priorities and goals, and it is vital therefore that they be judged accordingly.

Uncritical transfer

Many of the above examples illustrate problems concerning validity, fairness and bias in educational comparisons. These problems can become potentially dangerous if politicians use selective or partial information as a basis for policy reforms in the interests of 'quick-fix solutions or short-term political advantage' (Bartram, 2009: 30). Crossley and Watson (2003: 39) talk about the dangers of 'cherry-picking' practices deemed 'successful' in one country and recommending their adoption in another, as 'education … cannot be de-contextualised from its local culture'. Even though 'common problems may exist in different countries … solutions can rarely be found in the application of a common model across different cultures' (ibid.: 39). In this regard, Alexander (2001:41) was particularly critical of the Labour government's National Literacy Strategy that was introduced in the late 1990s in England, based on limited observations of practice elsewhere:

> … since the most striking pedagogical contrast was the much heavier use of whole-class teaching in the classrooms of the Pacific Rim and Continental Europe, it was assumed that a shift to this method in English primary schools would make the desired difference, reverse years of national decline and simultaneously propel Britain up the league tables.

For him, the implementation of this policy was founded on the rather simplistic assumption that high levels of literacy in these countries related to this form of pedagogy. His criticism focused in particular on the idea that such an assumption 'enables governments to legitimate their claim that questions of quality in education can be resolved by attaching pedagogy while ignoring structure and resources' (ibid.: 30).

Though there were certainly fierce advocates of the policy then and now, Alexander's point about attempting to fix a complex issue by focusing on one practice adopted from abroad remains a valid one, and many have contended that the strategy still works better in the Far East, where didactic forms of pedagogy still tend to dominate, as do larger class sizes and strong disciplinarian approaches. Furthermore, we should not forget that the educational experience of many children in the Far East is routinely supplemented by the widespread use of crammer schools in the evenings (see Chan et al., 2018 for a thorough discussion of this form of education often referred to as 'shadow education'). This practice, often regarded with some suspicion in the West because of the huge pressures it places on children, nevertheless has an impact on young people's learning, and partly explains the relatively higher performance of many Pacific Rim countries.

Many commentators (Auld and Morris, 2014; Bartram, 2018) are in fact highly critical of this form of opportunistic borrowing, selective contextual scrutiny and 'uncritical international transfer' (Crossley, 2006: 11), driven by political motives. As Robinson (1999: 223) makes plain, 'there is effectively no correlation between doing well in international tests … and overall economic performance'. And yet for all that, national governments appear to disregard the caution that many scholars have demonstrated is needed when interpreting complex comparative data. The work of Prais (2003) is regarded as seminal in offering a sophisticated analysis of the vagaries of international rankings, discussing some of the bias and sampling issues that raise significant questions about the results of the 2001 PISA survey. England's performance appeared relatively strong in this survey as far as mathematics was concerned, and yet a survey conducted by the Institute of Economic Affairs (IEA) only one year previously revealed a very different picture. Burghes (2018) offers some good examples of the ways in which issues of cultural bias can be especially important in such surveys, with suggestions that familiarity with test formats in certain countries (much has been made of a Japanese cultural bias towards exams, for example) may skew scores and therefore not provide accurate impressions of performance.

Conclusion

Summing up, then, it is clear that our interest in international and comparative education is unlikely to diminish, given the ways in which it can illuminate our understanding of education systems, and the growing political appetites for examining and learning from elsewhere. As the chapter has illustrated, comparative studies have long covered a wide range of issues, investigating them using quantitative and qualitative approaches, and for a range of purposes. This breadth and diversity makes international and comparative education a particularly rich and dynamic field of educational research. As we have seen, however, interest in attaining greater understandings of education has been driven in recent decades by quests for economic improvement and political point-scoring, as governments around the globe increasingly incline towards a human capital view of education – defining its importance predominantly in economic terms. Such a situation only heightens our need for caution and awareness – as demonstrated in this chapter, over-simplified use of comparison can severely undermine the value of any claims based on and lessons derived from comparative investigations.

Research task

In groups, investigate an educational issue in four countries. This might be an aspect of the curriculum, a phase of education, an aspect of teaching, learning or assessment, a funding or management issue, a school subject, approaches to inclusion, etc.

You may find it useful to search national government websites, and visit Eurydice, the EU's education database (www.eurydice.org), and the World Education database (www.ibe.unesco.org).

Make a set of justified recommendations for educational change in one of the countries on the basis of practice in the other three, whilst acknowledging your awareness of the various constraints (cultural, social, political, etc.) that might impede the successful implementation of your proposals for change. Present your findings to the wider group.

Summary

- International and comparative education is a diverse and expanding field of study and research.
- It enables us to understand how socio-cultural factors and global trends influence education differently in different parts of the world.
- As interest in the field grows, so does the need for a critical and questioning attitude when examining comparative studies, surveys and reports.
- Educational policies and approaches that work well in one context can rarely be easily and simply transferred elsewhere.
- National governments often make selective use of comparative data to justify their own ideologically-driven policy preferences.

Recommended reading

Bartram, B. (2018) *International and Comparative Education: Contemporary Issues and Debates*. Abingdon: Routledge.

Marshall, J. (2014) *Introduction to Comparative and International Education*. London: Sage.

Phillips, D. and Schweisfurth, M. (2008) *Comparative and International Education: An Introduction to Theory, Method and Practice*. London: Bloomsbury.

References

Alexander, R. (1999) Culture in Pedagogy, Pedagogy across Cultures. In R. Alexander, P. Broadfoot and D. Phillips (Eds), *Learning from Comparing*. Oxford: Symposium.

Alexander, R. (2001) *Culture and Pedagogy*. Oxford: Blackwell.

Alexander, R. (2014) Visions of Education, Roads to Reform: PISA, the Global Race and the Cambridge Primary Review. Lecture, University of Malmö, Sweden, 4 February 2014. Available at: www.robinalexander.org.uk/wp-content/uploads/2014/05/Alexander-Malmo-140204.pdf (accessed 18 March 2019).

Auld, E. and Morris, P. (2014) Comparative Education, the 'New Paradigm' and Policy Borrowing: Constructing Knowledge for Educational Reform. *Comparative Education* **50**(2), pp. 129–155.

Bartram, B. (2009) Comparative Education. In S. Warren (Ed.), *Education Studies: Course Companion to Themes and Contexts*. London: Continuum.

Bartram, B. (2012) *Attitudes to Language Learning: Insights from Comparative Education*. London: Bloomsbury.

Bartram, B. (2016) 'Career and Money Aside, What's the Point of University?' A Comparison of Students' Non-Economic Entry Motives in Three European Countries. *Higher Education Quarterly* **70**(3), pp. 281–300.

Bartram, B. (2018) *International and Comparative Education: Contemporary Issues and Debates*. Abingdon: Routledge.

Brubacher, J. (1966) *A History of the Problems of Education*. London: McGraw-Hill.

Budd, R. (2018) Higher Education – from Global Trends to Local Realities. In B. Bartram (Ed.), *International and Comparative Education: Contemporary Issues and Debates*. Abingdon: Routledge.

Burghes, D. (2018) International Comparisons in Mathematics: Perspectives on Teaching and Learning. In B. Bartram (Ed.), *International and Comparative Education: Contemporary Issues and Debates*. Abingdon: Routledge.

Chan, R., Hayes Tang, H. and Delaney, P. (2018) The Rise of Private Supplementary Tutoring: Contemporary Issues and International Perspectives on Shadow Education in China. In B. Bartram (Ed.), *International and Comparative Education: Contemporary Issues and Debates*. Abingdon: Routledge.

Cowen, R. (2005) Extreme Political Systems, Deductive Rationalities and Comparative Education: Education as Politics. In D. Halpin and P. Walsh (Eds), *Educational Commonplaces*. London: Institute of Education.

Crossley, M. (2006) Bridging Cultures and Traditions: Perspectives from Comparative and International Research in Education. A professorial address at the University of Bristol, 9 February 2006.

Crossley, M. and Watson, K. (2003) *Comparative and International Research in Education*. London: RoutledgeFalmer.

DfE (2010) *The Importance of Teaching*. London: DfE. Available at: www.gov.uk/government/publications/the-importance-of-teaching-the-schools-white-paper-2010 (accessed 5 April 2019).

Field, J. (2018) Comparative Issues and Perspectives in Adult Education and Training. In B. Bartram (Ed.), *International and Comparative Education: Contemporary Issues and Debates*. Abingdon: Routledge.

Grant, N. (1999) Comparing Educational Systems. In D. Matheson and I. Grosvenor (Eds), *An Introduction to Education Studies*. London: David Fulton.

Holmes, B. and McLean, M. (1989) *The Curriculum: A Comparative Perspective*. London: Unwin Hyman.

Lauwerys, J.A. and Tayar, G. (1973) *Education at Home and Abroad*. London: Routledge & Kegan Paul.

Marshall, J. (2014) *Introduction to Comparative and International Education*. London: Sage.

Morris, P. (2012) Pick 'n' Mix, Select and Project; Policy Borrowing and the Quest for 'World Class' Schooling: An Analysis of the 2010 Schools White Paper. *Journal of Education Policy* **27**(1), pp. 89–107.

Murray Thomas, R. (1990) *International Comparative Education*. Oxford: Butterworth-Heinemann.

Noah, H.J. and Eckstein, M.A. (1969) *Towards a Science of Comparative Education*. London: Macmillan.

Phillips, D. (1999) On Comparing. In R. Alexander, P. Broadfoot and D. Phillips (Eds), *Learning from Comparing*. Oxford: Symposium Books.

Phillips, D. (2000) Learning from Elsewhere in Education: Some Perennial Problems Revisited with Reference to British Interest in Germany. *Comparative Education* **36**(3), pp. 297–307.

Phillips, D. and Ochs, K. (2004) Researching Policy Borrowing: Some Methodological Challenges in Comparative Education. *British Educational Research Journal* **30**(6), pp. 773–784.

Prais, S. (2003) Cautions on OECD's Recent Educational Survey (PISA). *Oxford Review of Education* **29**(2), pp. 140–155.

Robinson, P. (1999) The Tyranny of League Tables. In R. Alexander, P. Broadfoot and D. Phillips (Eds), *Learning from Comparing*. Oxford: Symposium Books.

Chapter 9

Globalisation and populism

Why intercultural education failed

David Coulby

Introduction

It is the contention of this chapter that progressive education, and particularly intercultural education, has failed in many states. The evidence for this seems currently incontrovertible: the Brexit vote, the election of President Trump and that of other ethno-nationalists in a wide range of countries including Hungary, Poland, Turkey, the Czech Republic, Egypt and Brazil. If intercultural education over the decades had convinced pupils and students of its principles then they would surely have resoundingly rejected nationalistic policies and autocratic personalities. Behind this failure lies a set of theoretical weaknesses centring on the nature of globalisation and populism and their differential impact on states, cities and regions. At the theoretical level the temptations of economic and/or technological determinism are obvious: increases in inequality across many states have been accompanied by, and amplified by, the familiar irresponsibility of globalised social media and surveillance technologies (Baldwin, 2016). Undoubtedly these factors play a significant part, but globalisation is a human process: it may be halted, reversed or revised by human decision and impact. Further, its effects are highly geographically varied and stratified. So, whilst resisting the formulation of globalisation as inevitable and irreversible, it is reasonable to acknowledge that it has happened and is continuing to happen. Capital and technological expertise are being increasingly concentrated whilst the political institutions and movements which might be able to halt or even reverse this process seem, at least in the major Western countries, to be dormant or even moribund.

Among the impacts of increased globalisation have been enhanced climate change (see Chapter 12), massive environmental degradation and the inception of a new extinction event (Gelbspan, 2004; Maalouf, 2011: United Nations Development Programme, 2008). One example: 'According to official Chinese figures, more than 70 per cent of the country's groundwater in the North China Plain is so polluted that it is "unfit for human touch"' (Frankopan, 2018: 101). In economic terms, while poverty has been alleviated in many areas, severe inequality has increased in many states and regions. The role of advocate for globalisation, then, is not one that a social scientist would readily undertake. Nevertheless, in order to theorise the policies that have led to the failure of intercultural education and the forces that this failure has unleashed, it is necessary to acknowledge the overarching context is that of a steady increase in the movement of capital, products, people, ideas and services. This chapter looks first at the failure of intercultural education, then examines populism as one of the consequences of this failure, and concludes with suggestions for re-theorisation.

Intercultural education

History and forgetting are complex processes produced and reproduced in curricular systems of schools and universities highly differentially between states, and indeed between regions of the same state. The teaching of nationalism in schools and universities involves a range of subjects. History, language, literature and geography are all utilised by states and other educational actors, overtly or covertly, to enhance nationalist feeling in young people, variously described as 'patriotism' or 'citizenship'. Japan is portrayed as the enemy nation in China and North Korea (Harding, 2018). The avoidance of the embarrassments of imperial history involves significant gaps in the curricula of England and France (Fenby, 2015). The religion of the parish pump is not confined to religious institutions. The continuation of the synthesis of religion and education has survived the growth of scepticism and individualism even in European nations such as Norway, England and Wales and Greece. Schools and churches, mosques and other religious institutions operate in synchronised identity formation to embody belief systems that include gender roles, nationalism and xenophobia. Intercultural education has had little impact on these practices; indeed in some states, to the extent that it is operated as a marginal and marginalised activity, a brief survey of world religions, for instance, it is effectively complicit with them.

As education becomes more nationalised and narrowly technical, a space is opened for television and social media to become the major sources of information about culture and relativities. This is re-packaged, in the accepted ethos of individualism, through the simplistic 'personality'-based presentation so popular with broadcasters. So, Arab history or separatist movements in Europe, for example, are refracted through the presentation of whatever popular music singer or footballer the networks think will increase their ratings. Expertise is trivialised and demeaned: climate scientists and international trade lawyers are 'so-called experts', ignored or ridiculed by journalists and politicians. Particularistic culture is increasingly able to disregard any unpleasant counter-factual as 'fake news' (Heimans and Timms, 2018; Fountain, 2018). The formation of fetishised identity through television and social media is assisted rather than eroded by formal practices of intercultural education where massive cultural institutions and movements are presented as a matter of personal choice. The curricular framework of identity and individuality makes it virtually impossible for students in Savoy to understand the lives of their counterparts in the *banlieues* of Paris or Marseilles.

Languages are an area where curricular systems and identity formation interact. Actually this formulation itself is to an extent an Anglocentric issue. The point is that most of the Anglophone countries (except Australia) do not take foreign languages at all seriously. Not surprisingly they then also often do not take foreign people or their beliefs and cultures all that seriously either. In both the UK and the USA the lack of serious foreign language teaching isolates pupils within their own culture and diminishes their possibilities for interaction beyond their horizons. A non-marginal intercultural education in the nations of the UK or in the states of the USA might focus on the serious teaching of world languages rather than introductions to Sikhism or to Mexican food. In non-Anglophone states the predominant concentration on the learning of English, at the expense of other regional, national or neighbouring languages, can itself enhance cultural isolation as well as further legitimating the political authority of the hegemon. The lack of foreign language skills discourages international travel; it tends to focus cultural activity and enquiry within the bounds of one language/nation; it generates ignorance and prejudices about the people of other states even those separated only by the Rio Grande or the Pas-de-Calais. Foreign policy, even of rich and powerful states, is thereby distorted not only by the rise of populism but by the absolute shortage of expertise of other countries and their languages.

Intercultural education proclaimed the 'rights' of groups to be educated in the environment in which they were most comfortable. Interculturalists in England and Wales, for instance, argued that if Christians and Jews had distinct educational institutions then so should Muslims, Hindus, Buddhists, Sikhs and Greek Orthodox. This policy was implemented as part of the 'choice' rhetoric by the New Labour governments (1997–2010). (See Chapter 1.) Despite national curricular impositions this policy has resulted in particularistic schools, and, in some cases, universities. Over time these have served to reinforce rather than erode difference. Divisive schools have served to reproduce and reinforce divisions both within the locality and within the state. In many towns in the North of England Muslim children are educated in Islamic schools and non-Muslims in academies or local authority schools which are consequently predominantly white. Similarly, in Northern Ireland there remains a strict partition between Protestant and Catholic schools. In both cases ignorance about, and hostility towards, fellow-citizens are actually facilitated and even encouraged by the organisation of the education system.

Populism

What is commonly being called 'the rise of populism' was preceded by serious theoretical failures. These failures famously manifested themselves in the inability to predict or prevent the result of the EU referendum in the UK and that of the presidential election in the USA (Bremmer, 2018; Churchwell, 2018; Dumas, 2018; Eatwell and Goodwin, 2018). There are at least four aspects of this populism which may belatedly be addressed. They are isolated below for the sake of narrative clarity, but their power is enhanced by the way in which they compound with each other: nationalism, racism, the 'left-behind', the strong leader.

In 1945 nationalism, at least in Europe and Japan, had been thoroughly discredited. It was thought that it would disappear as a social and political force. But nationalism never really went away, even in Europe, as became evident in the wars that broke up Yugoslavia. Current notable manifestations of its resurgence include Hungary, Russia and Turkey, as well as, outside Europe, China and Saudi Arabia. But it never went away in Western European countries or the USA either. The rhetoric of the Cold War and of a unified West protected ample space for old-fashioned nationalisms to thrive: they survived in residual and marginal outposts such as football chants in England and Russia, Orange Day parades in Northern Ireland, national-day flag waving in Norway and Ireland, or Sunday morning sermons in the bible-belt. In Europe it has been small-area nationalism which has been the most vociferous and enduring. Scotland and Cataluña are the obvious examples, but also Flanders, Brittany, the Lombard League, Serbia, the Czech–Slovak split. Indeed, small-state nationalism, spreading from the Baltic States to Ukraine, was one of the forces driving the break-up of the Soviet Union (Conradi, 2017; Macaes, 2018). Paradoxically, small-nation nationalism may be one of the forces helping the coherence and continuation of the EU as movements such as the Scottish Nationalists see a place for themselves within a united Europe.

Racism appears in recent years to be not only more widely prevalent but also more readily and commonly legitimated. Why? Social media as explanation for everything objectionable provides a facile form of technological determinism. But there has been an increase in abusive rhetoric, even of threatening language, which has accompanied the development of political debate on social media (Franklin, 2017). It seems there has been, internationally, an increase in anger or at least in the desire to express anger. This anger and abuse can come from all colours of the political spectrum but an important component of right-wing vitriol is racism. The large-scale migration to the EU in the summer of 2016 had a massive popular impact, as did the political highlighting of migration to the USA from Latin America during the 2016 presidential election. Nationalism often carries with it incendiary racist overtones: the Hungarian and Polish definition of Europe as a Christian continent; the urge to mark borders and boundaries by fences and walls; the historicist and erroneous notion of indigenousness. A readiness, even eagerness, has been witnessed by mainstream politicians and media outlets to give voice to views previously considered marginal: the USA and UK provide ready and surprising examples. The BBC's cultivation of controversy (legitimated as neutrality) and thus persistent exposure of extreme views on climate change, the European Union, even vaccination can come as a regular shock. In the USA the move away from balance in broadcasting has given rise to radio and television channels of extreme, often racist, and sometimes violent views. Irredentism in China has been characterised by stigmatisation of the marginal (Xin Jian, Tibet) and perceived hostile (Japan) groups (Auslin, 2017; Kaplan, 2014; Rachman, 2016). This racism has also sometimes manifested itself in unexpected places: in Sweden far-right groups are increasingly involved in political coalitions at local level.

The 'left-behind' have become more prevalent and visible since the banking crisis of 2008–2009. Standards of living have frozen or declined for particular groups in particular places in the West: flyover America; UK and other European non-metropolitan areas. These have often been traditional (white) working-class towns and regions. Factors here are economic: stagnating wages and job opportunities in post-industrial areas contrast with booming economies for the internationally well-educated in, say, London and California. With no political or economic modes of address since 2009 this has resulted in a bitterness which has been manifested in them-and-us discourses, anti-elitism, municipalism and parochial triumphalism: Nord-Pas-de-Calais, North East England, rust-belt states (Tett,

2009). Old-fashioned class solidarity is being replaced by other forms of group identity focused around locality, racism, favoured news outlets, television programmes or social media selectivisms. A wilful ignorance is embraced, as manifest by the way that low migration areas, for example South Wales, Hungary, tend to be the most populist, anti-immigrant and anti-international.

The cult of the strong leader, almost always centres on a man (Bangladesh provides the exception with Sheikh Hasina). The cult of personality and celebrity in the West has contributed to this. Media have provided the megaphone: Trump, Johnson, Rees-Mogg have all been celebritised by television, thereby enhancing dubious political careers. Authoritarian regimes deliberately foster this cult: Russia, Egypt, China. Repeated real or contrived election victories appear to encourage it: Turkey, Bolivia, Uganda, Hungary. It is usually associated with the perceived failure of conventional, democratic politics and institutions and hostility towards metropolitanism or any form of expertise. It can be readily combined with taken-for-granted sexism, as in the US presidential election. This sexism along with anti-Semitism lurks in the UK Labour as well as the US Republican Party. Celebretisation and atomisation have been some of the cultural and psychological manifestations of globalisation. Ironically, when taken up as mass cultural pantomime via television or other media, they have led to the electoral rejection of globalisation itself, indeed of democratic procedures. It may be that, in the long run, the stress on individuality and the salience of identity in culture and politics is proving a force to break down previous modes of political and economic solidarity. The fragmentation of political parties in Spain and Italy, for instance, may represent the voting behaviour of the selfie epoch. But more widely this process has led to the hollowing out of the authority of states or their capture by demagogues, kleptocrats and comedians.

Taken together as populism these strands indicate that globalisation has given rise to the manifold of its opposite, especially in regions and classes of the self-perceiving dispossessed (self-perceiving because unemployed workers in the North of England are not normally compared with Syrian refugees in Anatolia). Education, including intercultural education, is implicated in the genesis of this populism, even though its practitioners may find themselves lamenting the outcomes.

Cynically one might echo German Chancellor Merkel or the *Daily Mail*: multiculturalism has failed. The celebration and resentment of this failure have been manifest in the politics of many regions of the USA and Europe, particularly those marked by high levels of relative poverty and inequality. Regional inequalities seem particularly successful in encouraging political resentment. Notions of somewhere and anywhere provide a simplistic explanation here, but an exploration of the factors inhibiting mobility – educational as well as geographical – might point to a more nuanced explanation. Advanced capitalist countries are witnessing a rigidity in their economic and cultural class structure. Elites have become increasingly successful at using educational certification and familial contacts to reproduce privilege. Resentment by the disadvantaged, now seen in terms of geography or educational level rather than those of social class, is far from without justification.

To re-theorise

Globalisation is the manifestation and conceptualisation of a unitary international economic system. It has carried with it a particular package of cultural institutions and activities and an international hierarchy of educational institutions and of workplace skills and knowledge. In this context, then, it is increasingly unreasonable to treat social, cultural or educational phenomena in the framework of the nation state. Educational elites across the globe send their young people to Harvard or London to acquire business or technical skills that will reproduce their privileged position into the next generation. The process of globalisation has not been to erode geography but to reinforce it, as business, technological and academic institutions are increasingly concentrated in particular locations. Furthermore, these locations are now stratified at an international level.

Factors inhibiting social and economic mobility have intensified in some regions in the post-recession phase of globalisation. Capital has been increasingly concentrated by the growth of the giant technical companies: Facebook, Apple, Alphabet, Amazon, Netflix and Google (FAANG). The global headquarters and substantial workforces of these corporations are in California. In this same phase, a handful of American banks have strengthened their grip on global trading and capital investment: J.P. Morgan, Citibank, Morgan Stanley, Goldman Sachs, Wells Fargo. Again, headquarters and workforces are concentrated, in this case in London and New York. The geographical implications of these concentrations are evident in the increasingly privileged position (house prices, infrastructure developments, cultural and sporting facilities) of these three areas, especially compared to the run-down regions of the rust belt or the de-industrialised areas of England, Wales and Scotland. The educational concentration is less visible but equally pervasive. Elite universities in the UK and the USA are overwhelmingly successful in international league tables. These universities are located in California and New England as well as London and Oxbridge. The schools that predominantly feed into these universities are largely located in privileged areas and are in many cases, especially in the UK, fee-paying. At neither school nor university level in these institutions is interculturalism a vital concern.

In global terms, culture is concentrated as well as dispersed. Seoul, Mumbai, Rio and Cairo all play significant roles in the globalisation of culture. But in terms of film, television, book publishing, news media, computer games and music, global cultural esteem remains focused in – surprise! – California, New York and London. The overlap of cultural and economic concentration magnifies patterns of inequality which are visible and resented not least in the USA and the UK themselves.

Global power distribution is currently uncertain and unsettled. Power no longer coheres with wealth and culture either socially or geographically (Auslin, 2017; Rachman, 2016). Change can be swift for both growth and decline in terms of both hard and soft power. The rise of China, its encroachment on the South China Sea and its ambitions in both its littoral region and central Asia are the most obvious uncertainties. They are paralleled by America's withdrawal, under both Obama and Trump, from its previously extensive global commitments. But Russia's mounting belligerence, in Syria as well as Ukraine and the rest of the near-abroad as well as its interference in US elections, provides another element of uncertainty, as does nuclear proliferation in the subcontinent, Iran and Israel as well as North Korea. The volatility of international power relations comes at a historical point when international cooperation is essential to combat climate change and associated human-created ecological disasters.

Practice and theory intertwine in economic discourse as well as that of intercultural education (Coulby, 2006). The paradoxes of intercultural education need to be more straightforwardly recognised. The stress on religious integrity often undermines the fundamental identities and medical and psychological integrity of women and girls. The attempt at cultural inclusiveness has resulted in superficiality and tokenism. Indeed, it can only result in this. It is not intellectually possible for an individual to inhabit a wide range of cultures. Without a massive commitment to language learning it is difficult to become competent in more than one. At the same time the core curricular objective of learning foreign languages is being casually neglected in many Anglophone countries. The idealism and idealisation of intercultural education is one of the normative processes that have separated school and university education from the workplace. In the context of globalisation this normative process has too often been differentially distributed. One set of children learn maths, English and Chinese, another set learn about world religions, ethnic music and dance, or, worse still, the inherent correctness of a particular theological text. The consequences for the reproduction of subsequent economic and social stratification are increasingly visible to both groups.

Conclusion

The theorisation of intercultural education needs to take account of these changes in global power, wealth and culture. Perhaps of particular importance is to examine the cultural fortresses of those disempowered and impoverished by these changes. Spectator sport, celebretisation, television, social media, popular music and dance all play their part, and, yes, nationalism and racism. Populism did not bloom because people were incapable of looking or thinking beyond their immediate environment. In the context of global and national recession, confronted by an apparently privileged and uncaring elite, too easily characterised as metropolitan or indeed intercultural, the solidarity of the campanile and those who offer it political and financial support, seems like a viable form of concerted sustenance and action. The discourse of the left long favoured social movements, indeed movements of almost any kind. In the face of movements from the right, the left appears to have no discursive response beyond time-warped Cold War rhetoric. Sanders in the USA and Corbyn in the UK seem unaware of the nature of the technological economy and the magnitude of its operators (Zuboff, 2019). Only by analysing the massive shifts in the accumulation of global technical and surveillance capitalism and the impact of these on impoverished people of all cultures, from Cape Town to Cardiff, will progressives be able to formulate understanding and policy initiatives to the benefit of the people they once thought they represented.

Intercultural education failed. Indeed the success of the educational enterprise itself is surely open to question. The voice of the revanchist right, long empowered by traditional media, has taken to the streets and the apps. We want our country back. If you are poor you vote out. Make America great again. America first, America first.

Questions for discussion

World religions tend to demean and control women. If intercultural education is to teach respect for all religions, how can it justify beliefs and practices which subordinate women and girls?

The chapter identifies three zones of Western prosperity, California, New York and London. Wells Fargo bank might seem to be an exception to the chapter's generalisations, but in fact its global headquarters are in San Francisco. What social indices might confirm or refute the prominence of these areas? Use the internet to check this out.

Summary

- The rise of populism and associated nationalism is an international phenomenon. The chapter asks why education and particularly intercultural education has done so little to mitigate this ascendancy.
- Globalisation signifies the rapid increase in the movement between states of people, goods, services, capital and ideas.
- Four characteristics of populism are identified: nationalism, racism, the voices of the 'left-behind' and the cult of a strong leader.
- The absence of strong provision for learning foreign languages is identified, in most Anglophone countries, as one of the sources of the failure of intercultural education.

Recommended reading

Bremmer, I. (2018) *Us vs Them: The Failure of Globalism*. London: Portfolio Penguin.
Eatwell, R. and Goodwin, M. (2018) *National Populism: The Revolt against Liberal Democracy*. London: Pelican.
Fountain, B. (2018) *Beautiful Country Burn Again: Trump's Rise to Power and the State of the Country That Voted for Him*. Edinburgh: Canongate.
Frankopan, P. (2018) *The New Silk Roads: The Present and Future of the World*. London: Bloomsbury.

Relevant journals

Intercultural Education – available online at www.tandfonline.com/loi/ceji20 (accessed 23 April 2019).
The Economist – available online at www.economist.com/ (accessed 23 April 2019).

References

Auslin, M.R. (2017) *The End of the Asian Century: War, Stagnation and the Risks to the World's Most Dynamic Region*. New Haven and London: Yale University Press.

Baldwin, R. (2016) *The Great Convergence: Information Technology and the New Globalisation*. Cambridge, MA and London: Harvard University Press.

Bremmer, I. (2018) *Us vs Them: The Failure of Globalism*. London: Portfolio Penguin.

Churchwell, S. (2018) *Behold America: A History of America First and the American Dream*. London: Bloomsbury.

Conradi, P. (2017) *Who Lost Russia? How the World Entered a New Cold War*. London: Oneworld.

Coulby, D. (2006) Intercultural Education: Theory and Practice. *Intercultural Education* 17(3), pp. 245–257.

Dumas, C. (2018) *Populism and Economics*. London: Profile Books.

Eatwell, R. and Goodwin, M. (2018) *National Populism: The Revolt against Liberal Democracy*. London: Pelican.

Fenby, J. (2015) *The History of Modern France: From the Revolution to the Present Day*. London: Simon and Schuster.

Fountain, B. (2018*) Beautiful Country Burn Again: Trump's Rise to Power and the State of the Country That Voted for Him*. Edinburgh: Canongate.

Franklin, D. (Ed.) (2017) *Megatech: Technology in 2050*. London: Economist Books.

Frankopan, P. (2018) *The New Silk Roads: The Present and Future of the World*. London: Bloomsbury.

Gelbspan, R. (2004) *Boiling Point*. New York: Basic Books.

Harding, C. (2018) *Japan Story: In Search of a Nation 1850 to the Present*. London: Allen Lane.

Heimans, T. and Timms, J. (2018) *New Power: Why Outsiders Are Winning, Institutions Are Failing, and How the Rest of Us Can Keep up in the Age of Mass Participation*. London: Picador.

Kaplan, R. D. (2014) *Asia's Cauldron: The South China Sea and the End of a Stable Pacific*. New York: Random House.

Maalouf, A. (2011) *Disordered World: Setting a New Course for the Twenty-First Century*. London: Bloomsbury.

Macaes, B. (2018) *The Dawn of Eurasia: On the Trail of the New World Order*. London: Allen Lane.

Rachman, G. (2016) *Easternisation: War and Peace in the Asian Century*. London: Bodley Head.

Tett, G. (2009) *Fool's Gold: How Unrestrained Greed Corrupted a Dream, Shattered Global Markets and Unleashed a Catastrophe*. London: Hachette.

Zuboff, S. (2019) *The Age of Surveillance Capitalism: The Fight for a Human Future at the New Frontier of Power*. London: Profile Books.

Chapter 10

Religion and worldviews in education

Denise Cush

Introduction

This chapter examines the place of religious and non-religious worldviews in education, in a world of religious and cultural diversity. It explains key concepts, provides a brief international overview, gives a summary history of religious education policy and practice in England, concluding with the recommendations of recent reports, and indicates a number of issues relating to religion in education, including the 'faith schools' debate.

Confessional/faith-based or non-confessional/inclusive Religious Education? Religion and Worldviews

'Religious Education' (RE) is an ambiguous term as it is used internationally to cover both traditional initiation into a particular religious tradition (called variously confessional, denominational, instruction, nurture, faith development), and the more recent non-confessional, multi-faith and multi-worldview academic subject, sometimes called 'inclusive' or 'integrated' RE.

The year 2019 marks the fiftieth anniversary of this innovative approach. In 1969, Sweden became the first country to legislate for RE which did not aim to promote a particular religion or religion in general, but which introduced pupils to a wide range of religions/worldviews. Also in 1969, the Shap Working Party for World Religions in Education pioneered such RE in Britain, and this soon became influential on practice, though not recognised in legislation until the 1988 Education Reform Act.

A recent report for England (CoRE, 2018) controversially recommended that RE should change its name. In spite of five decades of non-confessional, multi-faith RE, it still sounds like a 'religious' enterprise, especially as in some faith-based schools, to varying extents, it *is*. The name suggested is 'Religion and Worldviews'. 'Religion' in the singular, to imply the need to examine the whole concept, and 'Worldviews' plural, to encompass both religious and non-religious approaches to life. The term 'worldview' has a long pedigree in academic Religious Studies, and has wide currency internationally. This chapter will, however, continue to use the more familiar term 'RE'.

Terminology: religion, culture, worldview, secular, spirituality, plurality, diversity

Academic study soon reveals that terms in common use such as 'education' or 'religion' are actually constructed and contested: 'it depends what you mean by …'

'Religion' is notoriously difficult to define. Westerners, influenced by Christianity and the Enlightenment, tend to think of religion as being about 'beliefs' and centred on the existence of God, but elsewhere the focus may be more on practice, values or identity, and Buddhist, Jain and Pagan traditions are not about 'God'. Clearly distinguished 'systems' such as 'Hindu-ism' or 'Juda-ism' are seen by many as artificial constructs of nineteenth-century Western thinking, as in reality 'religions' are internally diverse, and the dividing lines between them are not clear, particularly in non-Western traditions. 'Religion' is often hard to distinguish from other markers of identity such as 'ethnicity', 'nationality' or 'culture'. Nevertheless, adherents do distinguish between religion and culture, and we can talk meaningfully of a religion/worldview adapting to a different cultural context. Can the 'religious' be separated from the 'non-religious'? Difficult, but we tend to use the term 'religious' to include a reference to some meaning or level of reality beneath or beyond that available to the senses and scientific enquiry. Most scholars continue to use the word 'religion' as a useful tool to refer to both the organised systems and institutions and personal approaches to life, while rejecting its referring to an actual 'thing'.

'Culture' is almost as hard to define as 'religion'. Generally interpreted as the learned aspects of being human, our language about 'different cultures' tends to reify distinct sets of language/customs/beliefs to which an individual belongs, or perhaps is 'torn between'. It is more helpful to see 'cultures' (like 'religions') as fluid, internally diverse and contested, influenced by and influencing other cultural streams, more like languages you learn than something you 'are'. So instead of being 'torn between' cultures, research with young Hindus and Sikhs in Britain (e.g. Nesbitt, 2004) shows them successfully navigating multiple cultural streams.

'Worldview' is used by the Commission on RE to refer to 'an overarching conceptual structure, a philosophy of life or an approach to life which structures how a person understands the nature of the world and their place in it' (CoRE, 2018: 72). However, several further paragraphs were needed to explain that it is not just cognitive beliefs, but includes emotions, values, ethical behaviour, everyday customs, and sense of identity and belonging. The term 'worldview' was chosen to encompass both religious and non-religious, and both institutional/organised traditions such as Islam or Humanism and individual, personal ways of making sense of life's experiences and deciding what is most important in life. Individual worldviews may be more or less consciously constructed or coherent, and may identify with one particular institutional worldview, or draw upon several, whether realising it or not.

The word 'secular' is often used as the opposite of 'religious', so that we could talk about 'religious or secular worldviews'. However, it can mean 'non-religious' or 'anti-religious' or 'not *officially* religious', or as 'treating diverse religions impartially'. The constitution of independent India was based on this latter sense. It is perfectly possible to be both religious and secular, as Turkey has claimed. If we use 'secular' to mean 'non-religious' it is still often difficult to decide what is religious and what is not, and some take a 'non-binary' approach and refuse to be labelled either religious or non-religious. Following the philosopher and sociologist Jürgen Habermas, some scholars talk about being in a 'post-secular' world, where religion has become an important factor again. There is perhaps more talk about religion in the public sphere and international affairs today, and in some places religions are growing, but on the other hand, fewer people in England and other European countries now identify with institutional religious worldviews. Research claims that identifying as 'non-religious' reached 50 per cent in England in 2015 (Woodhead, 2016), and even higher for young people; but what is meant by this is very varied, including what others might call 'spiritual' or even religious perspectives.

In recent decades the term 'spirituality' has become popular, generally for those who dislike the 'institutional' side of organised religions and wish to stress a more personal, inner commitment to something more than the material. 'I'm not religious but I am spiritual' is a common refrain, but again what is meant needs to be interrogated in each context, and some find the term unhelpful.

'Plurality' (of religions/worldviews) refers to the fact that human beings have many different views on the meaning and purpose of our lives, human nature and destiny, the nature of reality, reliable authorities and sources of knowledge, and ethical issues. 'Pluralism' is used to indicate a positive view of this situation. 'Diversity', often used in relation to gender, sexuality, ethnicity, class, or physical ability, can also be used to describe both the sheer variety of worldviews and the many different subgroups and interpretations of each tradition. Religion/worldview is one of the factors involved in 'intersectionality' (see Chapter 6) and one of the 'protected characteristics' of the 2010 Equality Act.

The international picture

The way in which state-funded education systems respond to the plurality of religions/worldviews is varied and complex, tied up with their history and sense of national identity, and is also constantly changing. However, there are three basic options which could be labelled 'confessional', 'secular' and 'non-confessional'.

Many countries take the traditional *confessional* approach to RE. Schools contribute to the nurturing of children within the faith tradition of their family, or what is deemed to be the heritage of the country. Confessional worldview education is not necessarily indoctrinatory, as it may (but also may not) encourage a critical and questioning approach to the tradition.

Such RE can be compulsory or optional, the syllabus can be decided by the state or the institutional religions/worldviews concerned or both. It can be taught by the ordinary class teacher or by paid or unpaid religious personnel. Where one particular tradition forms part of the dominant construction of national identity – Catholicism in Poland, Orthodoxy in Romania – that tradition forms the basis of the syllabus. Where there is more awareness of diversity, separate RE classes may be offered for the main traditions. In the majority of German Länder there is choice between Protestant and Catholic (and sometimes Muslim)

RE, and in Austria sixteen religious groups have the right to offer denominational RE. In Indonesia, confessional RE is possible for Christians, Hindus, Buddhists and Confucians as well as the Muslim majority. In Flanders, the majority attend state-funded Catholic schools, but there are also state schools where there is a choice of Catholic, Protestant, Anglican or Orthodox Christianity, Judaism or Islam (and coming soon, Buddhism). This can lead to very small classes in some schools and is becoming unsustainable as diversity increases.

In spite of the confessional label, many European educators in practice take a more open approach as they seek to connect with the actual worldviews and experience of their pupils; for example, in Germany many prefer to talk about 'denominational' rather than 'confessional' RE. In Flanders where it is recognised that, even in Catholic schools, the majority of students are not practising Catholics, they have developed the notion of the 'Catholic school of dialogue', open to the diverse perspectives of students, not proselytising but still centred on encountering a Christian faith position.

The *secular* option tries to leave religion out of schools, so that there is no subject like RE, and no religious activities on school premises. This can be because the state is officially anti-religious (such as the People's Republic of China, or earlier, the Soviet Union) or because there is a strict separation of 'church' and 'state' as in the USA, France and Japan.

In the USA the First Amendment to the 1787 Constitution sought to protect religious freedom by instituting a complete separation between 'church' and 'state'. This has been interpreted as meaning that no public funds can be used for teaching RE. An important ruling in 1963 made it clear that it is only promoting a particular religion that is ruled out, rather than teaching about religion(s). Some argue that religious freedom and choice can only really be guaranteed by learning about religions/worldviews. Increasing awareness of plurality has led several states, such as California, to include teaching about religions in the history or social studies curriculum. However, there is no discrete subject nor specialist trained teachers. In China, although the state is officially atheistic, and the teaching of Marxism/Maoism can be viewed as *confessional* worldview education, religious worldviews may be encountered in schools as an aspect of Geography, or as a part of 'ethnic education' for minority groups such as the Theravada Buddhist Dai people, the Tibetan/Mongolian Buddhists or the Muslim minorities, and Christian home-schooling, though illegal, is spreading. Religions are certainly studied in higher education in both the USA and China.

A growing number of countries take the *non-confessional* approach and provide RE that is open, balanced and impartial, and is seeking to educate children about religion and religions (and often non-religious worldviews), rather than promote a particular religion or religion in general. The countries with the longest experience of this are Sweden, England, Wales, and Scotland. More recently, they have been joined by Norway, South Africa and Namibia, and for students over 16 ('upper secondary') in Denmark, some Swiss cantons, and Quebec in Canada. South Africa calls the subject 'religion education' to emphasise that it does not have the aim of 'making people religious'. However, it is dangerous to generalise from labels. From 2012, a new RE course for pupils aged 10 in Russia is officially non-confessional, but only two of the six options ('world religious cultures' and 'secular ethics') appear to be so in practice. Jewish, Buddhist, Islamic and

Orthodox RE tend to be more like confessional RE, and the latter is increasingly being promoted as an aspect of Russian nationalism, and becoming the popular choice even with non-churchgoers.

Finland also illustrates how the situation is more complicated than the threefold typology allows. Until 2003, RE was technically confessional with three options of Lutheran, Orthodox or secular ethics, but in practice open to some teaching of a variety of religions, especially with older pupils in the majority Lutheran classes. Since 2003, it is described as 'non-confessional' but 'according to one's own religion'. The majority of pupils attend Lutheran RE or Ethics, a few are Orthodox, but there is also Muslim RE, and in more diverse urban areas a further choice of 'own RE' for those from Adventist, Baha'i, Buddhist, ISKCON (Hare Krishna), Anthroposophical, Catholic, Mormon and two other Christian backgrounds. It might be better described as 'weakly confessional'.

Although all three approaches can be found in Europe, the Council of Europe recommended in 2008 that all young people should receive inclusive and impartial education on the diversity of religions/worldviews, a decision supported by research showing that this is what most young people in Europe want. It is not well known that the foreign ministers of all forty-seven states signed their agreement to this (Jackson, 2016).

It is possible to construct arguments in favour of the confessional, the secular or the non-confessional approaches as being the best way to ensure human rights, freedom of religion and belief, and the promotion of social harmony rather than conflict. However, a world increasingly aware of plurality would seem to call for a non-confessional study of a wide range of worldviews, inclusive of all pupils, both academically rigorous and personally inspiring.

Question for discussion

Should RE be included in the school curriculum? If so, what should be its aims, content and methods?

Religious Education in England, a brief history: world class, but rather odd

RE has been a compulsory subject in the school curriculum since 1944 when it consisted of 'non-denominational' Christianity in most non-faith schools, and in one of the two categories of faith schools. The change to non-confessional and multi-faith RE came with the publication of the ground-breaking *Working Paper 36* (Schools Council, 1971) and was reinforced as part of the 'basic curriculum' in the 1988 Education Reform Act. This requires local authority RE syllabuses to 'reflect the fact that the religious traditions in Great Britain are in the main Christian, while taking account of the other principal religions represented in Great Britain' (repeated in 1996 Education Act, section 375.3).

Since the 1970s, British RE has been viewed as exemplary by the international academic community, but it rather lacks status here at home, and certainly has strange features compared with other curriculum subjects. RE is not part of the national curriculum (the two together form the 'basic curriculum') because it is organised locally. Each local authority must produce an 'Agreed Syllabus' for use in its schools. The parties agreeing the syllabus are the Church of England, other faiths and Christian denominations, teachers' representatives and elected councillors. The *local* nature of the syllabus allows for considerable 'grass roots' involvement, and the local Standing Advisory Council on Religious Education (SACRE) has been a forum for different faith communities to meet and work together. RE is the only subject (apart from sex education, but not relationships education) from which parents can withdraw their children, a right which is seen by some as anachronistic since RE became non-confessional, and by others as an important human right.

The local determination of RE has both supporters and critics. The latter have pointed out that the diversity of syllabuses is confusing and provides an uneven access to quality provision. There have been several attempts at more national uniformity. In 1994 two 'Model Syllabuses' were produced as guidance for local syllabuses (SCAA, 1994) and in 2004 the *Non-Statutory Framework for Religious Education* (QCA, 2004) was warmly welcomed by most professionals, the main faith communities, and some Humanist organisations. When the national curriculum for England and Wales was reviewed in 2013, no arrangements or funding were provided by the DfE for reviewing RE, so the Religious Education Council (REC) raised funding from charities to produce its own (REC, 2013).

A number of recent reports from Ofsted, the REC, and major research projects have identified strengths and weaknesses in English RE. Strengths include half a century's experience of non-confessional RE, an international reputation and influence, a major contribution to intercultural education, strong professional organisations, and the REC (a network of over sixty organisations where professionals from all levels of education and representatives of religious and non-religious institutions including Humanists UK, the Pagan Federation, the Board of Deputies of British Jews, the Muslim Council of Britain, the Church of England and the Catholic Education Service, all manage to work together, in a fine example of inter-worldview collaboration). The SACREs provide a similar opportunity at local level for teachers and faith communities to work together, for example on arranging visits to and visitors from different worldview communities, and local RE hubs and networks share good practice, funded by charities or on a voluntary basis. Nothing beats actually meeting people for deconstructing stereotypes, as experiments with school twinning across contrasting communities demonstrate. RE can be refreshingly countercultural in a qualifications-based, market-driven system.

However, inspection and research data reveal huge variations from excellent RE through inadequate RE to none at all, in spite of its compulsory status. RE has an image problem, not helped by the ambiguity of its name. It is rarely a priority for parents, schools or government, especially in a context which prioritises the economic need to serve the global labour market (though increasingly the soft skills of inter-worldview literacy are valued by employers). Research shows students generally enjoying RE and seeing its value, but usually they see it as less important than other subjects.

Statistics decade after decade reveal that RE has had the least funding, the most unqualified teachers, the least timetable time (teachers recently reporting being required to teach

GCSE classes in half the time of other humanities subjects), and fewest opportunities for continued professional development. Recent education policies have caused new problems for RE. The introduction of the 'English Baccalaureate', interpreted as a list of GCSE subjects that matter and upon which school are judged, omits RE as well as creative arts, leading to further deprioritisation of these subjects. The combination of cuts to local authority funding and the expansion of 'academies' and 'free schools', free from local authority control, has hit RE particularly. Academies do not have to follow the local RE syllabus and, in spite of technically still being required to provide RE, evidence shows that RE is often neglected or omitted in 'academies without a religious character'. Funding for SACREs, which is required by law, varies greatly, including none at all, and is generally decreasing. Initial teacher training in RE for primary teachers has deteriorated from its heyday in the 1990s and early 2000s to just a couple of hours in many cases. Secondary training bursaries for this under-recruiting subject have been restored after much campaigning, but to nowhere near the levels of, for example, Geography.

As well as these structural issues, the RE community has its own debates. A perennial one is whether to stress the academic, knowledge-rich learning about worldviews, or the contribution to the more holistic human development of students. There are arguments about whether to teach a few worldviews (or even just one) in detail and depth, or a wide-ranging selection of Abrahamic and Dharmic religions, newer movements such as Rastafari or Paganism, and non-religious worldviews. How far should RE be responsible for character development, ethical/moral education, community cohesion, citizenship, 'British values' or the Prevent agenda? Which of the many pedagogical approaches should be preferred? The existence of state-funded schools with a religious character, which may have their own denominational aims, further confuses the situation.

The 2018 Commission on Religious Education in England

The REC set up a major Commission on RE which spent 2016–2018 collecting evidence about the current state of RE in England and made recommendations for its future. The greatest concerns were the inequality of access to high quality RE, the problems caused by the increasing mismatch between legislation requiring local authority responsibility for RE and the academisation agenda (leading to ridiculous extremes where LAs are required to produce an RE syllabus which no schools are required to use as they have all become academies), and the changing religious landscape which requires paying more attention to the 'non-religious' and individual as well as institutional worldviews. The Final Report (CoRE, 2018) made eleven recommendations, of which the most important were changing the name, a statutory National Entitlement to the study of Religion and Worldviews, and developing non-statutory national programmes of study based on this. Other recommendations concerned changes to legislation, teacher education, SACREs, inspection, and review of the EBacc and right of withdrawal.

The two-page National Entitlement redefines the subject in terms of nine crucial aspects that need to be grasped to understand what worldviews are all about. These include key concepts; a focus on matters of central importance to adherents; diversity within and between traditions and change across time and context; influences across traditions, and that individuals may draw upon more than one institutional worldview in forming their personal worldview; the role of different categories of literature, ritual and the creative arts in forming and expressing worldviews and different interpretations thereof; how worldviews relate to questions of meaning raised by human experience(s); how worldviews influence the lives of both individuals and societies including behavioural norms; how worldviews have power and influence in society, culture and politics and appeal to various sources of authority; and the many ways in which worldviews can be interpreted and studied, including through a wide range of academic disciplines, and importantly by encounter and dialogue with adherents.

This National Entitlement is partly influenced by *Big Ideas for Religious Education* (Wintersgill, 2017, 2019), which applied international 'Big Ideas' theory of curriculum planning (influential on the science curriculum in the UK) to RE in order to solve some of the perennial problems of content selection, progression and assessment, and enabling students to see the point of education rather than gaining disconnected bits of random information.

Question for discussion

How does English RE need to change in order to ensure high quality provision for all pupils, improve its public image and gain government funding and support?

The 'faith schools' debate

One feature of the odd and complex picture of RE in England is the presence of state-funded 'schools with a religious character', some categories of which are allowed to provide their own *confessional* religious education.

Religious and non-religious worldviews have always influenced education worldwide, whether as providers, underpinning ideologies or curriculum content. Many countries, including the UK, have private schools independently funded by religious groups. Religious organisations such as Christian churches and Buddhist monasteries have in many countries pioneered education for the poor as well as the rich, and non-religious worldviews such as Maoism in the People's Republic of China have similarly influenced schooling. The Catholic Church is the biggest provider of schools worldwide. Such education was mostly aimed to pass on the beliefs, values, customs and sense of identity of the community or tradition providing the schools, and this tended to continue once states took responsibility for providing education. For example, in England and Wales, from 1870 until the late 1960s, a generalised 'non-denominational' Christianity was presumed and promoted even in non-church schools.

In 1870, when state education was introduced, it supplemented rather than replaced the voluntary provision by religious groups, and some state assistance was given to allow the voluntary schools to survive and meet basic standards. (See Chapter 1.) This is known as the 'dual system'. The 1944 Education Act established two categories of state-funded voluntary schools, a distinction which persists today, with the addition of foundation schools, academies and free schools. These are 'voluntary controlled' (VC) and 'voluntary aided' (VA) schools. The former is controlled by the local authority from which it receives all its funding. These schools must follow the non-confessional locally Agreed Syllabus for RE, but may conduct denominational worship. The VA category receives the majority of its funding from the LA, but in return for providing some of the funding itself, the religious body is allowed to provide RE of a denominational nature, as well as worship. Academies and free schools may have a faith-based foundation and RE and worship are determined by the relevant religious body or by the school itself.

Faith-based schools account for roughly one-third of state-funded primary schools, and one-sixth of secondary schools. Since 1998, a few Muslim, Hindu and Sikh schools have gained VA status, in addition to existing Jewish and Christian schools, though the vast majority are Church of England or Catholic. They are popular with parents and perceived as obtaining good academic results, but attacked as divisive and even as 'radicalising' students.

If we want a less divided society where diversity is respected, it might be better if all children from all backgrounds (including differences of wealth, ethnicity, special needs, gender, sexuality and religion) went to the same school. However, many faith-based schools are trying to make up for the disadvantages of segregation by making links with other schools, and by following multi-faith and multicultural curricula. In 2005 all the 'major faith communities' made a written agreement with the then Department for Education and Skills that it was important for schools with a religious character to teach about faiths other than their own. If the recommendations of the Commission for RE are implemented, including the National Entitlement, this might become a reality.

Question for discussion

What is the place of faith-based schools in a plural democracy? Should the state fund such schools?

Related areas: school worship

Religions/worldviews impact on school provision in other ways including practical issues relating to such things as food, dress, the arts and Physical Education. In England there is a legal requirement for schools to provide daily 'collective worship' which is 'wholly or mainly of a broadly Christian character'. Faith schools can provide their own denominational worship. There is the possibility of parental withdrawal from both kinds, and ways in which schools can be exempted, but it remains a difficult area, and often gets confused with RE.

Conclusion: plurality and 'positive pluralism'

The amazing diversity of religions/worldviews and their significant impact on individuals and societies requires that schooling enables children and young people to engage sensitively but critically in an informed way with this area of human experience. This is best achieved by having a discrete subject taught by well-qualified teachers. While confessional or denominational RE (of an open kind) is a human right for faith/belief communities and their schools, all students, whether at a faith-based school or not, should have access to an impartial, inclusive, non-confessional and multi-faith education in Religion and Worldviews.

This author coined a term, 'positive pluralism', in 1991 to describe an approach which views the plurality of religions/worldviews as a positive resource for humanity. Outlined in Cush and Francis (2001) it was developed from practical experience. It is based upon 'epistemological humility': your own sincerely held views, beliefs, values and customs need not mean that you have nothing to learn from others, even when their views differ greatly. Schools should respect the religious and cultural backgrounds of all pupils, whether religious or not, but also accept that these perspectives are open to debate and critical evaluation in the *public* forum that is education. This is *not* to maintain that all views/beliefs/traditions are 'equally valid', a position that does not withstand much scrutiny, or to teach *universalism* – the belief that all religions are the same really, just different paths to the same goal – as these are themselves confessional positions.

Summary points

- It is vitally important that young people are helped to live and work with people from diverse religious and non-religious worldviews, and also to reflect critically upon and develop their own personal worldviews.
- It is difficult to separate the 'religious' from the non-religious, the secular or cultural, but nevertheless 'Religion and Worldviews' is a distinct and necessary academic field.
- 'Factual' knowledge is needed, but is insufficient without understanding of the lived experience of individuals and communities, best gained from direct encounter, and a positively pluralist approach which combines sensitivity and respect with critical evaluation.
- Learning should focus on the 'Big Ideas' of the subject, such as avoiding generalisations about worldviews, or realising that they are about emotions, experience, values and identity and not just beliefs.
- Religious Education in England has a rather odd place in education policy and practice, but we can be proud of an innovative tradition much respected internationally.
- State funding of 'faith-based' schools is one example of a controversial issue at the interface between religion and education.

Recommended reading

Cush, D. (2007) Should Religious Studies Be Part of the State School Curriculum? *British Journal of Religious Education* **29**(3), pp. 217–227.

Grimmitt, M. (2000) *Pedagogies of Religious Education*. London: McCrimmons.

Jackson, R. (2004) *Rethinking Religious Education and Plurality: Issues in Diversity and Pedagogy*. London: RoutledgeFalmer.

Stern, J. (2018) *Teaching Religious Education*. London: Bloomsbury.

References

CoRE (Commission on Religious Education) (2018) *Final Report: Religion and Worldviews, the Way Forward: A National Plan for RE*. London: RE Council. Available at: www.commissiononre.org.uk/wp-content/uploads/2018/09/Final-Report-of-the-Commission-on-RE.pdf (accessed 28 March 2019).

Cush, D. and Francis, D. (2001) Positive Pluralism to Awareness, Mystery and Value: A Case Study in RE Curriculum Development. *British Journal of Religious Education* **24**(1), pp. 52–67.

Jackson, R. (2016) *Inclusive Study of Religions and Worldviews in Europe: Signposts from the Council of Europe*. Strasbourg: Council of Europe.

Nesbitt, E. (2004) *Intercultural Education: Ethnographic and Religious Approaches*. Brighton: Sussex Academic Press.

QCA (2004) *Religious Education: The Non-Statutory National Framework*. London: QCA.

REC (2013) *A Review of Religious Education in England*. Available at: http://resubjectreview.recouncil.org.uk/re-review-report (accessed 20 May 2019).

SCAA (1994) *Religious Education: Model Syllabuses*. London: SCAA.

Schools Council (1971) *Working Paper 36: Religious Education in Secondary Schools*. London: Evans/Methuen.

Wintersgill, B. (Ed.) (2017) *Big Ideas for Religious Education*. Exeter: University of Exeter.

Woodhead, L. (2016) Why No Religion Is the New Religion. Talk given at the British Academy 19 January 2016. Available at www.youtube.com/watch?v=hPLsuW-TCtA (accessed 23 May 2019).

Chapter 11

Education and climate change

David Hicks

Introduction

Why is it that all educators and learners need to understand the consequences of living in a climate-changed world? How can we help young people explore this extraordinary issue without losing their sense of direction and agency? This chapter sets out to clarify questions such as these and, in particular, explores:

- the various impacts of climate change and what the causes of these are;
- action that can be taken to both mitigate and adapt to climate change;
- the crucial role education can play in responding to this phenomenon.

The chapter begins by summarising the current *impacts* of climate change on both people and the planet. It then looks at the *causes* of climate change arising from our use of high-carbon fossil fuels over the last 250 years. Important responses come under two headings: *mitigation* (i.e. limiting climate change) and *adaptation* (i.e. ways in which society needs to change in order to stay safe).

Climate change

In 2018 the International Panel on Climate Change (set up in 1988) published its sixth report on the difficulties we face if prompt action is not taken. One headline reported: 'Huge Risk if Global Warming Exceeds 1.5C, Warns Landmark UN Report' (Watts, 2018). This chapter helps explain why.

Impacts

We all know what our weather looks like, but over the last few decades things have changed. We are now experiencing more variable and extreme weather, outside the normal range, due to a gradual rise in global temperatures. We have had extremes of weather in the past, but part of their increasing strength can now be attributed to climate change. The world is experiencing heavier rainfall, more frequent flooding and rising sea-levels. Heatwaves and fires have become more common and last much longer than before (Carrington,

2018). Storms are more damaging, winters more harsh, growing seasons more unpredictable. Make no mistake – this is the 'new normal' (Hicks, 2017). How this affects people in different parts of the world will vary, as does the damage that can arise.

Causes

By the 1980s it was clear these changes were caused by man-made greenhouse gases. This term was used because such gases act like the glass in a greenhouse, trapping heat within it. The three main gases are: i) carbon dioxide (CO_2) from the burning of fossil fuels – coal, oil and gas; ii) methane from the digestion systems of cattle – twenty-five times more powerful than fossil fuels; iii) nitrous oxide, a by-product of industrial processes – 300 times more powerful than CO_2. The progress brought by the nineteenth-century industrial revolution and technological developments of the twentieth century contained a terrible sting in their tail – global warming and thus climate change. Not something our ancestors could have ever foreseen or imagined. The task facing us all is to transition as speedily as possible from a dangerous high-carbon society to a more sustainable low- or zero-carbon one.

Responses

Mitigation

The action that enables us to play an active part in this cultural shift involves both 'mitigation' and 'adaptation'. Mitigation is any action that helps reduce carbon emissions, whether in school, at home or in the community. Essentially mitigation is about limiting one's 'carbon footprint'. This is a tool for measuring all the activities we partake in that cause carbon emissions. A good example is the Carbon Footprint Calculator (2018), where one can enter figures for oneself or one's family under headings such as house, flights, car, bus and rail, secondary. The secondary category includes everyday items such as food and drink, clothes, books and newspapers, computers, phones, restaurants, banking and recreation. Each aspect has its own footprint, which is then calculated in tonnes of CO_2 emitted. It is then possible to see where one's footprint needs to be reduced.

Adaptation

Adaptation refers to the changes that need to be made in school, home and community, to stay safe in the face of higher temperatures, increased flooding, rising sea-levels and dangerous storms. Adaptation is about what we need to do to stay both safe and as comfortable as possible in the face of climate change (Hicks, 2017). Some things are obvious. Although developers still build housing estates on flood plains, next to streams and rivers, the term is a give-away. If you have the choice, don't live near areas that might possibly flood. Learn what you need to do to stay safe in or near floods, particularly if children are involved. Learn what needs to be done in prolonged heatwaves. Old buildings will need retrofitting and new properties need to be based on climate-proof designs. Issues of mitigation and adaptation are both personal and local, but politicians, economists, and business leaders also have a major part to play, as do schools.

Denial

Many people find the whole notion of climate change difficult to comprehend. As a friend said, 'This cannot possibly be true!' Climate change is thus often seen as: someone else's responsibility; it doesn't feel really dangerous; we haven't got the whole picture; we can't imagine such a thing happening; it won't happen yet. Research by Oreskes and Conway (2010) found that many climate-change deniers work for the fossil fuel industries, or oppose any notion that neoliberal economics helps create climate change. Norgaard (2011) discovered how community norms are used to police discussion about climate change. Unwritten social rules thus ensure that some topics are just not up for public discussion. Climate change comes into this category because it turns our world upside down as well as feeling too big to comprehend. In a way denial is a logical response to an issue as complex as this. It feels too big to take in when there are other things that may urgently need our attention.

Revisioning

There is a powerful alternative to such negative responses. This is to understand the causes of climate change and then work: a) to limit its impacts (mitigation) and b) to stay safe from its consequences (adaptation). Both are equally important, at all levels of society, and this is where education has a crucial role to play. In short, we need to revise our views of what is 'normal' society. The old high-carbon story is dangerous and redundant. We, and future generations, need to understand, share and enact the new and safe zero-carbon story (Hicks, 2018). This doesn't mean climate change will go away – it will last for many generations – but it would mean we were pulling together towards a common goal. As educators we stand at the heart of such an endeavour (CAT, 2017). What steps does your school need to take now in order to begin envisioning and working towards such a future? Some schools are already beginning to engage in this work – sharing success stories, developing a sense of hope and agency in learners (Hicks, 2014).

Educational rationale

There is an argument, sometimes heard, that problematic issues should not be discussed in the classroom because they are too difficult and worrying for young minds to take in. The issue here is how we teach children about climate change and, in particular, whether we help them explore what their own concerns and hopes for the future might be. Of particular importance is helping young people see how they themselves can contribute to appropriate action for change. Winograd (2016) is a good resource in this context.

Contested terrain

But why should climate change have anything to do with schools and education? Climate change could be construed as too difficult to explore, too scary, needing specialist teachers, not belonging to any subject area, not part of the curriculum (except Geography), or there is no time for it. Its very complexity could make it difficult to teach, it could worry learners, it could be seen as irrelevant to everyday life. But it isn't any of these. What it does do is raise profound questions about the purpose and process of learning. It is crucial to recall that the purposes of education have always been contested: that is people have argued for a range of different purposes over time and across the world. For example, is it to pass on subject knowledge, to create a competitive workforce, to adhere to a religious tradition, to educate an elite, to bring out the best in all learners, to help change society for the better? Education is never neutral because its different forms embody the values and beliefs of its proponents, demonstrated by what is given emphasis in the curriculum, what is omitted and the very process of learning itself (Apple, 2006).

Neoliberal values

There was a time when teachers, as a professional body, were taken to be the experts on education. This shifted dramatically in the UK in the 1980s when politicians took control of teachers, schools and educational policy (see Chapter 1). At that time Conservatives were particularly taken by the philosophy of neoliberalism and its view of how the world worked best. Monbiot (2016) identifies some of its key beliefs as follows.

> Neoliberalism sees competition as the defining characteristic of human relations. It redefines citizens as consumers, whose democratic choices are best exercised by buying and selling, a process that rewards merit and punishes inefficiency. It maintains that 'the market' delivers benefits that could never be achieved by planning. Attempts to limit competition are treated as inimical to liberty. Tax and regulation should be minimised, public services should be privatised.

The impact of these beliefs on education has been elegantly dissected by Apple (2006). Currently many schools and curricula reflect such values: competition, hierarchy, privatisation, a mechanistic view of the curriculum, inadequate funding and marginalisation of social, political and environmental issues. This is not a good climate for education about climate change, or any other issue, to flourish in.

Holistic education

Traditional methods of learning are not sufficient on their own for the liberated learning that climate change requires. It can never be just about knowledge, because social and environmental issues are about both head and heart. Knowing how to think and analyse are vital but so also is the affective dimension of learning. What do I feel here? Is it really safe to share this? Do I trust this teacher/others in this group? Head and heart are two sides of the same coin; together they take us deeper, and need to be welcomed and respected. Climate change also requires that we become good decision-makers. What are the options we face here? Which is likely to be our most effective course of action?

There are those who believe this is where the boundaries of education should stop. One might have become knowledgeable about climate change but not be expected to actually act on this. But what is this learning worth if not directed into any form of positive action? One actually learns that meaningful action is inappropriate and nothing to do with school. Thoughtful action with others should be the end result of all education (Winograd, 2016). This is why whole-school policies on sustainability and climate-change safety improve the quality of learning and interaction between students and staff. We know what the problem is. We know what we want to do about it. We know who can help us and who we want to work with. This is active citizenship and participatory democracy at its best.

As Whitehouse (2016: 162–165) argues:

> The problem is that teachers can no longer educate for a future where the earth's climate is relatively stable … The moral imperative of doing something in response to the existential crisis of climate change, rather than only learning about something, changes the nature of teachers' work … no group's interests are as threatened by the climate crisis as are children's interests. The challenge is both political and moral.

Both children and students can develop a mature sense of agency in such contexts because they know what and how to contribute with support from others. Such participatory and holistic learning, when thoughtfully done, can diminish initial concerns that come up. Students are more likely to know what they want to do in life, they will have a trained eye on the future and be more ready for what is coming next down the line. Educating young people to contribute positively to a climate-changed world is one of the greatest gifts our generation can give. Not to do so would be to betray the future generations for whom as educators we have been given responsibility. Such learners will have a sense of hope rather than despair.

Good practice

Dimensions of learning

Whilst traditional learning focuses on the acquisition of information and skills, holistic learning takes a deeper and more multifaceted view of education. Climate change, as well as other issues, requires four dimensions of learning: knowing, feeling, choosing and acting. It isn't just about acquisition of knowledge (head), but also acknowledging feelings (heart). This is why emotional literacy and affective teaching have such an important part to play in schools. Where feelings are acknowledged supportively, both learning and relationships are deepened. When issues are being explored, learners also need to develop and hone their critical thinking skills, so they can clarify where they stand and how they might want to respond. An issue like climate change also requires active citizenship in school and community. There are but three possible educational responses to climate change: i) learn nothing, do nothing; ii) study climate change, take token action; iii) investigate climate change, working with others for the benefit of all in the community (Hicks, 2014).

In embarking on the latter course all four dimensions of learning are of equal import-ance. In exploring and intertwining these dimensions each has its own key enabling questions as follows.

> *Knowing:* What do we think we know/need to know about climate change? What are the main causes of climate change? What are the already occurring and future impacts of this?

> *Feeling:* What do I/we feel about climate change? What are the concerns/fears that we wish to share? What are the hopes and aspirations we have?

> *Choosing:* What appear to be the options facing us? What do I/we want to see happening? What should our school choose to do?

> *Acting:* What can we do to mitigate and adapt to climate change? What are others doing? Who can help us with what we wish to achieve?

Each dimension reflects a key element of both self and deeper learning. Knowledge needs to be interrogated and analysed for its ideological slant and its value to the community. Feelings, the affective domain, need to be supportively shared in a safe and respectful environment (see below). What we think and feel are two sides of the same coin, each affecting the other. The affective domain cannot be out of bounds in education, any more than it can in life. Thoughtful choosing is a vital decision-making skill. After weighing evi-dence and options, learners can then consider the best ways forward.

Working in groups

I have often found that young people and students feel uncomfortable when working in groups, a process which is vital to cooperative learning. The concern generally arises because no ground rules have been set out first. In my experience there are five essential ground rules which need to be set out as follows.

Speaking – Only one person should speak at a time, by putting a hand up or taking it in turns. *Listening* – Listen attentively to the speaker and do not interrupt. *Not judging* – Listen without making judgements, respecting the views and feelings of others. *Sharing* – No one person should dominate, no one should be left out, everyone should be encouraged to contribute. *Voice* – It is not necessarily about saying the right thing, but about finding one's voice and feeling supported by others.

I have many times seen acceptance of these ground rules transform an individual's experience of working in a group. Feeling one might be judged by others or that one has nothing to say can be debilitating in the extreme for some learners. Learning to work respectfully and cooperatively is at the heart of all effective learning.

Activity: Making climate change visible

An excellent resource for both schools and communities is Sheppard's *Visualising Climate Change* (2012), which approaches this issue through the four key themes used at the begin-ning of this chapter. His starting assumption is that learners often fail to recognise any evidence of the carbon chain around them. Thus his initial question, 'What are the tell-tale signs of carbon use in our community?'

Causes of climate change

Students are given a set of photographs to examine, all of which make visible the apparently 'invisible' carbon causes of climate change. Photos are clustered into groups; examples include the following. *Out of sight, out of mind*: offshore oil or gas rigs, coal mines, petrochemical refining, fossil fuel power plants. *Extreme events*: oil spills, refinery explosions, burst oil pipelines, televised clean-ups. *Local fossil fuel use*: low-efficiency homes, use of electricity meters, poorly insulated buildings, outside gas heaters. *Fossil fuels for transport*: petrol stations, cars and lorries, car adverts, extra wide streets, vapour trails in the sky.

Working in pairs, learners have to identify what each photo shows and how it is related to the carbon chain. High-carbon dependency is initially almost impossible to see, a 'landscape of guilt' that we do not wish to confront. An activity such as this can mark the beginnings of carbon consciousness and the ability to name it in the community.

Impacts of climate change

It might seem likely that the impacts of climate change are more readily identified in photos, given that this often involves damage and loss, but they can be misconstrued as natural processes or simply extreme weather. Example of photos Sheppard uses include the following. *Iconic and chronic*: melting ice-floes, retreating glaciers, the state of island communities, dust storms. *Extreme weather*: heatwaves, hurricanes, storm damage, dangerous flooding, severe ice and snow. *Gradual shifts*: early spring, new birds at the bird table, water restriction signs, forest die-back. *Multiple impacts*: bath-tub ring on lakes, increased run-off and erosion, landslides, wave damage.

Further photo sequences, as well as fieldwork, can be used to illustrate mitigation and adaptation initiatives in the local or other communities. It is as important to be able to identify solutions (mitigation and adaptation) to climate change as well as causes and impacts. Once students have learnt to actively see the carbon chain and the ways of breaking it, a basic climate literacy has been achieved.

Whole school: LESS CO$_2$

There are lots of things that can be part of whole-school policy too.

> *Are you a council working to reduce the energy use in your school estate? Want to engage and enthuse schools in your area about energy saving? Then talk to the LESS CO$_2$ team to see what we can do for you.*

Schools that have taken part in the free LESS CO$_2$ programme have gone on to save an average 14 per cent on energy costs and 17 tonnes of carbon each year. If you have challenging carbon reduction targets in your area, and are struggling for ways in which to reduce your emissions, then the LESS CO_2 programme could significantly help you reduce the emissions associated with the education sector and schools estate. The programme has worked closely with energy officers within local councils to help schools make significant reductions in their energy use, and hence save money on their ongoing energy bills.

> To register a cluster onto the programme the council needs to recruit up to 15 schools, ideally geographically close to one another, to work together in their cluster over the duration of the programme ... When the cluster is recruited and registered, the council then helps to secure the locations and venues for the four workshops through the year. These are: 1. Quick wins to save energy; 2. Engaging with your staff and students; 3. Linking sustainability into your teaching; 4. Being a sustainable school.
>   In between the workshops the schools have the opportunity to put into practice what they have learnt. This helps the programme become part of your school's culture and means you can start saving energy, and money on your bills, from day one. In subsequent workshops you share your experiences, challenges and successes with your peer group.
>   For details see: www.lessco2.org.uk/

Activity: Climate change reactions

Purpose: Critically reflecting on the impacts of climate change on people's lives in order to develop empathetic understanding of others.
Age level: 9–18
Time needed: 20–40 minutes
Resources:

- Computer/internet facilities to show an online video clip
- Online video clip on impacts of climate change on people's lives. For instance, teachers can choose a video clip from the 'climate witness video' section of WWF's website: http://wwf.panda.org/about_our_earth/aboutcc/problems/people_at_risk/ personal_stories/witness_stories/video2/
- Four slips of paper per student (create by quartering blank sheet of paper)

Procedure: In groups of six. After watching the chosen video clip, each individual writes four different reactions to what they have watched, one per slip of paper. This could be a brief paragraph, sentence or word. These are collected by one of the group, shuffled and dealt out as in a game of cards. Each group member looks at their 'hand', discarding into the centre any they wrote or don't relate to. They continue to discard and pick up from the pool until everyone has up to three reactions which i) they didn't write themselves and ii) they are in agreement with. Then in threes each reads their hand to the others, explaining why they chose those reactions. The whole group then collectively composes a reaction to the video clip, subgroups sharing and explaining their reactions before negotiating and writing a final whole-group reaction. Full class discussion follows.

Guidance: This activity is excellent for achieving a thoroughgoing sharing of reactions to a chosen story of how climate change impacts on people's lives. It helps develop empathetic understanding towards people in the story as well as towards participants. Students negotiate a joint agreed position or, if possible, clarify the nature of disagreements that emerge and their own perspectives and values.

To trigger *whole-class* discussion, questions such as the following will be useful:

- How did you first respond to the video clip and how did you express that response in your four reaction slips?
- Did the 'shuffling cards' process open your eyes to different ways of seeing the video clip?
- How challenging was the group writing of a joint reaction to the video clip? Does everyone feel their opinions were taken into account, or did you feel ignored at that stage?
- Looking at the reactions (personal, group, whole group), what values do they manifest? What change and action possibilities do they throw up?

Source: Abbreviated from Sustainability Frontiers (2013).
Available online at: www.sustainabilityfrontiers.org/

Conclusion

This chapter has set out the rationale for a curriculum which will help students think more critically and creatively about climate change. It highlights the need to understand both its causes and consequences as well as the crucial responses of mitigation and adaptation. It highlights the importance of positive action for change by teachers and students in schools and classrooms. Examples of good practice are given that embrace a holistic mode of learning, engaging both head and heart, leading to active citizenship in school and community.

But in 2018, Greta Thunberg (aged 15) walked out of school in Stockholm and began a strike outside the Swedish parliament because she felt neither schools nor politicians were paying attention to the gravity of the climate crisis. Other students rapidly joined in her protest which captured the imagination of young people who felt their concerns were not listened to. School climate strikes on Fridays spread like wildfire (www.fridaysforfuture.org). In March 2019 1.4 million students took part in such strikes in 128 countries and over 2,000 towns and cities around the world. Greta became a spokesperson for her generation, addressing both politicians and world leaders. Since it is the future of young people which is ultimately at stake it is unlikely this movement will dissipate. Are teachers and schools fit for this task or will they be found wanting in the dangerous days that lie ahead? Climate change requires a profound revisioning of schools, teaching and education before it is too late. What, in particular, do you think needs to change?

Questions for discussion

- How can you help to wean people off the redundant old high-carbon story?
- Who can help and support you in these endeavours?
- What is it you wish to be known for in the context of climate change education?

Summary points

- All schools should be thinking critically and creatively about climate change.
- This requires due exploration of its causes, impacts, mitigation and adaptation.
- Engagement of both head and heart helps develop a practical sense of agency.
- Learners thus respond to climate change through insightful active citizenship. How can you help learners to understand and enjoy the new zero-carbon story?

Recommended reading

CAT (2017) *Zero Carbon Britain: Making It Happen.* Machynlleth: Centre for Alternative Technology. Available at: www.zerocarbonbritain.org//images/pdfs/ZeroCarbonBritain-MakingItHappen. pdf

Hicks, D. (2014) *Educating for Hope in Troubled Times: Climate Change and the Transition to a Post-Carbon Future.* London: UCL IOE Press.

Hicks, D. (2017) *A Climate Change Companion: For Family, School and Community.* Chepstow: Teaching for a Better World.

Sheppard, S. (2012) *Visualising Climate Change: A Guide to Visual Communication of Climate Change and Developing Local Solutions.* London: Routledge.

Teaching for a Better World (2018) Available at: www.teaching4abetterworld.co.uk

References

Apple, M. (2006) *Educating the 'Right' Way: Markets, Standards, God, and Inequality.* London: RoutledgeFalmer.

Carbon Footprint Calculator. Available at: www.carbonfootprint.com/calculator.aspx (accessed 7 November 2018).

Carrington, D. (2018) Extreme Global Weather Is 'the Face of Climate Change' Says Leading Scientist. *The Guardian,* 27 July 2018. Available at: www.theguardian.com/environment/2018/jul/27/extreme-global-weather-climate-change-michael-mann (accessed 7 November 2018).

CAT (2017) *Zero Carbon Britain: Making It Happen.* Machynlleth: Centre for Alternative Technology. Available at: www.zerocarbonbritain.org//images/pdfs/ZeroCarbonBritain-MakingItHappen. pdf.

Hicks, D. (2014) *Educating for Hope in Troubled Times: Climate Change and the Transition to a Post-Carbon Future.* London: UCL IOE Press.

Hicks, D. (2017) *A Climate Change Companion: For Family, School and Community.* Chepstow: Teaching for a Better World.

Hicks, D. (2018) *Energy Matters: What Stories Do We Tell?* Available at: www.teaching4abetterworld. co.uk/docs/ENERGY%20MATTERS.pdf (accessed 7 November 2018).

LESS CO_2 (2018) Available at: www.lessco2.org.uk/ (accessed 7 November 2018).

Monbiot, G. (2016) Neoliberalism – the Ideology at the Root of All Our Problems. Available at: www.theguardian.com/books/2016/apr/15/neoliberalism-ideology-problem-george-monbiot (accessed 7 November 2018).

Norgaard, K. (2011) *Living in Denial: Climate Change, Emotions, and Everyday Life*. Cambridge, MA: MIT Press.

Oreskes, N. and Conway, E. (2010) *Merchants of Doubt: How a Handful of Scientists Obscured the Truth on Issues from Tobacco Smoke to Global Warming*. London: Bloomsbury.

Sheppard, S. (2012) *Visualising Climate Change: A Guide to Visual Communication of Climate Change and Developing Local Solutions*. London: Routledge.

Watts, J. (2018) Huge Risk if Global Warming Exceeds 1.5C, Warns Landmark UN Report. *The Guardian*, 8 October 2018. Available at: www.theguardian.com/environment/2018/oct/08/global-warming-must-not-exceed15c-warns-landmark-un-report (accessed 7 November 2018).

Whitehouse, H. (2016) The New Realism: A Rationale for Supporting Children's Climate Activism. In K. Winograd (Ed.), *Education in Times of Environmental Crises: Teaching Children to be Agents of Change*. London: Routledge.

Winograd, K. (Ed.) (2016) *Education in Times of Environmental Crises: Teaching Children to be Agents of Change*. London: Routledge.

Chapter 12

Education for sustainability

David Hicks

Introduction

Why is it so important for teachers to know about issues to do with the environment and human wellbeing? How can we help young people understand the urgent need for a more sustainable future for themselves and others? This chapter sets out to understand questions such as these and, in particular, explores:

- the rationale for a curriculum which explores issues of global sustainability;
- key debates about the meaning and nature of unsustainability/sustainability;
- educational initiatives illustrating good practice in education for sustainability.

Put at its most simple any human activity is *sustainable* if it can continue fairly indefinitely without causing harm to people or the planet. Alternatively, any human activity which results in ongoing harm to people or the planet is the opposite, *unsustainable*. Whilst this may sound an oversimplification, it also encapsulates a profound truth.

Recent reports on our impact on the natural world show that 'since the dawn of civilisation, humanity has caused the loss of 83 per cent of all wild mammals and half of plants' (Carrington, 2018). Damage on this scale is unsustainable because it is actually destroying the planet's life-support system. Research into human wellbeing shows that less equal societies are always marked by higher levels of stress, mental health problems and depression (Wilkinson and Pickett, 2018). This too is unsustainable. In the face of such facts we have no option but to explore more sustainable alternatives.

Educational rationale

Global awakening

The first photograph of the Earth taken from space in 1972 had a profound impact on human consciousness, our home planet like a 'blue marble' against the infinite blackness of space. All that we are, all that we care about, exists on that exquisite dewdrop of life. This awareness fundamentally altered humanity's view of itself, seen not as a random collection of individuals but rather a planetary community travelling through space. That decade also saw a growing awareness of global issues – damage to the environment, increasing global inequality, debates about the limits to growth – all interlinked and needful of attention. International organisations such as Friends of the Earth and Greenpeace sprang up to inform people about such matters.

Teachers felt young people needed to understand such issues too and by the 1980s educators were using terms such as global education, environmental education, education for sustainable development and education for sustainability (Hicks, 2008). These terms were seen not as related to a particular subject area, but rather as cross-curricular in importance. They often stressed education of the whole person, i.e. head and heart, knowing and feeling, as well as an active form of citizenship in which learners could participate and contribute to the wellbeing of their own communities in these matters.

Creating sustainable futures

Six fundamental building blocks which need to underpin any programme of education for sustainability are set out below.

The biosphere

The biosphere is that thin layer of life – atmosphere, rivers and seas, rocks and soil, flora and fauna, vegetation and living creatures – which makes our existence possible. Each of these elements needs to be in balance with the others for life to flourish. It is the biosphere which forms the planet's life-support system (Juniper, 2015). However, over the last two centuries the industrialised countries of the world have used the biosphere as an endless source of raw materials and a depository for all our wastes. Students therefore need to know why and how this came about and ways in which this situation can be sustainably resolved.

Human wellbeing

Over the last two centuries the richer countries of the world used their economic and military power to exploit and consume more than their fair share of the earth's resources. This contributed to growing inequality both within and between countries, as well as major migrations of peoples searching for a better life. Countries with the greatest inequality also have the highest incidence of social problems, poor health and mental illness (Wilkinson and Pickett, 2018). Students therefore need to explore and understand the ways in which these processes have led to extremes of wealth and poverty and ways in which this can be resolved sustainably.

Limits to growth

This prolonged exploitation of both people and the earth's resources, with its stress on constant economic growth, has led to a rampant consumerism in the rich world which now threatens all our futures. It has caused extreme damage to rivers and oceans, farmland and wilderness, despoliation through dumping and exporting waste, loss of flora and fauna, the extinction of many species, and damage to the atmosphere itself (Randers, 2012). Students therefore need to understand the limits to growth that exist in a finite world if the biosphere is to maintain its function as an effective life-support system (Hicks, 2014).

A new vision

This requires a 'new' vision of society and of the future, locally and globally. Such a practical vision was birthed back in the 1980s and has a long history (Visser, 2009). This participatory vision weaves together all the varying elements of a more sustainable future, from homes, schools and communities to work, leisure, farming and industry. Many of the pieces of this jigsaw are already available (Washington, 2015). Students therefore need to explore the history and lineage of this new low-carbon story, whilst developing skills of practical envisioning and action that can help lead to a variety of more just and sustainable futures.

Holistic thinking

Many of the problems we face today are the result of what is called a 'mechanistic' worldview, one in which we constantly break things down into their separate parts in order to make sense of the whole. Whilst this is vitally important, we then tend to see the world as if it is made up of innumerable separate parts. Even more important now is understanding whole systems and how they operate – for the sum is always more than the parts (Goleman *et al.*, 2012). Students therefore need to develop a more holistic or ecological view of their communities and the world by using the skills of 'joined-up', rather than fragmented, thinking.

Action for change

A number of global issues, such as environmental damage, climate change and energy use, will ensure the later decades of the twenty-first century are very different from today (Hicks, 2014). A curriculum which ignores the current state of the planet will fail to prepare students for the changes that lie ahead. Education for sustainability analyses the causes of unsustainable practices and explores new models of sustainability that support the well-being of both people and planet (Worldwatch Institute, 2017). Students therefore need to know about existing initiatives that are inspiring the action from which more sustainable lifestyles, schools and communities are emerging.

Debates

Economics versus ecology

The problem that underlies many global dilemmas is the question of how we can move from largely unsustainable ways of being towards more sustainable ways of living. This, however, is where the views of economists and ecologists generally collide (Barry, 2012).

Put at its simplest, economists tend to believe that there are no limits to growth, while ecologists acknowledge the finiteness of the earth's natural systems.

In the face of current global turmoil both economists and politicians continue to argue that the only thing that can save the world is increased consumption and economic growth. Commercial over-exploitation of global fish stocks is severe, war-torn areas are reduced to rubble and local populations flee, whilst climate change brings a whole raft of new hazards (Monbiot, 2016a). The assumption that economic activity is somehow independent from the biosphere has never been true. Growth, that is making an economy bigger, is not the same as sustainable development, which should aim to improve both human and environmental wellbeing.

Ecologists and others have long argued that: i) technological solutions on their own will not bring about a sustainable society; ii) exponential growth can lead to sudden catastrophes, economic, environmental and climatic; iii) problems cannot be resolved in isolation, but only when seen as part of an organic whole. Taking the biosphere as their model, ecologists insist that there are clear limits to growth and that our species needs to learn to live within these limits. As a result of such concerns, various authorities are arguing for a quite different view of economics, such as Washington's (2015) *Demystifying Sustainability* and Raworth's (2017) *Doughnut Economics*.

Impact of neoliberalism

Neoliberalism is the political belief system which underpins the current Western worldview. Among its core beliefs is the notion that human nature is basically competitive and that this is how the world works best. What follows from this is the notion of 'economic rationality': that competition between people, institutions and countries will bring material benefits to all. Governments should therefore not interfere with the process of the free market. This view has also deeply affected the way in which education is viewed and organised (Apple, 2006).

By contrast, what one might call a 'welfare-state' view of society stresses the importance of cooperation and responsibility for the welfare of others, especially the less fortunate. This view argues that the state has a key role to play in promoting the welfare of all in society. This would involve legislation ensuring state support for those in genuine need, which protected the environment and promoted sustainable development. Whereas neoliberalism leaves it to individuals and businesses to promote sustainability, if it is thought profitable, a welfare-state view stresses the need for governments to take the lead and actively encourage initiatives which will help create a more just and sustainable society (Monbiot, 2016b).

Contested meanings

The Brundtland Report (1987: 79) described sustainable development as 'development that meets the needs of the present without compromising the ability of future generations to meet their own needs'. While a useful starting point, critics might argue that neoliberal models of sustainable development focus narrowly on economic growth as a measure of progress and discount other costs. Thus actually: i) some people benefit at the expense of others; ii) people benefit at the expense of the environment; iii) people today benefit at the expense of future generations. This is patently unsustainable. A more radical and just notion of sustainability would emphasise: i) *human wellbeing*: increased levels of social and economic wellbeing for all, especially the least advantaged; ii) *environmental value*: increased emphasis on the need to protect the biosphere on which all life depends; iii) *future generations* should inherit at least as much wealth, natural and human, as we ourselves inherited.

Governments of rich countries often want poorer countries to take a more responsible attitude towards their natural environment. Poorer countries often see this as a luxury and want richer countries to help them eradicate poverty. Many poorer countries see imperialism and the strategies of the International Monetary Fund (IMF) as largely responsible for unsustainable development. They resent the suggestion that they shouldn't exploit their own natural resources for their own benefit. They also see the corporate neocolonialism of transnational corporations as a major factor in supporting unsustainable global business strategies.

Although sustainable development is part of international policy language, its meaning is still widely contested due to these fundamental ideological differences, and thus the term Education for Sustainable Development (ESD) is seen as suspect for many. When you come across the terms 'sustainable growth' and 'sustainable development' do not take them at face value. Read carefully between the lines to see which version of sustainability is being promoted.

Education for sustainability

Four key elements

One of the best models of sustainability is that put forward by UNESCO (2018) in *Teaching and Learning for a Sustainable Future*. It points out that a holistic or multidimensional notion of sustainability must encompass the ecological, economic, social and political dimensions of life. The *ecological* dimension requires care and protection of the biosphere as our essential life-support system. The *economic* dimension requires a society in which jobs and income are protected. The *social* dimension requires a society in which peace and equity are present and valued. The *political* dimension requires a democratic society in which power and decision-making are participatory in nature. Models such as this highlight the interconnectedness of all human experience and the ways in which the welfare of people and planet are inextricably intertwined.

Sustainable schools

It should be noted that party political differences always show up in educational documents. The Labour government (1997–2010) was very supportive of education for sustainability, whilst subsequent governments have not been. I cite below from several official documents of this period because they remain exemplary. For example, the role of education for sustainability in the curriculum was clearly set out in the original *National Framework for Sustainable Schools* and remains equally important today.

> Sustainable development is a way of thinking about how we organise our lives and work – including our education system – so that we don't destroy our most precious resource, the planet. From over-fishing to global warming, our way of life is placing an increasing burden on the planet, which cannot be sustained. Things which were once taken for granted such as a secure supply of energy or a stable climate do not look so permanent now. We need to help people in all parts of the world to find solutions that improve their quality of life without storing up problems for the future, or impacting unfairly on other people's lives. Sustainable development means much more than recycling bottles or giving money to charity. It is about thinking and working in a profoundly different way.
>
> (DCSF, 2007)

Whilst for ideological reasons political parties often play down the educational successes of previous governments, the guidelines on education for sustainability from the then Department for Children, Schools and Families (2007) are invaluable. The *National Framework* suggested that issues of sustainability could be explored through 'eight doorways': food and drink, energy and water, travel and traffic, purchasing and waste, buildings and grounds, inclusion and participation, local wellbeing, the global dimension. These doorways highlight the fact that, rather than issues of sustainability being another add-on, they are integral to the concerns of everyday life.

Good practice

Good practice in relation to education for sustainability should take place in the classroom, the whole school and the local community. It often begins in small ways and grows into a holistic endeavour involving children, teachers, management and ancillary staff. The eight doorways are a reminder that much of the curriculum can be approached in a way which highlights issues of sustainability. Where do our food and drink come from? What impact does its creation have on other people and the environment? How much energy and water do we use each day? Where do they come from and what impact does this have on others and the environment? Once the basic concepts of education for sustainability are understood, they can become woven into the fabric of everyday teaching and school life. Children know electricity comes at the press of a switch and water at the touch of a tap, but, if they are not taught to ask questions about the why and how of this, they will become yet another generation committed to unsustainable practices.

Food and farming 2050: a classroom activity

Here is a classroom activity, taken from *Sustainable Schools, Sustainable Futures* (Hicks, 2012), which encourages pupils to explore and debate a scenario illustrating possible aspects of a more sustainable food future. Each pupil needs a copy of the scenario and the numbered questions below.

Process

- Explain that visual scenarios are pictures of possible futures that could come about. They are not predictions, but used in order to prompt discussion and debate.
- Pupils work in small groups. First they individually write down their own responses to the questions below and then work to create a composite small–group response.
- Groups take it in turns to share their response with the rest of the class. Group responses or a composite class response can be put up for display.

Instruction

Look carefully at this scenario of what a more sustainable food future might look like. Imagine you are visiting this future with a group of friends to gather information about it. You can look around to see how things are different and also listen to what people are saying about life in this future.

Questions

1. What are the first three things you notice about this future?
2. How is this future different from today?
3. What are people doing and saying that is different?
4. What are the advantages of living in this future?
5. What questions do you have about this future?

This activity is an example of how one of the eight 'doorways' to sustainability (see above) can be explored. It would, of course, not stand alone but be embedded in a wider project on sustainable food and farming.

Sustainable schools: some research findings

L. Jackson (2007) *Leading Sustainable Schools: What the Research Tells Us*, National College for School Leadership.

What sort of leadership is found in schools committed to learning for sustainability? Here are some findings from a key piece of research into the characteristics of such leaders and their schools.

> From this study, it is evident that leaders who develop sustainability within their school do so with a passion and conviction, underpinned by personal values ... We found sustainable school leaders place sustainability at the heart of their school, providing an ethos which pervades all aspects of the school and its external relationships.

Successful schools are often inward looking, focused on attainment and good management, and the survey indicates that most school leaders place the global dimension relatively low on their priorities. However, sustainable schools look outwards to engage with their local communities and have a global perspective. This wider, more inclusive vision is also seen in the strong pupil voice and involvement of pupils in decision-making that we found in many of the case study schools.

From the case studies, schools are using sustainability to deliver the … curriculum in ways that are relevant and real to the students, leading to high levels of attainment or value-added progress. The survey results indicate that pupils are key in developing sustainability and there are several supporting comments endorsing their role in driving this agenda in schools.

The emerging model of green, or sustainable, school leadership builds on what we already know of effective school leaders, but has distinct additional characteristics based on the personal values of leaders who choose to embrace sustainable development. These include fostering participation in decision making, an outward orientation looking beyond the school gates and an optimistic world view.

Distributed leadership seems to be the model best fitted to fostering sustainability in schools, with different aspects of sustainable development being led by different members of the school community. By sharing out the tasks many are enabled to participate in the overall strategy, reducing the burden on the head and more deeply embedding sustainability across the school.

The key qualities of a sustainable school leader are that they are optimistic and outward looking. These leaders are conscious of the place of the school in the local and global community … These leaders have an integrated, systemic understanding of the world and their place in it and can communicate this to others. They understand the interconnectedness of society, the environment and individuals within these contexts.

Challenging plastic pollution: a whole-school project

What is the problem?

- It is estimated there is already 150 million tonnes of plastic in the oceans.
- A third of this is from microfibres released when washing our clothes.
- Ninety per cent of seabirds have plastic of some sort in their stomachs.

Where does it come from?

- Single-use plastic is plastic that is used once and then thrown away.
- Plastic bags clog up drainage systems and make flooding worse.
- Plastic drink bottles are often thrown away almost immediately.

What can be done?

- In 2016 Greenpeace UK set up a coalition of interested organisations.
- Lobby offending companies, e.g. Unilever, Nestlé, Procter & Gamble.
- Explore alternatives that can be used for different plastic items.

Finding out more

- One of the best basic reads is Will McCallum (2018), *How to Give Up Plastic: A Guide to Changing the World, One Plastic Bottle at a Time*, Penguin.
- Have a look at Greenpeace UK's website – '9 Ways to Reduce Plastic Use'. Available at: www.greenpeace.org.uk/9-ways-reduce-plastic-use/
- Research into how organisations, businesses and suppliers are changing from single-use plastic to other more sustainable materials.

Time to act

- Learners report back to their class about their different findings.
- In group discussion share what action one can take with others on this.
- As a class, draft a whole-school plan for a plastic-free school.
- How will you persuade other classes, teachers, the head, to support this?

Education for Sustainable Development: *an Ofsted report*

Ofsted (2009) *Education for Sustainable Development: Improving Schools – Improving Lives.*

What have official reports from the Office for Standards in Education had to say about good practice in education for sustainability? The points below arose from visits to schools over a three-year period to evaluate how effectively they developed pupils' understanding of sustainability and its wider impact on improving the life of the school. Here are some of the report's key findings which are of equal value today.

- Discussion with pupils showed that, over the three years of the survey, they developed a better understanding of the impact of their lifestyles on the sustainability of the environment.
- In the most successful schools, education for sustainability was an integral element of the curriculum and all pupils and staff contributed to improving the sustainability of their institution.
- Most of the headteachers found that, over the course of the survey, education for sustainability had been an important factor in improving teaching and learning more generally.
- Some school leaders identified links between particular pupils' involvement in sustainable activities and improvements in their attitudes and behaviour generally.

- Pupils responded particularly well to education for sustainability when it gave them the opportunity to take part in practical activities within and outside the classroom and enabled them to research, plan and implement projects that made a clear difference to the school and the local community.
- A common characteristic of the lessons observed … was the high level of engagement of the pupils in work they perceived as relevant to their lives and future wellbeing.
- The schools demonstrated how greater awareness of the need for sustainability can lead to reduced financial costs and better management of resources and estates.
- The knowledge and understanding that the pupils gained at school contributed to their leading more sustainable lives at home which, in turn, led their families to re-examine their lifestyles and use of resources.

Conclusion

This chapter has set out the rationale for and importance of an education that explores issues of sustainability throughout the school. It has looked at some of the debates that underlie notions of sustainability and the ways in which these are influenced by differing worldviews. Some key elements of education for sustainability have been set out and examples of good practice given in the classroom, as a whole-school endeavour, in relation to school leadership and school inspection. NB: The chapter should be read in conjunction with Chapter 11 'Education and climate change'.

It is also vital to recall that human damage to the biosphere has now reached dangerously critical levels. This has been marked by the emergence of a powerful new pressure group – Extinction Rebellion (XR for short) (https://rebellion.earth). XR describes itself as 'a socio-political movement which uses nonviolent resistance to protect against climate breakdown, biodiversity loss and the risk of human extinction and ecological collapse'. The movement has grown rapidly since 2018, organising a number of large-scale influential actions in London and elsewhere. Its demands to the UK government are: i) Tell the truth – by declaring a climate and ecological emergency, working with other institutions to communicate the emergency for change; ii) Act now – to halt biodiversity loss and reduce greenhouse emissions to net zero by 2025; iii) Beyond politics – create and be led by the decisions of a Citizens' Assembly on climate and ecological justice. Its process involves nonviolent direct action, i.e. it is peaceful in all action it engages in. It thus belongs in a long line of previous citizen movements committed to social change.

Summary points

- Any human activity causing ongoing harm to people or environment is unsustainable.
- Issues of environment (planet) and development (people) are key educational concerns.
- Ongoing ideological debates exist in relation to the meanings of sustainability.
- A four-dimensional model of education for sustainability recognises its holistic nature.
- Good practice embraces the classroom, the whole school, leadership and inspection, the community.

- Education for sustainability in schools can improve learning, behaviour and inspection, as well as the state of the planet.

Questions for discussion

- Why do you think that issues of sustainability, local and global, should be at the heart of the curriculum today?
- How do you think your main subject and other subjects can contribute to an education for sustainability?
- Which of the resources mentioned in different parts of the chapter do you find most valuable and why?

Further reading

Hicks, D. (2012) *Sustainable Schools, Sustainable Futures: A Resource for Teachers.* Worldwide Fund for Nature. Available at: www.teaching4abetterworld.co.uk (accessed 7 November 2018).
SEEd (2018) Sustainability and Environmental Education. Available at: http://se-ed.co.uk/edu/ (accessed 7 November 2018).
UNESCO (2018) *Teaching and Learning for a Sustainable Future.* Paris: UNESCO. Available at: www.unesco.org/education/tlsf/mods/theme_gs.html (accessed 7 November 2018).
Worldwatch Institute (2018) *EarthEd: Rethinking Education on a Changing Planet.* Washington, DC: Island Press.

References

Apple, M. (2006) *Educating the 'Right' Way: Markets, Standards, God, and Inequality.* London: Taylor and Francis.
Barry, J. (2012) *The Politics of Actually Existing Unsustainability.* Oxford: Oxford University Press.
Brundtland Report (1987) *Our Common Future.* Oxford: Oxford University Press.
Carrington, D. (2018) Human Race Just 0.01% of All Life But Has Eradicated Most Other Living Things. *The Guardian,* 21 May 2018. Available at: www.theguardian.com/environment/2018/may/21/human-race-just-001-   of-all-life-but-has-destroyed-over-80-of-wild-mammals-study (accessed 7 November 2018).
DCSF (2007) *National Framework for Sustainable Schools.* London: Department for Children, Schools and Families. Available at: www.se-ed.co.uk/sites/default/files/   resources/Framework%20Resource.pdf (accessed 7 November 2018).
Goleman, D., Bennett, L. and Barlow, Z. (2012) *Ecoliterate: How Educators Are Cultivating Emotional, Social and Ecological Intelligence.* San Francisco: Jossey-Bass.
Hicks, D. (2008) Ways of Seeing: The Origins of Global Education in the UK. Available at: www.teaching4abetterworld.co.uk/docs/download2.pdf (accessed 9 November 2018).
Hicks, D. (2012) *Sustainable Schools, Sustainable Futures: A Resource for Teachers.* Godalming: Worldwide Fund for Nature. Available at: www.teaching4abetterworld.co.uk (accessed 7 November 2018).
Hicks, D. (2014) *Educating for Hope in Troubled Times: Climate Change and the Transition to a Post-Carbon Future.* London: UCL IOE Press.
Juniper, T. (2015) *What Nature Does for Britain.* London: Profile Books.

Monbiot, G. (2016a) *How Did We Get into This Mess? Politics, Equality, Nature.* London: Verso.

Monbiot, G. (2016b) *Neoliberalism – the Ideology at the Root of All Our Problems.* Available at: www.theguardian.com/books/2016/apr/15/neoliberalism-ideology-problem-george-monbiot (accessed 7 November 2018).

Ofsted (2009) *Education for Sustainable Development: Improving Schools – Improving Lives.* London: Ofsted. Available at: https://dera.ioe.ac.uk/1089/1/Education%20for%20sustainable%20development.pdf

Randers, J. (2012) *2052: A Global Forecast for the Next Forty Years.* Chelsea Green, VT: White River Jct.

Raworth, K. (2017) *Doughnut Economics: Seven Ways to Think Like a 21st-Century Economist.* London: Penguin.

UNESCO (2018) *Teaching and Learning for a Sustainable Future.* Available at: www.unesco.org/education/tlsf/index.html (accessed 7 November 2018).

Visser, W. (2009) *The Top 50 Sustainability Books.* Sheffield: Greenleaf Publishing.

Washington, H. (2015) *Demystifying Sustainability: Towards Real Solutions.* London: Routledge.

Wilkinson, R. and Pickett, K. (2018) *The Inner Level: How More Equal Societies Reduce Stress, Restore Sanity and Improve Everyone's Well-Being.* London: Penguin.

Worldwatch Institute (2017) *EarthEd: Rethinking Education on a Changing Planet.* Washington, DC: Island Press.

Section 3

Knowledge and learning

Chapter 13

The sociology of knowledge
The intended and enacted curriculum

Rita Chawla-Duggan

There are a number of ways of thinking about curriculum, but how you define the term will influence how you plan for it, how you deliver it, and the messages you give to students about what it is to be a good learner and what learning is. Defining the term is important because educational settings carry messages about the curriculum, and sometimes what is planned may or may not be what is enacted; and conversely what is enacted may not be planned. Basil Bernstein's work is particularly useful in elucidating the kinds of messages sent out by educational settings through the intended and enacted curriculum. In this chapter you will learn:

- a definition of curriculum as intended and enacted;
- how knowledge is packaged and enacted in different curriculum types;
- how Bernstein's concepts of classification and framing are a conceptual language that helps to describe the messages that the intended and enacted curriculum carries in curriculum types;
- why exploring the intended and enacted curriculum is important for understanding learners and learning across national contexts.

Defining curriculum

The many ways of understanding curriculum

Look at the following definitions for curriculum and list them in order of preference. Discuss reasons for your choice.

Definition 1

Curriculum is such 'permanent' subjects as grammar, reading, logic, rhetoric, mathematics, and the greatest books of the Western world that best embody essential knowledge.

Definition 2

Curriculum is those subjects that are most useful for living in contemporary society.

Definition 3

Curriculum is all planned learnings for which the school is responsible.

Definition 4

Curriculum is the totality of learning experiences provided to students so that they can attain general skills and knowledge at a variety of learning sites.

Definition 5

Curriculum is what the student constructs from working with the computer and its various networks, such as the internet.

Definition 6

Curriculum is the questioning of authority and the searching for complex views of human situations. (Marsh, 2009: 5)

As the list demonstrates, there are many different ways to understand the term 'curriculum'.

The intended and enacted curriculum

In the opening sections of Hoadley and Reed's (2012) book on 'Curriculum', the authors describe two ways of examining the term: the intended and enacted curriculum. To illustrate the difference in the two ways, they present a school scenario in South Africa in which the teachers are struggling to make sense of curriculum changes being brought into their school. As a result, they are unsure about what they are expected to teach and how, so they enlist the help of a curriculum specialist in order to help them reflect on practice. Read the following discussion that demonstrates the teachers' perceptions of curriculum, reflecting on some of the differences in the ways they see the term:

MARGE: … the curriculum is a list of everything the Education Department wants us to teach our learners.

ROSE: Yes, it means the subjects we teach and assess, like Language and Maths and Science …

ZOZO: … curriculum isn't just subjects … it isn't a 'syllabus'. Do you follow exactly what is in the official curriculum? I don't … Sometimes I leave things out, and sometimes I do things a bit differently … I think the curriculum must be the official plan and what you as a teacher actually do in a classroom.

ZOLILE: … isn't there also a difference between what we think we're teaching and what the learners actually learn … We had to learn to be quiet in class unless the teacher asked you to speak. You had to take turns. You had to raise your hand to ask a question …

ANDILE: … I suppose all those things taught us something but it wasn't Maths or Science.

BEN: … but they were sometimes intended …

ANDILE: Not always, Ben! How much time was given to Maths? And Languages and History? What 'messages' did these arrangements convey to you about the relative importance of different subjects?

(Adapted from Hoadley and Reed, 2012: 27–28 and 47)

In the above conversation Rose and Marge understand curriculum as the list of subject content prescribed by their National Education Department in which teachers teach the curriculum exactly as the Department wants them to teach it, and learners learn exactly what teachers teach. Whilst their colleagues understand that a national department prescribes a curriculum, they have a broader understanding of the term curriculum; they argue that teachers do not simply teach it as it is; they reinterpret the curriculum and teach something slightly different. Rose and Marge focus on curriculum inputs (planned), and believe that these can be translated by teachers and learners, without difficulties, into what is learnt, the outcomes. Their colleagues, however, argue that the planned curriculum is changed during the teaching and learning process, and that some of what is learnt may or may not always be intended.

The intended curriculum sets out what has to be learnt (and sometimes how it should be taught). Forms of intended curriculum include:

- an official syllabus document or learning guide;
- a teachers' teaching plan from school;
- a textbook;
- a curriculum framework (or broad policy document).

All of these curriculum plans come from, or would probably be approved of by, the Education Department; and in this respect, the intended curriculum is often not contained in a single document. For a national curriculum, there may be a number of different documents that outline the content for learning areas and subjects. A national curriculum outlines a nation's educational priorities. It does the following:

- It defines school subjects and the knowledge included in them.
- It gives guidance on how this knowledge might be taught in the classroom.
- It serves as a guide for teachers in that it provides the minimum knowledge, skills and values that learners are required to learn.
- It provides a statement of the knowledge, skills and values that the curriculum designers believe are important for the individual learner and for society (Hoadley and Reed, 2012).

However, as the above teacher discussion demonstrates, what is set out in the intended curriculum may not always translate into practice; and this is what is called the 'enacted' (sometimes referred to as received) curriculum; that is, it is what is actually experienced and happens (Kelly, 2004).

... the fact that a government prescribes a curriculum, or that teachers receive a planned curriculum, cannot guarantee that:
Teachers will teach the curriculum in the manner in which planners may intend;
Learners will learn what has been prescribed in the curriculum, or even in the adapted
     curriculum.

(Hoadley and Reed, 2012: 45)

Amongst others, Bernstein's work demonstrates that there is always a gap between the intended and the enacted curriculum, and that an examination of the two and their relationship raises questions about messages we transmit and their consequences for learners.

Bernstein and the organisation of curriculum knowledge and pedagogy

Collection (performance) and integrated (competence) curriculum types

In Bernstein's (1975) seminal work on curriculum he distinguished between two broad types: a 'collection' type curriculum, and an 'integrated' type. In a collection type of curriculum '... the contents are clearly bounded and separated from each other' (ibid.: 80). For example, history would have a set time allocated to it in the week. The history classroom would be clearly marked out with wall displays relevant to that subject. It would be different from subjects such as maths or geography. Each of the subjects would use their own language, have different ways of teaching and learning and different ways of assessing. Answers would be based on clear externally determined criteria of what is right/wrong and the assessment would be formalised, for example, through an exam. A collection type of curriculum is associated with a performance model and content that is highly classified. Bernstein (1975) argued that on the whole in Europe the curriculum is of the collection type.

He juxtaposed the 'collection' type with a '... curriculum where the various contents do not go their separate ways, but here the favoured contents stand in an open relation to each other' (ibid.). That is, the subjects relate to one another in some way. He calls this curriculum the 'integrated' type. In this curriculum type, history, for example, would belong to the humanities, and students might be involved in developing a project based on their own experiences. There would not be a defined set of historical content to be mastered; instead, the content would be more related to relevant experiences in everyday life. We might recognise the content of this curriculum type in wall displays that would show themes/topics rather than history.

How is knowledge intended to be organised in the types? The concepts of classification and boundary maintenance

To explain how knowledge is packaged (or chunked up, so to speak) in the two curriculum types, Bernstein (1975, 2000) used the principles of 'classification' and 'boundary maintenance'. The principle of classification is concerned with the strength of the boundaries or the degree of insulation between categories, for example, between times, between spaces, between discourses, between agents and so on (Bernstein, 2000: 6). If we take the category of knowledge, it may be configured quite differently to suit what we believe to be the needs of young children, compared to when they are older, with perhaps a more collection/performance type curriculum as they get older. Strong classification aligns with this type because it assumes different kinds of knowledge must be kept apart; it refers to a curriculum that is separated into traditional subjects. Weak classification assumes they must be brought together. If classification is weak, boundaries between contents are blurred. Classification therefore refers to the degree of boundary maintenance between contents (Bernstein, 1975: 88). In a collection/performance type of curriculum there will be a *strong classification and strong boundary*. In an integrated/competence type of curriculum, there will be a *weak classification and weak boundary*.

How is intended knowledge enacted in the types? Translating knowledge and the concept of framing

When Bernstein discusses the pedagogical relationship he is referring to the *context(s)* in which knowledge is transmitted and received. In any pedagogical relationship (teacher and pupil, parent and child and so on), there is always an acquirer and a transmitter. Bernstein used the concept of framing to describe relations between 'acquirer' and 'transmitter', specifically being concerned with the degree of control exerted within this context, and how it relates to the strength of boundary. If the transmitter has the control, the framing is strong; but if the acquirer is given control, the framing is said to be weaker:

> Framing is the concept used to *describe relations between 'acquirer' and 'transmitter', is related to the strength of boundary*, and 'refers to the locus of control over the inter-actional and locationary features'.
>
> (Daniels, 1989: 125)

Bernstein identified how framing as control is made up of questions about who selects what knowledge the pupils learn, how it is organised in terms of its sequence, and how it is paced:

> Frame refers to the degree of *control* teacher and pupil possess over the *selection, organisation and pacing* of the knowledge transmitted and received in the pedagogical relationship.
>
> (Bernstein, 1975: 89)

Aspects of framing therefore include:

- Selection – what is chosen to be taught;
- Sequence – the order of taught learning;
- Pace – how quickly learning moves in the classroom;
- Evaluation – what is right and wrong.

Framing works with classification. Think of it as a container where framing is about the relationships in which the business of teaching and learning takes place.

Bernstein argued that in order to accomplish the relational idea of contents in the integrated type, the focus of its content has to be on general principles rather than particular knowledge, and this, he said, automatically affects pedagogy, in that:

> ... it will tend to identify ways of knowing rather than states of knowledge. If the underlying theory of pedagogy under collection is didactic, then under integration the underlying pedagogic theory is likely to be self-regulatory. Such a change ... in pedagogy is likely to transform the teacher-pupil ... relationship.
>
> (Bernstein, 1975: 83)

> ... the tension between curriculum of the collection type and the integrated type is not simply a question of what it is to be taught but a tension arising out of quite different patterns of authority, quite different concepts of order and control.
>
> (ibid.: 83)

Table 13.1 outlines some key differences in the way the curriculum type affects the enacted teacher-pupil relationship to teaching and learning.

A case example that applies theory to practice – pre-school education in the Indian Integrated Child Development Service (ICDS)

Initiated in 1975, India's Integrated Child Development Service (ICDS) was conceptualised in response to India's 1974 National Policy for Children, which maintained that focused,

Table 13.1 Curriculum type and associated pedagogy

	Integrated (competence) curriculum	Collection (performance) curriculum
Learner	Has control over the selection, sequence and pace of learning.	Has little control over the selection, sequence and pace of learning.
Teacher	Indirect role as facilitator of learning Control is personally negotiated.	Direct teaching role; control is hierarchical; the teacher decides.
Pedagogy	Focus on the learner.	Focus on the subject to be taught.
Knowledge	Subjects often integrated. Strong links to learner experience and everyday knowledge.	Subjects clearly demarcated from each other. Link between formal school knowledge and everyday knowledge not emphasised.
Assessment	General competence criteria. Focus on presences (on what learner knows and can do).	Specific performance criteria; there are clear rights and wrongs. Focus on absences (what the learner has left out).

child-centred interventions would address the interrelated needs (health, care and education) of women and children from disadvantaged communities. Also known as the *anganwadi* system, the ICDS is now estimated to be the world's largest integrated early childhood programme, with over 40,000 centres established nationwide. The programme covers over 4.8 million expectant and nursing mothers and over 23 million children under the age of 6. Of these children, more than half participate in early learning activities. The network consists of 3,907 projects, covering nearly 70 per cent of the country's community development blocks and 260 urban slum pockets (Awofeso and Rammohan, 2011). The ICDS policy works towards universalisation, with quality education (Government of India, 2012; Kaul and Sankar, 2009) throughout India, in line with global recommendations (UNESCO, 2000, 2007).

In the following study (Chawla-Duggan, 2016) I was interested in the pre-school education (PSE) aspect of the ICDS and how the pre-school curriculum was intended and then enacted in Indian slum school settings.

The intended child-centred ICDS model

Within the ICDS, it is the pre-school education component that is central to locating its educational discourse. The official, and therefore the intended, policy-related text describes the aim of PSE in the following way: 'Pre-School Education contributes to the universalisation of primary education, by providing to the child the necessary preparation for primary schooling ...' (Government of India, 2011: 26).

The PSE component is also central to locating the kinds of criteria used to judge a child's performance and whether they are ready for school:

> The activities which are undertaken as part of PSE include storytelling, counting numbers, free conversations to speak freely and apply their mind in order to organise small activities, painting, drawing, threading and matching colour related to fine muscle coordination and development, reading simple words, writing alphabets words, distinguish objects, recognise pictures etc. The constitution of the PSE kit may vary within a state/UT keeping in view the specific local needs and resources ...
> (Government of India, 2011: 26)

The pedagogic discourse associated with this [pre]schooling is 'child-centred':

> Under this, child centred play way activities, which is built on local culture and practices, using local support materials and developed by Anganwadi workers through enrichment training are promoted. It is considered the most joyous daily activity of the ICDS programme, which is visibly sustained for three hours a day ... [*sic*]
> (Government of India, 2011: 26)

Certainly 'child-centred' education is a well-cited pedagogic practice associated with 'quality' early childhood intervention programmes in the past. Seminal studies to support its value that are frequently cited include the longitudinal 'High/Scope Preschool

Curriculum Comparison Study' (Schweinhart *et al.*, 2005; Schweinhart and Weikhart, 1997) which involved young children living in poverty and at high risk of school failure. Carried out in Michigan, USA in the 1970s, its findings continue to support the conclusion that both the traditional nursery and the High/Scope models offer a powerful justification for high-quality PSE, with statistically significant advantages in the long term over DISTAR (a direct instruction model) on seventeen variables (Schweinhart and Weikart, 1997). Of relevance is the fact that the successful models cited encompass a notion of child-centredness described (at that time) in the following way:

> Within a permissive atmosphere, teachers expected children to show good manners, cooperate, and observe limits. Children had freedom to choose activities, move from one activity to another, and interact with adults and peers. The emphasis was on developing social skills rather than intellectual skills.
>
> (Schweinhart and Weikart, 1997: 121)

In India, there is a strongly espoused commitment to child-centred ideals within primary education (Alexander, 2001; Sriprakash, 2010), and child-centred intervention is positioned by education policy discourse as a way of addressing problems of pupil retention and achievement in rural government primary schools, serving the country's majority poor (Sriprakash, 2010: 297). In this respect, a notion of 'child-centred' is central to both the early childhood and primary education discourses for vulnerable children in India. The commitment to child-centredness in the Indian system of education is not without criticism. In fact, critics argue that the commitment bears no relation to practice or to established Indian pedagogic culture:

> There the espoused theory of teaching was strongly developmental, and Piaget featured fairly frequently in the teacher interviews. More common, however, were unattributed references, of a generally progressive kind, to 'discover', 'activity' and 'enquiry' methods …
>
> (Alexander, 2001: 546).

How is the ICDS enacted?

I collected data about six anganwadis in a Mumbai slum area. The anganwadis were observed using field notes, video and photographs. I also conducted semi-structured interviews with the child development project officer (CDPO) linked to the anganwadis, six anganwadi practitioners, two anganwadi supervisors, and key officials associated with the Ministry of Women and Child Development, with expertise in the intended purposes of the ICDS. What follows is an extract from observations of one of the anganwadis in order to demonstrate how the intended purposes of its PSE were enacted:

> The anganwadi occupies a room of approximately 3x3m. When we arrive the anganwadi worker (AWW) and co-worker are saying prayers with the children who are all dressed in pink uniforms. There are between 20–30 children present who are

between the ages of 3–5; but look much smaller (they look about my son's age – who is 18 months old). They do a minute of meditation and yogic exercise as part of their morning routine. There's a blackboard and displays are on the wall. They sing nursery rhymes; first teacher initiated and then class initiated followed by individual child contributions, initiated by the teacher. All the children clap after each child's presentation. The activity changes. The children are all given small slates and the practitioner tells me that they will now do numbers.

(Field notes. Anganwadi 1)

Anganwadi 1: strong framing and classification

In the analysis of scene 1 in the video data, which was entitled 'Munni behta' (the name of a Hindi nursery rhyme), two practitioners modelled (Bandura, 1977) what and how the Hindi poem should be recited, with all children following the practitioners' gestures and rhyme. The practitioners, as transmitters, demonstrated complete control in terms of gestures (hand movements), pace, rhythm, tone and sequence. The children, as acquirers or receivers, clearly knew what they were expected to do and therefore the criteria for performing well. They observed and modelled the rhyme in chorus, and the direction of the communication was from the adult to the child. There was strong framing in the interactional context of practice, where the rules of selection, sequencing, pace and criteria by which performance is judged were made explicit by the practitioners for children to realise.

The different observations about anganwadi 1 suggested that framing was strong generally in this and indeed the other anganwadis, because the boundary of what might be transmitted was fixed. The direction of control tended (in terms of the aspects of framing) to be located with the practitioners. The boundary of curriculum content was also strongly classified in anganwadi 1, in that there were mathematics/numeracy development (numbers on the blackboard and slate activity), language development (rhymes in scene 1) and scientific knowledge (science posters).

What questions does this raise about ICDS curriculum and the consequences for the learner?

The ICDS PSE proposed a child-centred discourse (Government of India, 2011). This is problematic when set against the more academic (school readiness) collection/performance type pre-school curriculum that was observed in the anganwadi settings. According to Bernstein the child-centred discourse is associated with the more 'progressive agenda' and its emphasis is upon 'everyday knowledge' rather than the 'academic', and an integrated type of curriculum. It has, in the past, been aimed, in England, at (apparently) empowering marginal groups in order to facilitate their access to academic knowledge. However, Bernsteinian researchers (e.g. Hoadley, 2006; Morais and Neves, 2011) have expressed the need for the classifications of everyday and school knowledge to be strong, due to the higher status of the latter.

In the ICDS settings that were video-filmed, the perhaps more Eurocentric view of the young learner as curious with an ability to direct his/her own learning, to be facilitated by the adult, is a stark contrast to the pedagogy that was observed. In the ICDS study, the predominant view of the young learner is of being a listener who acquires certain knowledge and way of behaving, to be transmitted by the adult practitioner, and this is all developed in a strongly regulated context. Of course, this view of the young learner requires a cultural context. Sarangapani (2004) examined learners who attend the middle stages of Indian schooling in order to understand teacher–pupil relationships. In demonstrating a framework for the key features of Indian schools – namely teacher authority and discipline – Sarangapani (2004) argued that whilst authority and discipline are seen as natural and central to school and learning in India, these characteristics are actually deeply rooted in a bias that lies outside of the school institution; it is a part of their everyday life. Thus, the local view of childhood and education has a framework that maps onto practices, and both children and teachers are able to use this as a point of reference from which to reproduce the framing of social relationship in schools. Authority is seen as natural and is used to maintain the moral order through behaviour and discipline that construct how teachers and pupils are seen by one another. Non-institutionalised relationships, whether adult–child or parent–offspring, that children experience before entering into the institution act as a basis of their relationships with adults – and by extension, with practitioners in anganwadi settings. This is essentially how Indian slum children come to learn their role in the social expectations of the particular relationship. When considering young children, families and AWW practitioners in the ICDS, we might therefore ask, 'how can a child-centred discourse associated with pre-school pedagogy acknowledge their framework of beliefs and respond in a language that they understand for the development of the pre-school curriculum?'

The central point that emerges from the case study cited is that the enacted pedagogy observed did not map onto the intended 'child-centred' pedagogy; in this respect, it was not aligned with the intended ICDS documentation relating to PSE. This raises questions about the possibility of shifting the meaning of child-centred pedagogy for the participants taking part in those settings, so that it is more context-oriented within the Indian pre-school and societal context.

Conclusion

This chapter has shed light upon the relationship between the intended and enacted curriculum and some consequences for learning and learners, illustrated with reference to a case study about the Indian PSE element of the ICDS. Through their everyday practices and processes, educational settings carry messages about the curriculum, so that what is planned may or may not be enacted; and conversely what is enacted may not be planned. Basil Bernstein's work continues to be particularly useful in elucidating the kinds of messages sent out by educational settings through the curriculum. Drawing on his concepts of classification and framing, the chapter has considered types of curriculum to examine how knowledge is packaged and enacted through everyday practices and processes, and the consequences for learning they can have, when children enter different kinds of educational settings.

Questions for discussion

- Think back to your own schooling. How was knowledge packaged?
- What sorts of things do you think you learnt that perhaps were not planned, but still shaped your behaviour and values and how you see yourself?
- How has your school experience differed from your experience in higher education?

Summary points

- It is important to recognise that there is always a gap between curriculum as intended/planned and what happens in practice.
- Looking at the intended and enacted curriculum in terms of Bernstein's concept of classification provides an understanding of how categories (such as knowledge) are organised in the classroom.
- Looking at framing in the various aspects of pedagogy (selection, sequencing, pace and evaluation) in the enacted curriculum helps us to see how knowledge is transmitted in the classroom.
- It important to understand how the intended curriculum is enacted because it gives a more complete view of teaching and learning so we can explain why learners learn different things that teachers teach them. It also encourages questions such as: 'Are teachers teaching certain kinds of knowledge/values without intending to?'

Recommended reading

Bernstein, B. (1975) On the Classification and Framing of Educational Knowledge. In B. Bernstein, *Class, Codes and Control. Vol. 3*. Chapter 5. London: Routledge & Kegan Paul.

Bernstein, B. (1975) Class and Pedagogy: Visible and Invisible. In B. Bernstein, *Class, Codes and Control. Vol. 3*. Chapter 6. London: Routledge & Kegan Paul.

Daniels, H. (1989) Visual Displays as Tacit Relays of the Structure of Pedagogic Practice. *British Journal of the Sociology of Education* **10**(2), pp. 123–140.

Hoadley, U. and Reed, Y. (2012) *SAIDE Curriculum: Organising Knowledge for the Classroom*. Southern Africa: Oxford University Press.

Kelly, A.V. (2004) *The Curriculum: Theory and Practice* (5th edn). London: Sage.

Marsh, C.J. (2009) *Key Concepts for Understanding Curriculum* (4th edn). London: Taylor and Francis

References

Alexander, R. (2001) *Culture and Pedagogy: International Comparisons in Primary Education*. Oxford: Blackwell.

Awofeso, N. and Rammohan, A. (2011) Three Decades of the Integrated Child Development Services Program in India: Progress and Problems. In K. Śmigórski (Ed.), *Health Management: Different Approaches and Solutions*. Croatia: InTech.

Bandura, A. (1977) *Social Learning Theory*. New York: General Learning Press.

Bernstein, B. (1975) *Class, Codes and Control, Vol. 3: Towards a Theory of Educational Transmissions*. London: Routledge & Kegan Paul.

Bernstein, B. (2000) *Pedagogy. Symbolic Control and Identity: Theory, Research, Critique*. Lanham, MD: Rowman & Littlefield Publishers.

Chawla-Duggan, R. (2016) Pedagogy and Quality in Indian Slum School Settings: A Bernsteinian Analysis of Visual Representations in the Integrated Child Development Service. *Research in Comparative and International Education* **11**(3), pp. 298–321.

Daniels, H. (1989) Visual Displays as Tacit Relays of the Structure of Pedagogic Practice. *British Journal of the Sociology of Education* **10**(2), pp. 123–140.

Government of India (2011) *Evaluation Report on Integrated Child Development Services*. Planning Commission. New Delhi: Government of India.

Government of India (2012) *Draft National Early Childhood Care and Education (ECCE) Policy*. Ministry of Women and Child Development. New Delhi: Government of India.

Hoadley, U. (2006) Analyzing Pedagogy: The Problem of Framing. *Journal of Education* **40**, pp 15–34.

Hoadley, U. and Reed, Y. (2012) *SAIDE Curriculum: Organising Knowledge for the Classroom*. Southern Africa: Oxford University Press

Kaul, V. and Sankar, D. (2009) *Early Childhood Education and Care in India*. New Delhi: National University of Educational Planning and Administration (NUEPA).

Kelly, A.V. (2004) *The Curriculum: Theory and Practice* (5th edn). London: Sage.

Marsh, C.J. (2009) *Key Concepts for Understanding Curriculum* (4th edn). London: Taylor and Francis.

Morais, A.M. and Neves, I.P. (2011) Educational Texts and Contexts That Work: Discussing the Optimization of a Model of Pedagogic Practice. In D. Frandji and P. Vitale (Eds), *Knowledge, Pedagogy and Society: International Perspectives on Basil Bernstein's Sociology of Education*. London: Routledge.

Sarangapani, P. (2004) Childhood and Schooling in an Indian Village. *Childhood* **10**(4), pp. 403–418.

Schweinhart, L.J and Weikart, D.P. (1997) The High/Scope Preschool Curriculum Comparison Study through Age 23. *Early Childhood Research Quarterly* **12**(2), pp. 117–143.

Schweinhart, L.J., Montie, J. and Xiang, J. (2005) *Lifetime Effects: The High/Scope Perry Preschool Study through age 40*. Ypsilanti, MI: High/Scope Press.

Sriprakash, A. (2010) Child-Centred Education and the Promise of Democratic Learning: Pedagogic Messages in Rural Indian Primary Schools. *International Journal of Educational Development* **30**(3), pp. 297–304.

UNESCO (2000) *The Dakar Framework for Action. Education for All: Meeting Our Collective Commitments; Including Six Regional Frameworks for Action; Adopted by the World Education Forum*. Dakar, 26–28 April. Paris: UNESCO.

UNESCO (2007) *EFA Global Monitoring Report 2006/7 – Strong Foundations: Early Childhood Care and Education*: Paris: UNESCO.

Chapter 14

The social psychology of learning

Cathal Ó Siochrú

Introduction

In this chapter we will be exploring the educational insights achieved through the application of social psychology. For those unfamiliar with it, social psychology represents that portion of psychological theory and research concerning the study of groups and interpersonal relations. You may be wondering how social psychology relates to educational psychology. Educational psychology is not a distinct sub-section of psychological theory in the way social or cognitive psychology are. Instead, educational psychology is the application of any psychological theories to understanding or influencing the process of education.

The reason for focusing on the application of social psychology is that education is an intensely social activity. While it is possible to learn entirely by yourself, this tends to be the exception rather than the rule. It is far more common to learn with the support of others and in the company of fellow learners. This means that the classroom is a social context where relations and interactions between teachers and learners or among learners are as important in determining the outcome as teaching technique or study skills. Moreover, the classroom exists as part of a larger social context where learners and teachers are influenced by family, friends and beyond. Many of these social forces have a critical impact on learning and understanding them can be useful to learners or teachers.

What is a group?

A key concept in social psychology is the 'group', but before we can start talking about groups and how they function we first need to establish the nature of a 'group' as far as psychology is concerned. In everyday language, a group is any gathering of two or more people. But to social psychology not all such gatherings would qualify as a group with a well-defined identity. Conversely, from a psychological perspective once a group identity has been formed then the group still exists and functions even when the people in the group are separated.

A group identity is formed out of certain key qualities which all groups have to some degree but which vary from group to group in terms of how well defined or frequently the quality is demonstrated. Listed below are examples of some of the key qualities which define the nature of a group.

- Interactivity – the extent to which the group members meet or communicate with each other;
- Shared goals/values – the degree to which group members want the same things;
- Consistency – the extent to which group membership remains stable over time;
- Boundaries – the degree to which it is clear who is or isn't part of the group;
- Interdependence – the extent to which group members rely on each other or are affected by the experiences of the other group members;
- Self-awareness – the degree to which group members view themselves as a group.

From this list it should be obvious that these are qualities which vary along a continuum rather than being all or nothing. A group identity is also on a continuum with some groups having a stronger or more well-defined identity than others. This quality is sometimes known as the group's 'entitativity', those qualities that make a group appear to be a coherent entity (Campbell, 1958). A group's level of entitativity will have relevance later on as we see that a stronger group identity is often associated with higher levels of group cohesiveness, which can mean that group has a greater importance to its members and thus a bigger effect on their behaviour.

Questions for discussion

Place the following groups in order in terms of their entitativity, the strength of their group identity, from highest to lowest entitativity:

- Bus queue
- Family
- Football team
- Left-handers
- The English
- Women

Consider how the entitativity of any of these groups might vary in response to context or events. Would the entitativity for a rural bus queue be different from an urban bus queue? How might a parent's divorce and remarriage affect the entitativity of their family?

Group norms and in-groups/out-groups

When we consider groups that have a stronger, more well-defined identity it is important to note that this identity persists mainly through the force of group norms. Norms are the expectations of the group with regard to its own members (Sherif, 1936). They can cover everything from what the members are expected to do, to what they wear, what they say and even what they are expected to believe. Some norms have been laid down as formal rules, others are held as informal (but no less powerful) traditions, habits, beliefs or fashions.

To join the group you need to adopt the norms of the group and in this way the group identity remains relatively stable. While there is usually some flexibility regarding how much each individual must follow all the norms of the group, the range of flexibility, what is or isn't considered 'normal', has limits. As we will see, those who champion the norms invite reward and those who deviate from them risk punishment and rejection.

Naturally, only those people who are in the group are expected to follow its norms. Thus, the world could be divided into group members (the in-group), who are expected to follow the norms, or outsiders (the out-group) who are allowed and even expected to deviate from those norms. Assigning someone to the in-group or out-group can completely change the way in which we perceive them. With in-group members we focus on our similarity to them but with the out-group we tend to focus on our differences. In this way we find it much easier to like in-group members since similarity between us and them is a big part of what we find appealing about other people (Byrne, 1971).

An important thing to note here is that in times of stress or crisis we look for comfort from the groups we belong to. One thing that comforts us is the feeling that we are close to others in our group. Often, in order to feel closer we subconsciously focus on similarities with other members of the in-group and overlook or downplay any differences, known as the 'accentuation effect' (Tajfel, 1959). By contrast, when we view the out-group under these circumstances, we focus on their differences from the in-group, known as the 'metacontrast principle' (Turner, 1987). The intention is not malicious; emphasising the difference between in-group and out-group in this way creates a clearer boundary around the group which also makes the group feel more stable and thus more supportive to us as in-group members. However, these distortions in our perceptions of both in-group and out-group open the door to problems such as stereotyping and prejudice.

Prejudice can be characterised as an unjustified negative attitude toward a group, typically a group to which we don't belong. Stereotyping this group is an integral part of prejudice in order to construct the image of the others as threatening or unworthy, so as to rationalise the prejudice in the eyes of the beholder. Therefore, anything which promotes the separation of people into distinct groups with minimal contact between groups has the potential to produce stereotyping and prejudice. This has direct relevance to education as many favour a school system with parallel but separate schools, segregated by gender, religion or even ethnicity. The problem with such systems is not just that such segregation can serve to exaggerate accentuation and metacontrast processes leading to prejudice, but that the prejudice may then lead to further segregation in other areas of life (Schlueter et al., 2018).

What can educators do to avoid the potential harm of segregation? Solutions vary, some favouring top-down approaches such as integration, mainstreaming or affirmative action, but all of these options come with their own complications. For example, in the United States there is a long-running debate over the merits of affirmative action. Affirmative action describes the practice by which universities seek to facilitate entrants from minority ethnic groups that are under-represented through quotas or special requirements for applicants from those groups. Putting the debate in psychological terms, advocates of affirmative action argue that it ensures that the in-group is seen as multi-ethnic, avoiding the automatic association of certain ethnicities with the out-group, thereby reducing stereotypical or prejudicial views (Gorodzeisky, 2011). Another argument in favour of affirmative action is that it has the potential to change the norms of all groups involved, making the attendance of higher education a norm for all groups irrespective of ethnicity. Critics, however, highlight research which appears to show that simply mixing different groups together without meaningful cooperation doesn't reduce prejudice (Sherif, 1956). Furthermore, joining any group has certain entrance requirements or costs and the requisite for all members to meet those requirements represents an initiation which 'earns' you membership (Galanter, 1999). Anyone who has not met those requirements won't have passed the initiation and so affirmative action students may not be seen as legitimate group members. While this review of the psychology on both sides, unfortunately, does not offer a direct resolution to the debate, it does offer some useful insights. For example, based on this research you could argue that headstart programmes, which seek to boost higher education (HE) attendance of disadvantaged groups through increased support at secondary level, are likely to trigger fewer of the negatives we have discussed compared to the current quota system.

Roles and status

Although the members of the in-group will generally be expected to follow the group norms, it does not mean that the group views its members as interchangeable and homogeneous. Within the in-group there will be a number of different identities, known as 'roles', and each group member will have a role. Some of these roles are formal positions within the group, often referred to as 'task-oriented' roles since they focus on particular tasks that person is expected to complete (Bales, 1958). An example of a task-oriented role in education would be a teacher, a classroom assistant or an administrator. The other type of role is more informal, known as 'relations-oriented', based on the impact that person has on other group members (Bales, 1958). For example, someone who makes people laugh would be seen as the comedian in the group, others may be known as the troublemaker or the conscience of the group.

One very important quality associated with any role is its 'status'. The status of a role typically refers to its position in the hierarchy of the group, with the best example of a high-status role being the group's leader. However, the status of a role is not just conferred by a formal hierarchy, it can also be derived from the prestige, respect or admiration afforded to that role by the group members, usually as a result of the perceived qualities of the specific person occupying that role. Thus, you can have a high-status role which has no formal position in the hierarchy or which exists in a group with no formal hierarchy at all. A good example of this can be seen in higher education, where researchers found that most academics saw effective leadership coming more from informal (highly respected) leaders than formal leadership (management) sources (Bolden et al., 2012).

There are a number of ways to gain status within a group. You will gain status if you are seen to defend the group, enhance its wellbeing or embody the norms of the group.

For example, Santee and VanDerPol (1976) found that students held their instructor in higher esteem and viewed them as having more value to the college if the instructor was seen to match the norms expected of someone in that role. The need to closely follow the group norms can be considered to be one of the duties of high status, as deviation from the norms will typically cause you to lose status (Festinger *et al.*, 1950). Consequently, it is interesting to note that although high-status individuals are expected to embody the norms of the group, they are permitted to deviate very noticeably from some norms (typically the less important ones) if they are seen to very closely adhere to the more important norms, a phenomenon known as 'idiosyncrasy credit' (Hollander, 1958). In return for their enhancement of the group and embodiment of its norms, high-status individuals benefit from greater access to resources of the group and higher levels of influence on the group and its norms.

Norms are not the only thing guiding our behaviour in the role we occupy within the group. Sometimes when we enter into a new role we may already have our own set of expectations of what the role involves based on what we have heard about that role and other people we have seen who were in that role or similar ones. These personal beliefs and expectations are known as a role 'schema' (Bartlett, 1932). A schema can be thought of as a collection of all the things we know about some specific thing, place, person or situation. Our role schema can be an important guide to our initial behaviour in a new role. For example, Hamilton (2018) found that a new teacher's set of beliefs and expectations were critical in predicting their behaviour as a teacher, such as their willingness to adapt to curricular reforms taking place around them. However, as we will see later when we consider stereotyping, our role schemas can mean that being assigned to a role can become a label which we can't remove and which constrains or even defines our behaviour.

Questions for discussion

- To what extent is a teacher's behaviour constrained by the expectations of their students?
- What responses is a teacher likely to face from students if they don't conform to the norms of their teaching role?
- How might a teacher go about getting their students to accept them changing or challenging those norms?

Role schemas are just one example of the way we mentally organise social information to make it easy and quick to access. We also have schemas for groups and locations which help us to figure out what is going on and what we should do, even in new and unfamiliar situations. One way we do this is by taking the small things we learn about someone when we first meet them and using those fragments to assemble a mental picture of who they are, usually by placing them in one or more roles or groups, a process known as 'social categorisation'.

Social categorisation and stereotyping

From the moment we meet someone, when we learn things like their gender, job, nationality or even their hobbies we use this information to categorise them, linking them to one or more schemas based on a role or a social group. Linking them to a role or group schema in this way helps to reduce the demand on our mental facilities, known as 'cognitive load' (Sweller, 1988). Furthermore, once we categorise someone we can apply all the things we know about the associated schema to that person, anticipating things about their personality, beliefs and behaviour. It means we don't need to figure out each person we meet from scratch, we can use the schemas to which we have associated them as a rough guide to help us fill in the blanks with educated guesses. Used properly, this social categorisation is an automatic and benign process which helps us to get by on limited information. As long as we remember that a real individual will never completely match their associated schema (no actual teacher is ever going to be a perfect fit for our schema of a teacher) then no harm is done. Stereotyping, on the other hand, occurs when we over-apply the characteristics of a group or role schema to an individual (von Hippel et al., 1995). We make the assumption that the schema is a perfect fit and stop paying attention to the differences. Often we interpret the behaviour of the individual to fit our schema, becoming more likely to notice and recall things that fit our expectations. This is known as 'confirmation bias' (Anderson et al., 1980; Gilovich, 1991) and it is a key element of how we maintain a stereotypical view of someone, sometimes even in the face of contradictory evidence.

One area where these role schemas and stereotypes can have a profound impact on education is in relation to gender roles. Our schemas for the two gender roles, known as 'gender schemas' (Bem, 1981), can determine the expectations that both teachers and students have about students' academic abilities and suitability to study various subject areas. For example, research has found that students of both genders and their teachers expect female students to outperform male students on reading tasks (Retelsdorf et al., 2015). The research showed that this expectation stemmed from the belief that good communication is a more important ability for women than men, and thus female students will be more motivated to study language-related subjects. By contrast, the association of scientific, technological, engineering and mathematical (STEM) subjects with traits that are deemed to be masculine, such as logic, can lead teachers to have higher expectations for male students in those subject areas (Ó Siochrú, 2018).

Another place where role schemas can affect us is when they expose us to 'stereotype threat'. Stereotype threat describes the anxiety and pressure an individual experiences as a result of the stereotypical expectations of others (Steele and Aronson, 1995). Those stereotypical expectations can be associated with the schema for the group the individual belongs to (for example ethnicity, gender or religion) or the role they occupy. An example of this can be found in McGee's (2018) exploration of the experiences of black and Asian students in the USA who study STEM subjects. Black students felt they were expected to occupy the role of a 'problem student', while Asian students felt they were expected to occupy the 'star student' role, particularly in relation to STEM subjects. McGee found that both students suffered from stereotype threat. The black students sought to defy the expectations associated with their role, pushing themselves to succeed to such a degree that it caused stress and emotional distress. By contrast, the Asian students felt pressured by their stereotype to excel at all times, and that anything but the highest marks would be perceived as an 'Asian fail'. They also felt pressured by the stereotypical association between their race and STEM such that they believed that they must study a STEM subject or face disapproval from family and friends. This shows us that a stereotype can be harmful irrespective of whether it contains positive or negative expectations associated with the role.

Questions for discussion

- What can we do to help students that we believe are facing stereotype threat or other negative consequences of stereotyping?
- Is simply telling people about the harm of stereotyping likely to produce lasting change?
- Are there ways in which we can challenge such stereotypes? Who needs to be involved in this process?

Self-categorisation and conformity

An interesting point to consider is that we might apply this process of social categorisation to ourselves as much as to other people. Self-categorisation theory (Turner, 1985, 1991) suggests that in any given social situation we tend to identify ourselves with a specific group. The group we choose to identify with does not have to be physically present at the time (I might identify myself as a student even if I am the only one of my class that is present), but our choice of which group to identify with will be influenced by various features of the social situation. For example, Stoppa and Lefkowitz (2010) found significant changes in the way that mature students in HE identified as religious, which the researchers attributed to the fact that HE studies can often cause students to re-evaluate their identity.

Of course, it is one thing to categorise yourself to be part of a group, but it is a very different issue as to whether the group itself accepts you as a member. As we saw earlier, membership of the group can be contingent on following the group's norms. The pressure to do this, under threat of group censure or expulsion, is what creates the form of social influence known as 'conformity'. Conformity can be defined as any change in a person's behaviour, beliefs, attitudes or values which happens in response to the norms of a group they belong to. There are a number of reasons why we change our behaviour based on what others in our group are doing, but the two main ones are informational influence and normative influence.

We often use other people as a source of information; in fact, one of the reasons we join a group is to make use of the group's shared resources which includes information.

Thus, in situations where we are not sure what do, the beliefs and behaviours of others in our group have an informational influence (Deutsch and Gerard, 1955) and become the basis for our beliefs and behaviours. However, even in a situation where we feel confident we already know what to do, we may still do what everyone else is doing in order to fit in. This can result in a normative influence where we conform to gain the approval of others in the group and avoid punishment (Deutsch and Gerard, 1955). Some researchers have rejected the idea that we conform out of fear of punishment though. Instead, they argue that when we notice any difference between ourselves and other in-group members we either try to rationalise those differences away or we seek to change ourselves to become more like the others in the group as an expression of our group membership (Turner, 1991).

One issue in education where these concepts play an important role is in the practice of excluding students from school. From the perspective of self-categorisation and conformity we could represent this as an attempt by the school to use the punishment of exclusion from the group to encourage everyone to conform to the norms of school behaviour. But, it is possible that the tendency for the disruptive individual not to self-categorise themselves as a member of that group (school students) is at the root of their non-conformity (Turner, 1987). This is likely to be driven, in part, by their perception that they have a low status in the group and as such are not valued. Consequently, exclusion may only serve to increase the time they spend identifying with other groups outside of school where they feel more valued, thus further reducing the extent to which the student identifies with the school. That would lessen the importance of the school's norms, making non-conformity and disruptive behaviour more likely rather than less. An alternative approach was explored by Burton (2006) who found that getting disruptive students to work in specific groups within school, learning to manage their own behaviour, was far more effective than exclusion. Working in a group of students with similar issues helps to normalise feelings or behaviours by showing a pupil that they are not the only one who feels or acts like that. In essence, the working group becomes a new social group for the students to self-categorise into: a group where they will identify more with the group norms and feel of equal status to the others. Working with the group also requires them to adopt certain rules, such as mutual respect and cooperation, which are initially presented as rules of the working group but which mirror the norms of the larger group (the school). Consequently, when the students from the working group re-integrate with the main school they already find its norms are more compatible with their values, thus increasing the likelihood of them self-categorising as members of the school group.

One interesting question raised by self-categorisation and conformity is the relationship between these changes in one's behaviour and one's identity. If I'm a hard-working student to my teachers in school but a lazy son or daughter to my family at home, which one is the 'real me'? The intriguing answer is that there may be more than one 'me'; according to some psychologists we may do more than just vary our behaviour in different social situations, we could take on entirely different social identities.

Social Identity Theory (SIT)

If you are asked to identify yourself you are likely to offer your name. If pressed, you might even produce an official identification document like a work ID or a passport. One thing to note is that all of these identify you as belonging to a group; your name places you in a family and your ID documents place you in a business or a country. This means our identity has a social element: we are who we are (in part) because we belong to certain groups. It also raises the interesting possibility that we may have more than one identity since we belong to more than one group.

This was the idea developed by Tajfel (1972) in his Social Identity Theory. In Social Identity Theory a person has not just one 'personal self', but rather has multiple 'social identities' which are derived from membership of social groups. We occupy a role and internalise the norms in each group we belong to, with each group membership and role representing a separate social identity. Any one person can have multiple social identities and these identities are not exclusive, they co-exist within the individual. As we saw in the section on self-categorisation, different social contexts may cause us to identify with one of the various social groups we belong to, causing the same individual to think, feel and act differently in different social situations (Turner, 1987). In this way you may be the 'baby' of your family at home, the 'chatterbox' to your teachers in school and the 'comedian' to your friends.

It is worth noting that not all social identities will be equally important to us. The importance of any one of our social identities is likely to be a function of the cohesiveness of the group and the status associated with our role in that group. 'Cohesiveness' is a term used to describe how well integrated and interactive the group is. Higher levels of cohesiveness in a group make that social identity appealing because they make us feel secure in our group membership (Festinger et al., 1950). The higher degree of interaction in a cohesive group is of particular value in education-related groups since interaction, in the form of mutual support in shared information, is an important element of learning (Waltonen-Moore et al., 2006). Another reason we might value a social identity is because group membership carries with it certain benefits, such as access to the group's resources and support. However, level of access to group resources depends on our status in the group. This is one of the reasons why a group where we have a higher-status role represents a more important social identity.

The existence of multiple social identities can give rise to problems such as role conflict (Bakker and Geurts, 2004), which describes the difficulty faced by a single individual in satisfying the demands of multiple roles in different groups. An example of this in an educational context would be the challenges faced by mature students returning to education, who take on the role of 'student' while simultaneously trying to maintain their existing roles in their family and workplace (Johnson and Robson, 1999). A more dramatic example of role conflict can be found in those cases of teachers who face disciplinary proceedings or even termination of employment as a result of their political beliefs or sexuality, even if those things are only visibly expressed outside of the classroom (Maxwell, 2018). Here the perception of a role conflict comes from others who question whether a teacher can have another role (with associated values) which is seen as incompatible with the expected norms and behaviours associated with their role as a teacher.

Conclusion

In this chapter we have explored a small portion of the insights on education that have been achieved through applying research in the field of social psychology. Throughout we have offered examples of the ways in which social psychology can help us to better understand a variety of educational issues. These issues have ranged from the link between segregated schools and prejudice to the relevance of status in understanding the limitations of school exclusions. Whether it is the part played by schemas in producing stereotype threat for minority students or the impact of role conflict on mature students, we can see the value that a greater understanding can play in improving the lives and educations of many.

Finally, as our discussion on affirmative action demonstrates, although social psychology may not have any 'silver bullet' solutions to the challenges we face in education, it can make a difference while simultaneously offering a foundation for future study.

Summary

- A group identity is formed out of certain key qualities which all groups have to some degree, but which vary from group to group.
- All groups have norms, the expectations of the group regarding the behaviour of its members, with adherence to the norms being rewarded and deviation being punished.
- We divide the world into in-group and out-group, and our attempt to emphasise the difference between in- and out-group can lead to prejudice toward the out-group.
- Within the in-group there are a number of identities, known as 'roles', with any role having a status representing the prestige or respect associated with that role.
- We socially categorise everyone, associating them with a group or role, but going too far in expecting them to match the group/role schema can lead to stereotyping.
- We self-categorise ourselves into certain groups, which results in us having multiple social identities which can shape our behaviour and even conflict with each other.

Recommended reading

Festinger, L., Schacjiter, S. and Back, K. (1950). *Social Pressures in Informal Groups*. New York: Harper.
Tajfel, H. (1959). Quantitative Judgement in Social Perception. *British Journal of Psychology* **50**, pp. 16–29.
Turner, J.C. (1991). *Social Influence*. Milton Keynes: Open University Press.

References

Anderson, C.A., Lepper, M.R. and Ross, L. (1980) Perseverance of Social Theories: The Role of Explanation in the Persistence of Discredited Information. *Journal of Personality and Social Psychology* **39**(6), pp. 1037–1049.

Bakker, A.B. and Geurts, S.A. (2004) Toward a Dual-Process Model of Work–Home Interference. *Work and Occupations* **31**(3), pp. 345–366.

Bales, R.F. (1958) Task Roles and Social Roles in Problem-Solving Groups. In E.E. Maccoby, T.M. Newcomb and E.L Hartley (Eds), *Readings in Social Psychology* (3rd edn). New York: Holt, Rinehart and Winston.

Bartlett, F.C. (1932) *Remembering: A Study in Experimental and Social Psychology.* Cambridge: Cambridge University Press.

Bem, S.L. (1981) Gender Schema Theory: A Cognitive Account of Sex Typing. *Psychological Review* **88**(4), pp. 354–364.

Bolden, R., Gosling, J., O'Brien, A., Peters, K., Ryan, M., Haslam, A. Longsworth, L., Davidovic, A. and Winklemann, K. (2012) Academic Leadership: Changing Conceptions, Identities and Experiences in UK Higher Education. Available at: https://ore.exeter.ac.uk/repository/bit-stream/handle/10871/15098/academic_leadership_v1_19312.pdf (accessed 17 April 2019).

Burton, S. (2006) 'Over to You': Group Work to Help Pupils Avoid School Exclusion. *Educational Psychology in Practice* **22**(3), pp. 215–236.

Byrne, D. (1971) *The Attraction Paradigm.* New York: Academic Press.

Campbell, D.T. (1958) Common Fate, Similarity, and Other Indices of the Status of Aggregates of Persons as Social Entities. *Behavioural Science* **3**(1), pp. 14–25.

Deutsch, M. and Gerard, H.B. (1955) A Study of Normative and Informational Social Influences upon Individual Judgment. *The Journal of Abnormal and Social Psychology* **51**(3), pp. 629–636.

Festinger, L., Schacjiter, S. and Back, K. (1950) *Social Pressures in Informal Groups.* New York: Harper.

Galanter, M. (1999) *Cults: Faith, Healing, and Coercion* (2nd edn). New York: Oxford University Press.

Gilovich, T. (1991) *How We Know What Isn't So.* New York: Free Press.

Gorodzeisky, A. (2011) Mechanisms of Exclusion: Attitudes toward Allocation of Social Rights to Out-Group Population. *Ethnic and Racial Studies* **1**, pp. 1–23.

Hamilton, M. (2018) Pedagogical Transitions among Science Teachers: How Does Context Intersect with Teacher Beliefs? *Teachers and Teaching* **24**(2), pp. 151–165.

Hollander, E.P. (1958) Conformity, Status, and Idiosyncrasy Credit. *Psychological Review* **65**, pp. 117–127.

Johnson, S. and Robson, C. (1999) Threatened Identities: The Experiences of Women in Transition to Programmes of Professional Higher Education. *Journal of Community & Applied Social Psychology* **9**(4), pp. 273–288.

Maxwell, B. (2018) When Teachers' Off-Duty Creative Pursuits Conflict with Role Model Expectations: A Critical Analysis of *Shewan*. *Interchange* **49**(2), pp. 161–178.

McGee, E. (2018) 'Black Genius, Asian Fail': The Detriment of Stereotype Lift and Stereotype Threat in High-Achieving Asian and Black STEM Students. *AERA Open* **4**(4).

Ó Siochrú, C. (2018) Boys Do Maths, Girls Do English: Tracing the Origins of Gender Identity and Its Impact in Education. In C.Ó Siochrú (Ed.), *Psychology and the Study of Education: Critical Perspectives on Developing Theories.* Abingdon: Routledge.

Retelsdorf, J., Schwartz, K. and Asbrock, F. (2015) 'Michael Can't Read!' Teachers' Gender Stereotypes and Boys' Reading Self-Concept. *Journal of Educational Psychology* **107**(1), pp. 186–194.

Santee, R.T. and VanDerPol, T.L. (1976) Actor's Status and Conformity to Norms: A Study of Students' Evaluations of Instructors. *The Sociological Quarterly* **17**(3), pp. 378–388.

Schlueter, E., Ullrich, J., Glenz, A. and Schmidt, P. (2018) From Segregation to Intergroup Contact and Back: Using Experiments and Simulation to Understand the Bidirectional Link. *European Journal of Social Psychology* **48**(1), pp. 17–32.

Sherif, M. (1936) *The Psychology of Social Norms.* New York: Harper.

Sherif, M. (1956) *In Common Predicament: Social Psychology of Intergroup Conflict and Cooperation.* Boston, MA: Houghton Mifflin.

Steele, C.M. and Aronson, J. (1995) Stereotype Threat and the Intellectual Test Performance of African Americans. *Journal of Personality and Social Psychology* **69**(5), pp. 797–811.

Stoppa, T.M. and Lefkowitz, E.S. (2010) Longitudinal Changes in Religiosity among Emerging Adult College Students. *Journal of Research on Adolescence* **20**(1), pp. 23–38.

Sweller, J. (1988) Cognitive Load during Problem Solving: Effects on Learning. *Cognitive Science* **12**(2), pp. 257–285.

Tajfel, H. (1959) Quantitative Judgement in Social Perception. *British Journal of Psychology* **50**, pp. 16–29.

Tajfel, H. (1972) Experiments in a Vacuum. In J. Israel and H. Tajfel (Eds), *The Context of Social Psychology: A Critical Assessment*. London: Academic Press, European Monographs in Social Psychology.

Turner, J.C. (1985) Social Categorization and the Self-Concept: A Social Cognitive Theory of Group Behaviour. In E.J. Lawler (Ed.), *Advances in Group Processes: Theory and Research*, Vol. 2. Greenwich, CT: JAI.

Turner, J.C. (1987) *Rediscovering the Social Group: A Self-Categorization Theory*. New York: Basil Blackwell.

Turner, J.C. (1991) *Social Influence*. Milton Keynes: Open University Press.

von Hippel, W., Sekaquaptewa, D. and Vargas, P.T. (1995) On the Role of Encoding Processes in Stereotype Maintenance. *Advances in Experimental Social Psychology* **27**(C), pp. 177–254.

Waltonen-Moore, S., Stuart, D., Newton, E., Oswald, R. and Varonis, E. (2006) From Virtual Strangers to a Cohesive Online Learning Community: The Evolution of Online Group Development in a Professional Development Course. *Journal of Technology & Teacher Education* **14**(2), pp. 287–311.

Chapter 15

Philosophy and education

Tom Feldges

Introduction

In the preface to a book about Philosophy and Education Ward (2019) explains that Philosophy, along with the other contributory disciplines of Psychology, Sociology, Economics and History, serves as a theoretical basis for the academic discipline of Education Studies. Ward's position puts Education Studies into a subsidiary position, being – at least partially – dependent upon the theoretical framework of other academic disciplines. This has practical implications as such a claim means that everyone studying Education Studies should engage with these contributory disciplines and their theoretical frameworks. It thus looks as if the acceptance of these fundamental contributory disciplines increases the workload of those who engage with Education Studies as a wider set of theoretical frameworks have to be learned, understood and applied. One could thus critically question the justification for such an ordering, leaving Education Studies in a dependent relationship to other academic disciplines.

Before it is possible to clarify some aspects of the relations between these other disciplines and Education Studies it is first the multi-dimensionality of Education Studies that needs attention. This issue manifests itself in that it is perfectly possible to describe, account for, and probably even explain, what education does upon a multitude of different levels. Education Studies, and with that the application of a theoretical perspective upon the act or the practice of education, can approach educational practice upon the following levels:

a) a psychological/psycho–social level, concentrating upon the transitional and transformative relationship between tutor and student in which learning is supposed to unfold;
b) a sociological level, focusing on the educational system by contextualising the social function that education as a whole is supposed to accomplish within a society;
c) an organisational level, contextualising the interplay between the administration and management of educational organisations and the parts of the organisation that are supposed to perform the actual educational tasks;
d) a historical level, capturing the genesis of the current educational system in relation to its historic context and thus revealing potential constraints and possibilities for future development.

However, there is also, and probably in a more fundamental manner, the academic discipline of Philosophy. At this point the question may emerge: What has philosophy got to do with it all? By carving up the concept of education in such a way that it becomes comprehensible upon various levels, a first step into a philosophising engagement with education has already been made. Taking this further it becomes evident that education is essentially about the transfer of knowledge and skills via educational efforts to evoke learning, and that necessitates:

a)   a secure stock of practical skills and theoretical knowledge about how to achieve learning;

b)   alongside a secure stock of knowledge about what is supposed to be taught/learned.

Knowledge in both forms is crucial to Education Studies, However, every knowledge transfer stands invariably in relation to the society which defines what *counts as* a worthwhile set of skills and desirable knowledge. And these questions of *why* and *how* to teach *what* and to *whom* are the sort of questions that fall into the philosophical remit. It is best to start with some general remarks about Education and Philosophy first.

Philosophy, Education and the Philosophy of Education

To engage in a genuine philosophising attempt, the three related concepts of 'Philosophy', 'Education' and 'the Philosophy of Education' need initial clarification.

When being asked the question 'What is Philosophy?' it is difficult to provide a short and straightforward answer. That is because what Philosophy takes itself to be has changed over time and is now no longer what it used to be. In that respect it might be a good idea to start with what Philosophy used to be about 2,500 years ago when all that which we know now as 'Western Philosophy' started in ancient Greece. Back then the aim of Philosophy was to:

a)   provide a universal orientation that contributed to the human ability to understand the world.

The goal was to develop explanations that reached beyond previous accounts which had to make recourse to the working of the gods and/or magic, while

b)   equally trying to make sense out of human life.

These attempts were characterised by thought that followed a rule-governed, logical and methodical pursuit to understand the world, and to answer the question of how to live a *good life* while striving to be a *good person*.

However, the discipline of Philosophy developed further and nowadays it applies itself to a wide range of problems. Cottingham (1996) for example lists the questions of knowledge and certainty, being and reality, mind and body, self and freedom, science and method, morality and the good life. It is obvious that these diverse foci have resulted in current

Philosophy becoming a much broader discipline when compared with its early beginnings. Nevertheless, Philosophy went even further. In the eighteenth-century Enlightenment, Philosophy started to take the critical aspects that Philosophy had developed so far and subject them to further critical scrutiny by applying its own enlightened methods. But this 'critical Philosophy', as it became known, adds yet another domain to what Philosophy understands itself to be and what it aims to achieve. As it is difficult to clearly define the complete extent of the concept, it is probably best to stick with its main characteristics, i.e. to perceive Philosophy as a (mostly) thought-based endeavour applying itself to a variety of problems in a logically coherent, rule-governed and methodical manner.

The question of what education actually is remains one that is rarely asked, but to gain clarity about the relevant concepts it is necessary to capture the essence of education by drawing a wider picture.

Already in the 1920s Scheler (2009) developed the idea that human beings are essentially born unready to survive their environments. He claims that the most characteristic trait of humankind is its helplessness. Other animals from birth are stronger, can run faster, have better senses and are quickly independent. He suggests that human survival is secured by the ability to reason about how to overcome environmental demands or obstacles. However, the use of this *tool of reason* has to be learned and exercised in relation to emerging or existing surrounding cultures. It is this cultural aspect that ensures that every new-born human does not have to start at *square one*. Humans can be initiated into the stock of culturally accumulated knowledge and practice, and use it as their own starting point to develop further. However, the stock of knowledge transmitted to the learners, initiating them to become the new members of a society or culture, is not only a process of knowledge transmission; it also turns learners into different persons: teaching is *transformative* in nature. Viewed in such a way, education supplements the new-born, biological human body with cultural achievements and turns it into a human being. As Misawa (2019) pointedly explains, education sits between the natural (biological) and the social (cultural) dimensions of human life. We can thus, and in the most general manner, attempt to define education as the sum of all wilful attempts to bring about an enculturing, transformative accomplishment to supplement new generations with the achievements of the culture that surrounds them.

With the clarification of the concepts of 'Philosophy' and 'Education' it is now possible to conceive the *Philosophy of Education* as the application of philosophical methods and understanding to educationally relevant problems (Griffith, 2005). While accepting this most general definition it remains nevertheless possible to develop a reasoned argument about the question of what already-existing philosophy could or should count as educationally relevant.

Question for discussion

The Philosophy of Education consists of the application of philosophical thought and method to the practice and theory of education. Can you develop an argument for an active – philosophising – engagement with a specific aspect of education?

This difference between *learning about the Philosophy of Education* as opposed to *philosophising about education* has been developed elsewhere (Feldges, 2019) and here it might be best to develop this attitude by considering an example.

On liberty and freedom

The focus of the previous section was the mediating role of education, connecting the natural with the social. Education establishes this connection by establishing cultural practices into the developing biological-neuronal layout of the learner (Hebb, 1949), preferably, as Dewey (1916) urges, to educate autonomous individuals into the continuity of social life within a democratic society. Dewey envisages the overall goal of education as the means to secure a continuous democratic, societal life, with free and rational agents. Hence, individuals must have the space and the freedom to choose based upon their own reasons, and to enact these choices. This necessitates a certain amount of freedom as the precondition for autonomous individuals: autonomy cannot exist in a merely rule-governed environment where everything is fixed and pre-determined.

John Stuart Mill (1859/1985) formulated the enlightened idea of individual *liberty*, or 'freedom' as one would say today, as a principle whereby men and women should be free to do as they please, as long as they do not cause harm to others. Mill's principle sounds as if it could be the basis for a universal application, i.e. one that would hold for everyone and at any time, while equally securing the needed space that Dewey's individuals require to be autonomous. But things are not so easy. Mill's concept of freedom has at least three problems:

a)   Mill left freedom as a relational concept whereby individual freedom finds its limitations when it harms another person. This seems sensible, but it remains difficult to draw an objective border according to which one can rightfully claim that such harm has happened, and that a supposed harm is not merely a superficial inconvenience.

b)   Of course, these boundaries are sometimes defined with the help of the law, regulating what would need to be tolerated and what would be a definite harm. And it is here that freedom reveals its societal grounding: it is dependent upon what societies perceive as an acceptable/unacceptable individual exercise of freedom. A totalitarian regime, such as communism, might define tighter borders than a liberal democracy would do. It is exactly this possibility of different and/or changing social interpretations that leaves Mill's concept of freedom as culturally situated: dependent upon the society which applies it.

c)   However, Mill's concept of freedom involves a further cultural situated-ness with direct implications for education. Mill's ideas were supposed to hold for 1850s Great Britain, and probably even for the developed Western world of that time. He argued that, within these liberal-democratic societies, liberty was supposed to find a broad application regardless of what other societies would allow or not allow their citizens. However, at the time when Mill wrote his treatise on liberty, the state of India was still governed as a colony of the British Empire. And it is here that Mill's concept of liberty shows another aspect of cultural situated-ness. Mill explains that his concept of liberty does not at all hold for India or its inhabitants. He saw the Indians in terms of their civilisation, if not for their race, to be inferior (Said, 1978). Hence, Mill is drawing another border. With recourse to biological markers (ethnicity) Mill attempts to justify the withholding of individual freedom. This does not only show how much individual freedom is subject to social convention, it also reveals how the then British society enabled Mill to draw a distinguishing border between human beings based upon a scientifically flawed conception of race. It was thus possible for everyone to argue for a limited or lacking entitlement to individual liberty for some humans who happened to be born on the wrong side of this divisionary line. (See Chapter 3.)

This social situated-ness disguises the concept of freedom as a social construct (Berger and Luckmann, 1991) whereby a given society applies its traditions, common practices and its established rules to fix the extent of freedom (Brady, 2019). And it is here that we might want to follow the earlier-mentioned critical turn that philosophy has accomplished by turning its own methods upon itself. The 1985 Swann Report (DES, 1985) on the education of minority ethnic pupils in Britain pointed to the fact that the pluralistic make-up of British society had not resulted in equal access to life and educational chances, and that inequality and prejudice towards minority groups remained prevalent. These considerations are currently echoed by Dorling and Tomlinson (2019), linking educational inequalities to a tacit stereotyping whereby educational entitlement – i.e. the freedom to choose one's educational pathway – depends at least partially on a learner's ethnic background. This tacit sorting exercise limits some learners, while leaving others' choices unrestricted. The tacit und underlying social construction of educational freedom remains hidden and invisible to the observer, as long as educationalists do not critically engage with the relevant concepts of autonomy and freedom in the first place. But once the arbitrary and socially-dependent reach of individual freedom has been revealed, it becomes clear how 'freedom' could mean different things to different individuals. The next section examines the contributory disciplines in education.

Education and the 'contributory disciplines'

Chapters in this book (e.g. 13 and 14) offer more detail on the relation of the various contributory disciplines with education. What follows here is to capture the relationship between these academic disciplines in a philosophical and critical manner.

Psychology and education

The commonly shared assumption regarding our ability to explore the world revolves around the fact that we actively or passively receive sensory information which somehow allows us to have the mental content to navigate our world. We hear the roar of the tiger and seek shelter, we see the inviting red of the strawberries and we move to get them. However, the mere availability of sensory information at our sense-organs cannot in itself be sufficient to guide our behaviour. Hence, establishing a stimulus-response chain would not leave much room for individual autonomy or the individual application of what Scheler (2009) called 'the tool of reason'. Some further sorting and processing of sensory information is needed to arrive at perceptions and object-recognition. Capturing these sorting and processing steps is the task of Psychology, i.e. the provision of a scientific description and explanation of what is happening within a brain and/or mind, based upon empirical evidence. This is a difficult call to make as we tend to imagine that our thought processes are not available to anyone outside of our own head. However, if education, as outlined earlier, is supposed to alter, modify and extend some of these thought processes, then it becomes immediately clear that education depends upon a very close relationship with Psychology. Psychology tries to infer what is going on in the mind by presenting specified stimuli and by observing resultant behaviours (Feldges, 2018a). These psychological results can be applied to the instructive relationship between teacher and learner; that then forms the close relationship that allows education to utilise psychological knowledge and theory to make sense of educationally relevant matters of fact in the form of teaching, learning and the assessment of educational success.

However, quite a number of educationally relevant contents remain elusive to attempts to capture such a direct link between quantified stimuli and observed responses. One of these elusive concepts is the earlier discussed notion of 'freedom'. As a social construct, this concept is not easily captured because the perception of freedom, or its absence, appears to be something that is much more dependent upon where one is located socially. Available educational choice may be overwhelming and limitless for some, while others may perceive their own individually available freedom to choose as one that is characterised by a limited range of only a few alternatives. Hence, too simple a psychological focus upon the processing of sensory data, supposed to spark off subsequent behavioural displays, may not be able to capture the full picture. What could easily be missed here would be the individual experience, the question of 'what does this mean to me?' or 'how does that make me feel?'

Of course, the space for such an individual interpretation of available sensory data increases as soon as socially constructed concepts are concerned. Nevertheless, the general idea of an individualised perceptual accomplishment holds, even for the simple perception of an object like a school desk. While such a desk may be perceived as a mere piece of classroom furniture by a teacher, a student may experience it as something similar to the rowing-benches of a slave-galley, confining the student to tedious boredom (Pieczenko, 2019). Hence – and that is the overall point here – as much as the various other disciplines can contribute to the academic discipline of education, all of these contributory disciplines come with their own tacit underlying assumptions. These discipline-specific underpinnings may at times not quite fit the underlying assumptions of education.

Question for discussion

Psychological behaviourism as formulated by Watson (1913: 158) rests on the assumption that Psychology is 'a purely objective, experimental branch of natural science', one that 'must discard all reference to consciousness' and 'never use the terms consciousness, mental states [and] mind …'. How successfully do you think a modern educator could work without utilising these concepts that Watson rejected?

Education, Sociology and Economics

It is of course possible to decry the influences of societal demands upon education in the form of an increasing marketisation and an increasing need for educational institutions to compete with each other in neoliberal societies. (See Chapter 1.) Education, when viewed in such a way, opens itself up to be contextualised in terms of a variety of sociological theories that make sense of the relationship between education and society. However, the relation between education and society is a multifaceted one, encompassing the field of politics and economics in a mutually dependent and interdependent relation where one field gains social approval from the others, and vice versa (Lyotard, 1979). Although it appears undisputed that sociology can help to capture education's social function, it also looks as if too strong a focus upon the social function of education may lead to the educational encounter between teacher and learner being rendered as a secondary feature. That is, too strong a sociological conceptualisation of education may draw the life-blood out of education, and education may lose its very own reason for being (Feldges, 2018b). Questions of this sort could critically engage with how much actual freedom a Marxian concept of education as an institutionalised effort to replicate pre-existing class structures would be able to allow its educators and learners (Ashwin, 2012). This sociological perspective upon the dichotomy between a constraining structure, as opposed to individual freedom and agency, has undoubted benefits in that it allows a clear view of specific problems. However, although these dichotomies consist of the opposing endpoints of a spectrum, the endpoints are not mutually exclusive by necessity. As Ritzer (2014) explains, one can live within the constraints of sociological structures while nevertheless retaining one's agency and freedom, at least partially.

It is here that Luhmann's (2010) concept of the education system as related to the overall social system unfolds its explanatory power. Luhmann explains that every sub-system, as part of an overall system, must produce something of worth for the overall system. Were that not the case, these sub-systems would be starved of resources and eventually cease to exist. Luhmann calls this the '*Anschlussfähigkeit*' (or connectivity) of education: i.e. the capacity of educated individuals to connect to societal demands and to perform along the social expectations in relation to the educational qualifications obtained.

There is a growing view that societal demands do by now reach so far into the educational systems that Giroux (2014) finds it appropriate to speak about a neoliberal war that is waged on UK higher education. Newman *et al.* (2004) state that the marketisation of education leads institutions to place emphasis on revenue rather than on knowledge transfer. Hence, there is an apparent concern about increasing managerial control regimes and accountability. These concerns do not only focus upon the education system's wider environment. What seems at stake here is the fact that these regulatory constraints of the neoliberal agenda are becoming more and more a part of the education system itself, i.e. that education almost becomes a streamlined process with an aim to effectively produce learners displaying the needed '*Anschlussfähigkeit*'.

This is a more extensive concern than the one discussed earlier when social function and instructive relationship were pitched against each other. The discussion about inter-educational, managerial control regimes is one that revolves around the students perceived either as partners in genuine learning collaborations with shared responsibilities, or students perceived – and perceiving themselves – as 'customers', with the learning relationship along the cash nexus. It appears obvious that teaching based on purchasing power and the exchange of goods would limit educators' professional freedom.

The philosophical engagement with the notion of an academic's freedom to influence the character of the instructive relationship has revealed that education is – in its core – not at all under threat by the mere fact that any such relation would have to serve a social function as well. What seem much more of a threat to education are increasing control regimes to safeguard productivity, efficiency and accountability by neoliberal managerial means. However, to trace the development of these influences, it is necessary to have a brief look at one more remaining contributory discipline: History.

Education and History

Since Socrates' idea of the educator as a midwife to the learner's thoughts, more than 2,400 years have passed and education and educational ethos have obviously changed. Tracing changes as they occurred over time, and accounting for these changes in relation to the relevant actors, is the task of the academic discipline of History. History can be applied to any process with a temporal dimension, capturing what has been before, if and how it has changed and what it is now. If, as Misawa (2019) argues, education sits in a mediating position whereby human beings are equipped with a cultural background to form them into social beings, then education exists at least as long as there are cultures instructing their new members.

Returning to the concept of 'freedom', Kant (1784/2015) traced changes to what the concept of freedom could entail. While a priest may demand: *Do not reason, but believe!* Kant recommends that people should find the courage to utilise their own reasoning powers. This caused a conflict with the Prussian King Frederick the Great, and Kant paraphrases the king's advice to the citizens: *Reason as much as you like and about whatever you like, but obey!* It does not need further argument to show that the pre-Enlightenment (religious) concept of freedom is very different from the one that was the concern in Kant's debate with his king. Although in 1784 reason as such was at least permitted and not totally suppressed, Frederick's concept of freedom to reason is a far cry from the concept as we developed it earlier. That was the concept that did not only permit the individual exercise of reason, but also entailed the freedom to *act* accordingly. In that respect the concept of freedom reveals its dependency on the social and cultural circumstances in which it is used.

When running these changes of the concept of freedom against Mill's concept and against Dewey's idea of educating the new members of a society, it is easy to lose the ground under one's feet. All of a sudden the concept of freedom is increasing over time in terms of what it entails (religious choice, sexual self-determination, etc.) and what it did not entail at an earlier time. While the concept of schooling is changing (exclusive private tuition, religious schooling, state schools and compulsory attendance requirements), the concept of what we understand to be a child has also changed (cheap industrial labourer, small adult, or a human being during its developmental journey). By trying to provide an account of how schools do and did educate the children to exercise their freedom in a reasonable way, one has to rely on these concepts of 'freedom', 'children' and 'schooling' to get the historical narrative going. But if the concepts used to capture change are themselves subject to change, things get very difficult.

Discussion

Try to engage with the changing concept of *family* and think about how a change from a pre-industrial 'extended family' to a post-war 'nuclear family' and to modern 'patchwork families' may affect your ability to relate educational issues to the concept of the *family* over the centuries.

Conclusion

Philosophy, as a way of thinking and a method to investigate issues, can find a multitude of applications for educational purposes. In that respect it is important not to treat the Philosophy of Education as a mere intellectual history to be learned, but rather as an active way to engage with educational problems. Of course, when doing so, it is important to develop a secure stock of knowledge about Philosophy and the Philosophy of Education as it helps to avoid covering already-charted ground. However, education does not only need the critical, philosophising attitude to ensure that it is doing what it is supposed to do; it also needs to rely on the theoretical frameworks of the contributory disciplines. The philosophising discussion within this chapter has shown that these contributory disciplines may lend some of their theoretical underpinnings to education. But it is always up to the educationalist to challenge these foundations and to assess the suitability and compatibility with the educational problem under consideration. In that respect the Philosophy of Education is not merely about what one can learn about what was thought before: it is the individual development of a disciplined and critical – a *philosophising* – engagement with educational matters.

Summary points

- Education is a social practice and it serves a social function.
- To theorise about educational practice, a wide range of theoretical frameworks from contributory academic disciplines are used.
- However, these disciplines may have theoretical foundations that are not compatible with the educational problem under consideration. Therefore, a clear and critical assessment of these frameworks is needed.

- Education, in its institutionalised form, will always entail the instructional relationship and a social function which it serves for a surrounding society. Fulfilling these social expectations should not be the first purpose of education, but it is the necessary precondition for an instructional relationship.
- Changes in organisational structures may lead to a decreasing space for the teaching profession to engage in a meaningful instructional relationship.
- A genuine philosophising attitude will make educational professionals and academics aware of tacit and emerging problems. This can help to sort out some of the difficulties, or at least to see the problem from a different perspective and – if no answer is forthcoming – to try to develop different questions to understand the problem better.

Recommended reading

Feldges, T. (2019) *Philosophy and the Study of Education*. London: Routledge.
Kenny, A. (2012) *A New History of Western Philosophy*. Oxford: Oxford University Press.
Dorling, D. and Tomlinson, S. (2019) *Rule Britannia: Brexit and the End of Empire*. Oxford: Blackwell Publishing.
Although Dorling and Tomlinson's book is about the British secession from the European Union, it can equally be read as a book about the workings of tacit societal influences upon an educational system and how that – in return – influences a society.

References

Ashwin, P. (2012) *Analysing Teaching-Learning Interactions in Higher Education: Accounting for Structure and Agency*. London: Continuum.
Berger, L. and Luckmann, T. (1991) *The Social Construction of Reality*. London: Penguin.
Brady, A. (2019) The Teacher-Student Relationship: An Existential Approach. In T. Feldges (Ed.), *Philosophy and the Study of Education*. Abingdon: Routledge.
Cottingham, J. (1996) *Western Philosophy: An Anthology*. Oxford: Blackwell Publishing.
DES (1985) *Education for All (The Swann Report)*. London: HMSO.
Dewey, J. (1916) *Democracy and Education*. New York: Macmillan, 1916, republished in 1942.
Dorling, D. and Tomlinson, S. (2019) *Rule Britannia: Brexit and the End of Empire*. Oxford: Blackwell Publishing.
Feldges, T. (2018a) Motivation and Experience versus Cognitive Psychological Explanation. *Humana Mente* **11**(33), pp. 1–18.
Feldges, T. (2018b) Review: Education and Philosophy – An Introduction by A. Allen and R. Goddard. *Educational Futures* **9**(2), pp. 110–112.
Feldges, T. (2019) Introduction: Philosophy and Education. In T. Feldges (Ed.), *Philosophy and the Study of Education*. Abingdon: Routledge.
Giroux, H. (2014) *Neo-liberalism's War on Higher Education*. Chicago: Haymarket Books.
Griffith, J.P. (2005) Problems of the Philosophy of Education. In T. Honderich (Ed.), *The Oxford Companion to Philosophy*. Oxford: Oxford University Press.
Hebb, D.O. (1949) *Organization of Behaviour*. London: John Wiley.
Kant, I. (1784/2015) *What Is Enlightenment?* London: Penguin.
Luhmann, N. (2010) *Das Erziehüngssystem der Gesellschaft*. Stuttgart: Suhrkamp.
Lyotard, J.F. (1979) *The Postmodern Condition: A Report on Knowledge*. Minneapolis: University of Minnesota Press.
Mill, J.S. (1859/1985) *On Liberty*. London: Penguin.

Misawa, K. (2019) The Social, the Natural and the Educational. In T. Feldges (Ed.), *Philosophy and the Study of Education*. Abingdon: Routledge.

Newman, F., Couturier, L. and Scurry, J. (2004) *The Future of Higher Education: Rhetoric, Reality and the Risks of the Market*. San Francisco: Jossey-Bass.

Pieczenko, S. (2019) Educational Phenomenology: Is There a Need and Space for Such a Pursuit? In T. Feldges (Ed.), *Philosophy and the Study of Education*. Abingdon: Routledge.

Ritzer, G. (2014) *The McDonaldization of Society*. London: Sage Publications.

Said, E.W. (1978) *Orientalism*. London: Penguin.

Scheler, M. (2009) *The Human Place in the Cosmos*. Evanston, IL: North Western University Press.

Ward, S. (2019) Editor's Preface. In T. Feldges (Ed.), *Philosophy and the Study of Education*. Abingdon: Routledge.

Watson, J.B. (1913) Psychology as the Behaviorist Views It. *Psychology Review* **20**, pp. 158–177.

Chapter 16

Creative pedagogy for empowerment

Holistic learning through expressive arts

June Bianchi

Introduction

Though the commitment to progression within traditional core academic subjects remains a central tenet within contemporary curricula, opportunities for children and young people to develop their holistic capacities are internationally recognised as pivotal in enabling them to participate as citizens within transitional societies. Arts educationalists challenge the continued dominance of cognitive domains of learning within education, citing the importance of creative and cultural pedagogy to empower diverse learners with the holistic knowledge and skills required to contribute to contemporary global political, economic and cultural shifts.

While creative and cultural learning can potentially occur across the curriculum, the expressive arts offer an interdisciplinary focus where the generating of qualitative outcomes provides an alternative to prioritisation of test and examination scores. Recognition of the holistic value of creative and cultural experiences challenges the endemic shift towards early specialism, with its consequent narrowing of focus potentially impoverishing young people's life experiences, restricting their access to wider knowledge, skills and aspirations.

This chapter explores the potential of expressive arts in empowering learners, building key interdisciplinary skills to support holistic learning agendas of equity, pluralism and citizenship. It will initially discuss key policies and literature impacting on the role of expressive arts education within contemporary curricula. An overview of previous policies and practice provides a framework of the role of arts education in promoting interdisciplinary holistic learning. Case-study evidence based on interdisciplinary cultural partnerships models creative pedagogical strategies for inclusion and empowerment within an international context.

Expressive arts within a test-based curriculum

The relative value of disciplines and subjects within the curriculum is contested, with debates around the political and social adjustment elicited by governmental changes. Consensus on what constitutes a balanced curriculum is culturally and ideologically constructed amidst wider concerns about economic and social stability, and growth (see Chapter 13). Global comparisons of educational systems are disseminated through statistical data evaluating the impact of countries' educational systems on their population. *The International Education Database*, which measures and ranks the impact of global education systems 'in stabilizing their economy, and in developing their social environment' (2019), ranks the United Kingdom (UK) as 21st in a global evaluation of over two hundred countries based on meeting economic and social targets. UNESCO's statistics (2015) evaluating countries' achievements based on indices of equality and access related to its Education Development Index (EDI) are based on four indices: primary education, adult literacy, quality of education and gender.

While international data on educational quality are predicated on wider indices of value, the UK governmental requirement is to quantify and evidence students' attainment within the core academic subjects, prioritising the demonstration of learners' cognitive and deductive capacities. Standard Attainment Tests (SATs) provide assessment data for English, Mathematics and Science at 7 and 11 years, at the end of Key Stages 1 and 2. Research by the National Union of Teachers critiqued this testing and accountability culture as instigating a narrow curriculum, 'a loss of creativity; an emphasis on uniformity; a decline in the quality of personal relationships' (Hutchings, 2015: 10). The Education Select Committee's Primary Assessment Report found that links between test results and the accountability system pressurised the progress and attainment of students. It claimed 'the high stakes system can negatively impact teaching and learning, leading to narrowing of the curriculum and "teaching to the test", as well as affecting teacher and pupil well-being' (House of Commons Education Committee, 2017: 3).

Despite such concerns, SATs results are promoted as a prerequisite in identifying children's capacity to meet required standards for their age range. Conservative Secretary of State for Education, Damian Hinds (2019), argued that SATs tests assessed the competence of schools, 'to check up on the system – and those who oversee it on your behalf'. Both parents and professional associations expressed concerns over subjecting children to a regime of testing under the guise of monitoring the quality of the education system. Parents responded by boycotting their children's test attendance, and teachers' associations balloted members for agreement in formally boycotting the 2020 SATs (Weale, 2019).

At secondary level the English Baccalaureate (EBacc) (Gov.UK, 2019) measures students' performance in government-funded schools at GCSE level (16 years) in five core academic subjects: English, mathematics, history or geography, sciences, and a language. While schools can additionally offer creative and cultural subjects, technology and religious education, nearly 90 per cent of school leaders argued that the privileging of traditional academic subjects in the EBacc narrows the curriculum (ASCL, 2015). The campaigning movement *Bacc for the Future* (2019), supported by creative businesses, education bodies, organisations and over 100,000 individuals, criticises EBacc's devaluing of creative, artistic and technical subjects. It contends they are essential for the economy, and that holistic learning and wellbeing should be given parity with core subjects. It argues that EBacc effectively excludes arts, creative and technical subjects from counting towards the government's secondary schools' monitoring and accountability system: Progress 8 and Attainment 8.

The Progress 8 system provides a metric for evaluating performance of the prescribed EBacc curriculum across a range of schools and contexts. It purports 'to prompt and promote self-improvement, to inform the public and stakeholders, and to provide credible information to enable action in cases of underperformance' (DfE, 2019a: 6). However, its quantitative approach to assessing students' achievement through 'subject buckets' with reduced weighting allocated to subjects listed as non-academic and unapproved has been critiqued as reductionist, lowering the status of creative and technical subjects, and impacting on their recruitment. *Bacc for the Future* cites statistical data, gathered by the Joint Council for Qualifications, indicating a 34 per cent decline in the number of state pupils taking arts and creative subjects at GCSE since 2010. These figures are supported by the Department for Education's data on EBacc organisation in schools, indicating that continuation of arts education is managed by 'Allocating less curriculum time to non EBacc subjects ... offering them through enrichment or after school sessions, not necessarily studied to GCSE' (DfE, 2019b: 18). Educationalists like Mary Bousted, joint general secretary of the National Education Union, called for the scrapping of EBacc, describing it as 'a straitjacket' (Smulian, 2019).

Questions for discussion

- What is your view of current educational monitoring and testing procedures?
- What impact do you feel SATs and EBacc requirements have on children and young people's holistic learning?

Creative revolution: expressive arts for holistic learning

Sir Ken Robinson (2016: 112) has repeatedly challenged this standards-driven ethos, calling for a creative revolution, with disciplines equally balanced within the curriculum, to address 'major areas of intelligence, cultural knowledge and personal development'. The reduced status of the arts, culture and creativity is contested by extensive evidence supporting its significance. Cultural Learning Alliance's (CLA) international research data substantiates the role of the arts in combating inequality and supporting school improvement. It argues that 'the arts and heritage are an intrinsic part of how we come to know and understand the world and how we express ourselves as individuals, communities and a nation' (2017: 2). Distilling its findings into ten key areas, CLA's research indicates that engagement with the arts empowers participants across holistic indices of health, well-being and achievement with benefits including: improvement of cognitive abilities and academic attainment; improved participation through to degree level and beyond with significant positive impact on retention and response amongst children from low-income families; enriched levels of societal contributions on social and political levels. The British Council charts the rise of the creative economy, asserting that 'policies to promote and protect creativity will be the crucial determinants of success in the twenty-first century'

(Newbigin, undated). Data indicated a rise in value from £94.8 billion in 2016 to £101.5 billion in 2018 with growth in creative and cultural industries 'at nearly twice the rate of the economy since 2010' (Department for Digital, Culture, Media, and Sport, 2018).

While success stories support the role of arts, culture and creativity, a commensurate rise in the status of expressive arts subject disciplines within the curriculum has not occurred. Privileging of cognitive deductive intelligences is arguably endemic within Western culture and education, but holistic educationalists like Howard Gardner campaign for a more inclusive paradigm, celebrating shared enterprise, social relationships, spatial skills and physical ingenuity. Gardner's (2011) influential theory of Multiple Intelligences (MI) posited intelligence as multi-perspectival, incorporating traditional spectrums of intelligence such as mathematics and linguistics with: visual and spatial; musical and kinaesthetic; naturalist; interpersonal, intrapersonal; spiritual and existential consciousness. The continued reluctance to create disciplinary parity within international curricula must reflect contemporary societies' underlying ethos, indicative of their dominant ideologies, values and aspirations.

Such meaning systems are disseminated implicitly and explicitly throughout a society's entire cultural milieu (Williams, 1958 cited in Higgins, 2001: 11) with cultural institutions bestowing value on artists' production, reinforcing stratification of value by their patronage. Yet challenges to cultural hierarchies, colonialism, gender and class emerge from feminism, queer theory, post-colonialism and anti-globalisation, with post-modernism proposing multiple narratives, countering traditional paradigmatic structures. The ability to operate across the spectrum of cultural production, understanding its nuances of meaning and function, is known as 'cultural capital' (Bourdieu, 1984). While not conveying fiscal wealth, it ascribes 'symbolic profit' (ibid.: 230), social confidence and esteem. As CLA (2017) find, creative and cultural learning can positively impact upon holistic learning, wellbeing, health, and sustainability, empowering a stronger sense of identity, critical thinking and citizenship. This does not occur in a vacuum; as Robinson (2016) claims, creativity is an acculturated, not an individualistic phenomenon, predicated on socio-cultural conditions. It requires acknowledgement of learners' diversity of experiences and perspectives within increasingly heterogeneous global societies and contexts.

Pedagogies of empowerment through expressive arts: a policy and practice heritage

The need for a broad spectrum of learning experiences within a balanced curriculum can be charted in education policy over half a century. This section examines the advocacy of creative and cultural aspects of education encapsulated through expressive arts, highlighting a range of key policy documents within the UK. Concerns raised over this period are equally relevant in addressing contemporary societal and curricular change.

The Plowden Report (1967) provided a comprehensive review of primary education and secondary transition at a time of educational change. The Labour government's commitment to egalitarianism instigated replacement of the grammar school system with comprehensive education, superseding streaming with a focus on children's individual needs. Espousing a liberal view of child-centred learning, informed by Piaget's theories of development, Plowden argued for equitable, inclusive provision across a spectrum of socio-economic need. Learning through the arts was promoted as a key curriculum component, as a means of expression, and an essential attribute for the developing child and a healthy society, affecting 'all aspects of our life from the design of the commonplace articles of everyday life to the highest forms of individual expression' (Plowden, 1967: 246).

Following their Education Reform Act of 1988, the Conservative government established the national curriculum, to ensure commonality of provision across the state sector. Schools within primary and secondary phases were required to provide a core curriculum of subjects. Art and Design and Music were identified as single-subject areas, while Drama and Dance were part of the English and Physical Education subjects respectively. This curriculum provision has remained, for state-funded schools in the UK, during consecutive governments, while schools within the private and academy sectors regard it as advisory or discretionary (Gov.UK, 2014). Continued concern at the perceived lack of balance in the curriculum instigated two influential educational reports examining the role of expressive arts in education in the 1980s and 1990s, both edited by Sir Ken Robinson.

The Arts in Schools Report (Robinson, 1989) reiterated Plowden's emphasis on the relevance of expressive arts in education, pinpointing societal conditions as key factors in the profile of the arts within education. Robinson suggested that socio-economic challenges should be addressed by an education system not merely addressing immediate employment needs, but also generating 'intuition, creativity, sensibility and practical skills' (ibid.: 5), prerequisites for generating new employment opportunities and adaptation to societal change. The report advocated a curriculum balanced between logical deductive skills and expressive capacities, arguing that cultural and creative qualities develop flexibility, and understanding of pluralist perspectives and values. Such heterogeneity of thinking enables citizens to respond positively to the benefits and challenges of living within an increasingly culturally diverse world, and to contribute effectively to it. Robinson described our own society and the wider world as a cornucopia of differences to be understood, celebrated and assimilated, an analysis which continued to hold resonance over the following three decades.

Ten years later the National Advisory Committee on Creative and Cultural Education (NACCCE) published their report on arts in education, *All Our Futures: Creativity, Culture and Education* (1999), placing creativity and cultural education as interrelated components fostering skills, knowledge and understanding to respond to societal change. Defining creativity as 'imaginative activity fashioned so as to produce outcomes that are both original and of value' (NACCCE, 1999: 30), the report presents a democratic perception of creative engagement as attainable across the spectrum of subject disciplines. It construes cultural learning, in its most democratic sense, as taking place across 'shared values and patterns of behaviour that characterise different social groups and communities' (ibid.: 47). Emerging from these findings, the *Creative Partnerships* initiative provides opportunities for young people in deprived areas to develop their creativity and experience, working collaboratively with a range of partners and multi-disciplinary agencies: schools, arts practitioners, creative organisations and businesses. Its mission statement promotes the potential of the arts to:

> empower young people and the adults in their lives to imagine and question how the world can be improved, giving them the capability to solve individual and collective problems, to create and innovate and to build confidence and a positive attitude towards their future learning and lives.
>
> (*Creative Partnerships*, 2019)

Though its funding stream was reduced by later Coalition and Conservative governments, *Creative Partnerships* continues to generate a lasting legacy, inspiring young people to be innovative, risk-taking, adventurous and cooperative members of society, alongside facilitating regenerative connections between educationalists, arts professionals and institutions.

Every Child Matters (ECM) legislation (DfES, 2004) similarly promoted a holistic approach, supporting young people's spiritual, moral, social and cultural needs (SMSC), alongside physical, emotional and intellectual personal development. The five ECM outcomes addressed learners' health, safety, achievement and enjoyment, ability to contribute to society, and economic wellbeing. ECM recognised the socio–cultural factors placing additional pressure on schools in meeting both academic and holistic outcomes, with schools in deprived environments struggling to meet students' social needs alongside academic targets and league tables. Arts subjects contribute to wider creative and cultural learning, while potentially developing economic growth, alongside providing empowering leisure activities for young people. Reduction of their status is regarded by arts educationalists as detrimental to the employment and social needs of future citizens, particularly those vulnerable to unemployment and cultural exclusion. CLA (2017) continues to campaign for the significance of expressive arts, demonstrating that: 'Learning through and about culture is a human right enshrined in international law' with 'compelling educational, employment and civic benefits delivered by cultural learning' (ibid.: 2).

Such evidence informed the independent review *Cultural Education in England* (Henley, 2012), commissioned by the 2010 Coalition government. Henley argued for universal access to cultural and creative educational opportunities across statutory education, 'ensuring that all children and young people in England, no matter what their background, circumstances or location, receive the highest quality Cultural Education both in school and out of school, in formal and in informal settings' (ibid.: 4). Henley challenged EBacc's curriculum balance, advocating mandatory inclusion of one expressive arts subject to be studied to GCSE level. Sorrel, Roberts and Henley (2014) then published a manifesto arguing for the holistic impact of the arts in four key areas: knowledge, critical and analytical skills, designing and making skills, and understanding the historical breadth of human experience. They contend that the arts develop young people's 'sense of their own identity and a shared understanding and appreciation of the environment in which they live and their own personal role within that environment' (2014: 28). Such holistic pedagogy regards education as a means of empowering young people as engaged citizens, not merely a process of cognitive training.

Questions for discussion

- How do policies, literature, and research data provide evidence for developing the role of expressive arts within curricula?
- What impact does engagement in holistic learning through the arts have on individuals and society?

International case study: fostering empowerment and holistic learning through expressive arts

A foremost issue of our time, for global citizens and educationalists committed to promoting equal access to education, is the increasing challenge to provide for the influx of young migrants seeking refuge in the UK and Europe from civil unrest, war and economic destitution. Approximately 10 per cent of the EU population were born in a different country from their place of residence; children under the age of 15 constitute 5 per cent of this group (Jante and Harte, 2016). Although the pattern varies by country, data indicate that children with a migrant background tend towards lower educational achievement and are more likely to leave school early than their counterparts from a native background, particularly when refugee status is combined with economic deprivation (Population Europe, 2014). Social integration is recognised, within international policy agendas, as crucial for cohesion and economic growth, yet lack of training and resources may hamper educators in responding effectively to increased academic, linguistic, and social diversity within their classrooms.

As humans we build our sense of self, and relationships with others, through social, cultural and political environments. Our identity is constructed through interaction with familial, social and cultural networks, informed by community, nationality, ethnicity, religion, gender, generation, class, sexual orientation, abilities and needs. Article 27 of the United Nations' Universal Declaration of Human Rights (1948) declared that 'Everyone has the right freely to participate in the cultural life of the community, to enjoy the arts and to share in scientific advancement and its benefits.' Integration through arts education is a tested practice that has yielded positive results in improving the performance of disadvantaged children and their families, enriching cultural and social interconnections. The European Commission (2017) identified key foci for effective integration of migrant communities as:

- Empowerment: recognising migrants and refugees as individuals with knowledge, skills and cultural experience;
- Intersectional connections: engaging educational, economic, cultural, and welfare partnerships in programmes integrating migrant and local communities.

Empirical responses to the European Commission's report include their funding of international arts educational initiatives like the international project *Arts Together: Integrating*

Migrant Children through the Arts (2019). *ArtsTogether's* partnership team draws from academic, educational, charitable, cultural and social welfare sectors of five European countries: Austria, Belgium, Greece, Italy and the UK. Building on good practice from research data and exemplars, it develops and tests a curriculum based on expressive arts activities. Collaborative approaches equip teachers in responding to socio-cultural and linguistic diversity, fostering mutual understanding and respect among their students and the school community, while improving the educational performance of migrant students. Supporting these aims is the *ArtsTogether Inclusion Curricula* (2019), developed by the current author and UK partnership team at Bath Spa University. Providing an empirical focus for disseminating and celebrating shared creative, cultural and social experiences, it fosters understanding and respect for our shared humanity through the theme 'Our Stories, Our Communities'.

ArtsTogether promotes an inclusive pedagogy, supporting integration of migrant children and their families through creative, intercultural engagement across the wider family and school community. Interdisciplinary active learning experiences foster holistic collaborative pedagogy and practice, enriching cognitive and affective development. Curriculum resources explore and celebrate the theme 'Our Stories, Our Communities' across a wide range of cultural contexts. Learning activities encourage children and young people from migrant and host communities to reflect on their own and others' cultural experiences and contexts, sharing and celebrating both common and contrasting experiences. *ArtsTogether* resources and Learning Activities stimulate curiosity and empathy in relation to diverse and shared cultural backgrounds, with intercultural understanding enhanced through universal themes such as: the migratory journeys of all species; global stories exploring personal, social and cultural identity; the environments we inhabit; the seasonal celebrations and festivals which illuminate and enrich our annual calendars. Interdisciplinary learning takes place within five interconnected *ArtsTogether Modules*, each supported by an explanatory Guide, PowerPoints and resources (2019):

1. Journeys
2. Global Stories
3. Performing People
4. Our Shared Environment
5. Celebration

ArtsTogether enriches children's experiences, supporting safe sharing, and promoting development of resilient and creative identities to sustain them within different cultural environments. The *ArtsTogether Inclusion Curricula* features a repertoire of creative and artistic resources and collaborative activities that highlight an inclusive approach to cultural identity, diversity and difference, fostering mutual understanding and respect to support individuals' wellbeing, social development and integration. Initial pilot studies of *ArtsTogether* materials within migrant camps, centres, nurseries and schools in Greece and Italy, indicate that the *ArtsTogether Inclusion Curricula* provides a global model of affective and holistic learning for transitional learning contexts. This positive approach is based on valuing and supporting individual learning within a changing community context, helping migrant and host communities to develop resilience and work together towards an integrated society.

Conclusion

Partnership is a unifying factor within the policies and projects discussed here, and is widely regarded as a valuable attribute in challenging limitations and prejudice, restricting learners' potential. Henley (2012) regards partnership as central to creative and cultural education, with contributions from 'government departments, non-departmental government bodies, the National Lottery, local authorities, schools, cultural organisations, voluntary organisations, the creative and cultural industries, conservation practitioners, business sponsors, charities and philanthropists' (ibid.: 8). Evidence indicates that partnership-based arts projects can build self-esteem and promote human rights, extending understanding and appreciation of diversity.

While current educational paradigms are predicated on notions of Western society as post-industrial and systems-based, evidence suggests that global societies are in flux, struggling to respond to political, economic, environmental and socio-cultural challenges. Literature and data signal the issues impacting upon education, and policies and strategies must address the widening challenge of global educational agendas. Shifts towards creative- and knowledge-based societies demand new educational legislation and approaches; governments are being challenged to recognise the potential of expressive arts pedagogies in evolving educational policy. Expressive arts practitioners and theorists passionately believe the arts are transformational tools, engaging learners in creative and cultural activities facilitating extrinsic and intrinsic benefits to themselves and their communities. Educators need such strategies and opportunities to develop knowledge, skills and expertise to empower children and young people in their care with the creative, holistic capacities to embrace and address future societal change.

Questions for discussion

- How can expressive arts pedagogies contribute to learners' sense of empowerment and to societal integration?
- How can cultural and educational institutions foster expressive arts education locally, nationally and internationally?

Summary

- Arts educationalists challenge narrow subject hierarchies and over-emphasis on testing, advocating pluralist educational perspectives to foster holistic learning.
- Current and past policy and approaches explicate the need for expressive arts to be recognised as pivotal in learners' and societal development.

- Cultural and creative partnerships promote key knowledge and skills, empowering learners to contribute to twenty-first-century life.
- Expressive arts education provides strategies to address holistic national and international educational agendas.

Recommended reading

Bresler, L., O'Toole, J. and Fleming, M. (2015) *The Routledge International Handbook of the Arts and Education*. Abingdon: Routledge.

Cultural Learning Alliance (2017) *Key Findings: The Case for Cultural Learning*. Available online: https://culturallearningalliance.org.uk/wp-content/uploads/2017/08/CLA-key-findings-2017.pdf (accessed 8 June 2019).

Hatton, K. (Ed.) (2015) *Towards an Inclusive Arts Education*. Stoke-on-Trent: Trentham Books.

Sorrel, J., Roberts, P. and Helnley, D. (2014) *The Virtuous Circle: Why Creativity and Cultural Education Count*. London: Elliott & Thompson Limited.

Acknowledgements

Thanks to the *Arts Together Inclusion Curricula* Bath Spa University writing team: Dr Penny Hay, Geraldine Hill-Male, Dr Michael Riley, Fiona Hunt and the EU *Arts Together* Project team.

References

Arts Together (2019) Available online: www.artstogether.eu/ (accessed 6 June 2019).

Arts Together Inclusion Curricula, Bianchi, J., Hay, P., Hill-Male, G. and Hunt, F. (2019) Available online: www.artstogether.eu/work-packages-no-2 (accessed 6 June 2019).

ASCL (2015) Nearly Nine in 10 School Leaders Oppose Compulsory EBacc in Its Current Form. Available online: www.ascl.org.uk/news-and-views/news_news-detail.nearly-nine-in-10-school-leaders-oppose-compulsory-ebacc-in-its-current-form.html (accessed 6 June 2019).

Bacc for the Future (2019) Available online: https://baccforthefuture.com/ (accessed 10 August 2019).

Bourdieu, P. (1984) *Distinction: A Social Critique of the Judgement of Taste*. London: Routledge & Kegan Paul.

CLA (2017) Key Findings: The Case for Cultural Learning. Available online: https://culturallearningalliance.org.uk/wp-content/uploads/2017/08/CLA-key-findings-2017.pdf (accessed 6 June 2019).

Creative Partnerships. Available online: www.creativitycultureeducation.org/programme/creative-partnerships/ (accessed 6 June 2019).

Department for Digital, Culture, Media and Sport (2018) Britain's Creative Industries Break the £100 Billion Barrier. Available online: www.gov.uk/government/news/britains-creative-industries-break-the-100-billion-barrier (accessed 6 June 2019).

DfE (2019a) *Analytical Associate Pool: Summary of Recent Smallscale Research Projects*. London: DfE. Available online: https://assets.publishing.service.gov.uk/government/uploads/system/uploads/attachment_data/file/802600/Analytical_Associate_Pool_-_summary_of_projects_March_2019_-_002.pdf (accessed 6 June 2019).

DfE (2019b) *Secondary Accountability Measures: Guide for Maintained Secondary Schools, Academies and Free Schools*. London DfE. Available online: https://assets.publishing.service.gov.uk/government/uploads/system/uploads/attachment_data/file/783865/Secondary_accountability_measures_guidance.pdf (accessed 6 June 2019).

DfES (2004) *Every Child Matters: Change for Children in Schools*. London: DfES.

European Commission (2017) *How Culture and the Arts Can Promote Intercultural Dialogue in the Context of Migratory and Refugee Crisis: Report with Case Studies by EU Member States*. Brussels: European Union.

Gardner, H. (2011) *Frames of Mind: The Theory of Multiple Intelligences* (3rd edn). New York: Basic Books.

Gov.UK (2014) *National Curriculum for England*. Available online: www.gov.uk/government/collections/national-curriculum (accessed 6 June 2019).

Gov.UK (2019) *English Baccalaureate*. London: DfE. Available online: www.gov.uk/government/publications/english-baccalaureate-ebacc/english-baccalaureate-ebacc (accessed 6 June 2019).

Henley, D. (2012) *Cultural Education in England: An Independent Review by Darren Henley*. London: DCMS.

Hinds, D. (2019) Education Secretary Sets out the Importance of Testing in Primary School. London: Gov.UK. Available online: www.gov.uk/government/news/education-secretary-sets-out-the-importance-of-testing-in-primary-school (accessed 6 June 2019).

House of Commons Education Committee (2017) *Primary Assessment*. House of Commons Publishing. Available online: https://publications.parliament.uk/pa/cm201617/cmselect/cmeduc/682/682.pdf (accessed 6 June 2019).

Hutchings, M.E. (2015) *Exam Factories: The Impact of Accountability Measures on Children and Young People*. London: National Union of Teachers. Available online: www.teachers.org.uk/files/exam-factories.pdf (accessed 6 June 2019).

International Educational Database (2019) Available online: https://worldtop20.org/education-database (accessed 6 June 2019).

Jante, B. and Harte, E. (2016) *Education of Migrant Children: Education Policy Responses for the Education of Children in Europe*. Santa Monica: Rand. Available online: www.rand.org/pubs/research_reports/RR1655.html (accessed 6 June 2019).

National Advisory Committee on Creative and Cultural Education (1999) *All Our Futures: Creativity, Culture and Education*. London: DfES. Available online: https://developingcreativelearnerssite.wordpress.com/the-naccce-report/ (accessed 6 June 2019).

Newbigin, J. (n.d.) *What Is the Creative Economy?* London: British Council. Available online: https://creativeeconomy.britishcouncil.org/guide/what-creative-economy/ (accessed 6 June 2019).

Plowden, B. (1967) *Children and Their Primary Schools: A Report of the Central Advisory Council for Education*. London: HMSO.

Population Europe (2014) Available online: www.population-europe.eu/pop-digest/why-immigrant-children-dont-do-well-school (accessed 6 June 2019).

Robinson, K. (1989) *The Arts in Schools: Principles, Practice and Provision*. London: Calouste Gulbenkian Foundation.

Robinson, K. (2016) *Creative Schools: Revolutionizing Education from the Ground Up*. London: Penguin.

Smulian, M. (2019) Non-EBacc Subjects Pushed into After-School Sessions. *Times Educational Supplement*, 17 May 2019. Available online: www.tes.com/news/non-ebacc-subjects-pushed-after-school-sessions (accessed 6 June 2019).

Sorrel, J., Roberts, P. and Helnley, D. (2014) *The Virtuous Circle: Why Creativity and Cultural Education Count*. London: Elliott & Thompson Limited.

UNESCO (2015) *Education for All 2000–2015 Achievements and Challenges: EFA Monitoring Report*. Paris: UNESCO. Available online: https://unesdoc.unesco.org/ark:/48223/pf0000232205 (accessed 6 June 2019).

UNESCO (n.d.) *Global Education Monitoring Report*. Paris: UNESCO. https://en.unesco.org/gem-report/ (accessed 6 June 2019).

United Nations (1948) *Universal Declaration of Human Rights*. New York: UN. www.un.org/en/universal-declaration-human-rights/ (accessed 6 June 2019).

Weale, S. (2019) Primary Teachers to Be Balloted on Boycotting Sats. *The Guardian*, 15 April 2019. Available online: www.theguardian.com/education/2019/apr/15/primary-teachers-to-be-balloted-on-boycotting-sat-exams (accessed 6 June 2019).

Williams, R. (1958) Culture Is Ordinary. In J. Higgins (Ed.) (2001) *The Raymond Williams Reader*. Oxford: Blackwell.

Chapter 17

Information Technology and learning
The shifting identities of learners and educators

Kyriaki Anagnostopoulou

Introduction

Every new technology is hailed as having the potential to revolutionise education for the better and simultaneously destroy traditional well-regarded educational systems and establishments. For example, it was only a few years ago that the rise of Massive Open Online Courses (MOOCs), offered on online platforms such as Coursera, EdX and FutureLearn, was signalling the death of universities in favour of high-quality free higher education for all, irrespective of who or where you were in the world (Whyte, 2015). However, from the outside, it appears that education is still awaiting its technological revolution, partly because traditional modes of education co-exist alongside new ones.

Nonetheless, education today is very different from that experienced by previous generations. The role of the learner has evolved from being a passive participant to becoming a co-creator of their educational experiences. Furthermore, the identity of the educator has changed from being a knowledge/subject expert to being a facilitator and co-learner and, instead of using technology to support learning, individuals are now manipulating technology to offer high degrees of personalised experiences. Access to education and how learning happens have been transformed, although changes in learner and educator identities take time, as does the embedding of technology in personal and professional aspects of life. As such, engagement with the various waves of technological movements has facilitated the evolution of education, rather than its revolution.

This chapter scopes the field of educational technology and presents three examples of technological innovations that are having a disruptive influence on the role of the learner, the role of the educator, and on education systems more generally. Through these examples, this chapter explores current practice, highlights concerns for the future and poses pertinent questions that need to be considered further in the field of Education Studies.

AI-powered learning

This chapter was written at a time when artificial intelligence (AI) has become prevalent in our homes, through small, inconspicuous speakers, and is available through personal mobile devices. Alexa, Siri and Google Assistant are examples of AIs that have quietly become part of the family. With regard to embodied AI, it is noteworthy that the first AI robot has been enrolled in school, in Japan, and is learning alongside human children (RT World News, 2016), robots are working alongside humans in shops and a robot has even gained citizenship in Saudi Arabia (Griffin, 2017).

AI is where computing science, psychology and educational research converge. It is increasingly prevalent in education, spanning from K–12/nursery through to university, and includes teaching robots, intelligent tutoring systems, and adaptive learning systems (Chassignola *et al.*, 2018). A number of research studies further extol the benefits of such systems, which range from being able to facilitate higher academic achievement (Karacı *et al.*, 2018) through to enabling accelerated learning by using more efficient machine tutoring (Aravind and Refugio, 2019).

The definition of AI is slippery, as every time an advancement in AI is made, the boundary between human/natural intelligence and artificial intelligence shifts, and this is partly due to a lack of a robust definition of intelligence itself (Marx and Anagnostopoulou, 2018). Generally, definitions of AI include the ability of a machine to mimic/simulate the intelligence of a human, which includes deciding how to complete tasks, being context aware and being able to learn. However, distinctions are being made between what is currently achievable (narrow, domain-specific AI) and what may yet come (AI capable of redesigning and improving itself) (Luckin, 2018). Indeed, not all AIs are made equal and some are more sophisticated than others, as illustrated by the examples below.

Example 1

In the field of education, at one end of the AI spectrum there is the Knewton online virtual learning environment (VLE), onto which educators upload educational content, such as videos, diagrams, research articles and podcasts, and label them accordingly. For example, this content may be labelled introductory level or may be more appropriate for advanced learners, it may support the achievement of one specific learning outcome or teach a particular skill. By including this descriptive metadata, alongside the data the system already holds and analyses about each user, through diagnostic testing and previous interactions, this VLE recognises its learners' preferences and creates a bespoke learning experience for each learner. It automates personalised instruction by measuring learners' prior knowledge and assigns tailored lessons based on its findings (Lapowsky, 2015). In this example, the technology is effectively taking on the role of the teacher/curriculum designer, who understands the strengths and weaknesses of their students. It diminishes the educator's role to one of content expert and multimedia resource identifier.

Example 2

At the more context-aware area of the spectrum of AI, intelligent robot tutors are able to detect schoolchildren's emotional and cognitive states (i.e. whether they are concentrating, distracted or inactive) when interacting with the educational software. Depending on its findings, the AI devises and makes pedagogic interventions to improve the learning experience, by offering support or engaging them in more interesting ways (Cuadrado *et al.*, 2016). In this instance, the technology is receiving and responding to real-time learner feedback, similar to what a teacher might be doing to support individual learners in the classroom, through monitoring and tailoring their lesson plan.

Example 3

Finally, at the more sophisticated end of the spectrum there is IBM Watson. This is an AI that learns from all the information and databases to which it has been connected and, coupled with its sophisticated analytics software, it replicates humans' ability to answer questions. It is being used successfully in a number of universities to create a 24/7 online student advisory system; early pilot projects demonstrated that almost half the students were not aware that the email support they were receiving was from an AI and not a faculty member at the university (Deakin University, 2015; Goel and Polepeddi, 2017). In this instance, the AI completely replaced those education-related roles that provide information and clarifications to support student learning.

Questions for discussion

- If a robot/AI can learn in class with humans, and an AI system can design personalised learning experiences whilst enjoying civic rights, what does this mean for education and education systems now and in the future?
- What might the increased use of automation technologies mean for the role of the educator?

AI is deemed to be one of the UK government's 'grand challenges', alongside concerns about the ageing population, clean growth, and the future of mobility. The new Industrial Strategy (HM Government, 2017) aims to position the UK at the forefront of the AI and data revolution, and sector deals are boosting the UK's global position as a leader. However, one might ask whether schools and universities are geared up to develop the workforce of the future.

Luckin (2018: 95) states that 'Educators' lives are going to change in significant ways, not because their roles are likely to be automated away but because they will need to teach a different curriculum and probably teach in a different way.' However, it is evident from the examples provided in this section, that a degree of automation is already underway. Therefore, it is imperative that we take the time to carefully manage the transition, not only of how we introduce AI into teaching, but also how we educate new generations of teachers to take advantage of the technological affordances and to focus on the more human aspects of the profession.

However, there is little consensus on what knowledge, skills and expertise will be needed by teachers and what should be taught to learners (Luckin, 2018). A number of education providers extol the virtues of teaching the '4 Cs', critical thinking, creativity, collaboration and communication, as twenty-first-century skills, whilst the World Economic Forum (2015) highlights these alongside foundational literacies (e.g. numeracy) and other skills that support learners in engaging with their perpetually changing contexts (e.g. persistence, adaptability, and leadership). Also noteworthy are the new literacies that are discussed by Aoun (2017) in his book about 'robot-proofing' education to promote employment readiness.

Alongside the cognitive capacities that need to be nurtured, which Aoun (2017) identifies as critical thinking, systems thinking, entrepreneurship and cultural agility, he states that there are three new literacies:

- Technological literacy, including mathematics, coding and basic engineering principles, that enable us to manipulate technology and develop it further.
- Data literacy is required in order to be able to analyse and make correlations between large data sets, focusing on their interconnectedness, to enable us to answer questions of how and why particular patterns emerge.
- Human literacy, including appreciation of diversity, ethics, grace and beauty, communication, collaboration, negotiation skills, collective decision-making. A deep understanding of what makes us human will enable us to differentiate ourselves from the technology.

It is this 'human literacy' that is of particular interest. Often we equate higher education with increasing employability prospects; so in this world of increased automation, it is important to understand what jobs can, and most likely will, be automated and which aspects of our jobs are distinctly human. If we can predict what jobs might be automated, then, as educators, it would be imperative to limit the teaching of their associated knowledge and skillsets. Otherwise, we might be preparing students, the employees of the future, for a job market that places them in direct competition with technology, for jobs that can be done more effectively and efficiently by machines. So what are the distinctly human aspects that we need to be focusing on in the curriculum?

Lee (2018), a technology executive and AI expert, places all jobs on a spectrum. At one end of this spectrum, he situates the jobs that relate to optimisation. These are repetitive and routine (e.g. telesales, truck-driving, customer support, news-reporting) and he predicts that they will be automated within the next decade. At the other end of the spectrum Lee places the jobs that require creativity and strategic thinking. These jobs are more complex (e.g. CEO, artist, scientist) and require distinctly human engagement, and specifically human compassion. He asserts that unless education prepares learners for jobs at the creative/strategic end of the spectrum, it will be doing them a disservice. This means that educators urgently need to accept that the future will be increasingly automated and to re-examine how they fulfil their responsibility to develop learners' skills to work alongside machines. Lee (2018) asserts that supporting the development and harnessing the power of human compassion for employment purposes is imperative. Depending on how much compassion is required by future jobs, the workforce of the future may be working *alongside* AI, carrying out work *informed by* AI or even enhancing and *surrounding* AI outputs by adding the human touch. Each of these modes of working will require a knowledge base and skillset that is fundamentally different from what currently is being offered in schools and universities.

The global classroom

In 2012, there was intense media coverage surrounding Massive Open Online Courses (MOOCs) and their potential to democratise and open up higher education for all. MOOCs get their name because they are:

- *Massive.* Some MOOCs have hundreds of thousands of learners registered to take the course at any one time.
- *Open.* Motivation is all that is required to register for a MOOC, as these courses are open to all, irrespective of who they are or where they are based. They are free at the point of delivery, past educational achievements are irrelevant and formal education qualifications are not required. Some even come with Creative Commons open education licences that enable users to adapt and reuse content for their own purposes.
- *Online.* These are completely online courses, facilitated asynchronously, but may have synchronous events included, such as live question and answer sessions.
- *Courses.* These courses are offered by high-ranking universities and are 'courses' in the sense that they have a beginning and an end, lasting 2–10 weeks approximately. However, full participation is not compulsory, they may not be assessed, and the vast majority do not offer university credit.

Born out of the open educational resources (OER) movement, top universities in the USA initially, and later across the world, invested heavily and are continuing to do so in order to provide these free online educational opportunities (Bersin, 2016; Conole, 2013). They do this for a variety of reasons, which include a desire to showcase and promote their teaching and research activities, a need to offer taster sessions in support of widening access agendas, a means of attracting high-calibre international applicants to their fee-paying courses, and, more altruistically, to give back to society and provide MOOCs for the social good (Conole, 2013).

As an extension of traditional distance learning courses, what makes MOOCs simultaneously powerful and weak as a learning experience, is the large number of learners. They are powerful, because they potentially offer experiences that money cannot buy. For example, the University of Bath's MOOC on cancer genetics brought together thousands of participants from more than ninety countries. In line with research, the majority of MOOC participants already had a first degree (Zhenghao *et al.*, 2015), and approximately one-third of participants were researchers, medical practitioners, and professionals in allied fields. A further third were students, from pre- and post-16 education, all the way through to PhD researchers who were seeking clarification and inspiration, as well as exploring what the university has to offer. The final third were members of the general public and those with an interest in cancer genetics. These included cancer-sufferers and carers, as well as friends and family of people affected by cancer who were seeking explanations and answers. They came together into a single online space to gain access to up-to-date expertise and worldwide perspectives from professionals and high-ranking university academics, whilst hearing about real-world, authentic accounts of those experiencing cancer. At the same time, MOOC learners were developing their digital literacies and independent learning skills, whilst engaging in professional networking at an international level.

Evans *et al.* (2006) discuss learning environments as being on an 'expansive-restrictive spectrum' and claim that 'expansive' environments can afford transformational learning experiences, which alter existing frames of reference, rather than just the accumulation of information/knowledge. Indeed, this MOOC environment was as 'expansive' as it was creative, dynamic, constantly evolving through participants' contributions, and offered maximum opportunities for learning. One might say that the global classroom experience offered online was much richer than that offered in a traditional university lecture theatre. The latter can be more 'restrictive', as it is limited and confined by boundaries that do not permit the flow of discussion between various areas of expertise.

In this example, new technological initiatives are offering free, informal education that is potentially a superior learning experience to that offered by esteemed educational establishments, which command high tuition fees and result in significant financial student debt. Indeed, a number of student unions nationally queried the reasoning of universities in offering MOOCs, as it was their fees that were being used to provide free, possibly better, experiences to those who were not officially part of their academic community. Staff and students' unions expressed concern that, if MOOCs were to offer credits, this might result in the downsizing of university campuses and dilution of the quality of higher education (Smith, 2013). Indeed, less than seven years after their initial inception, MOOCs platform providers are offering entire, online degrees, for credit, and subscription models for businesses who wish to offer professional development opportunities to their staff (Morrison, 2016). Although this places MOOC providers in direct competition with universities, MOOCs cannot currently exist independently of them, as they do not currently have the capacity to offer expert content, support and accreditation without university partners.

However, simultaneously, by traditional measures, the MOOC experience can be deemed weak and impersonal, as the teacher-student ratio is nothing like that, which is valued, in traditional higher education. Anonymity and large learner numbers are not associated with the personalisation of learning and meaningful student engagement. Indeed, certain established practices that are known to lead to meaningful engagement, such as those offered by Salmon (2000), are no longer feasible. For example, it is not possible to welcome online learners individually to a course to help build confidence and rapport when they are with thousands of enrolments. Also, the phenomenally high dropout rate of MOOCs (Onah *et al.*, 2014) means that the vast majority of learners do not complete the full course. As there is no formal invigilated assessment at the end of the course, there is a lack of evidence as to whether learning has taken place. Nonetheless, the cancer genetics MOOC had some of the highest satisfaction rates, rates that would be the envy of many academics teaching in a traditional setting. As such, MOOCs continue to challenge notions of quality of experience in online learning delivery.

Questions for discussion

- How does a teacher effectively teach more students in a single online cohort than the total number of students they would teach face-to-face in their entire career?
- How do they establish presence in a classroom of thousands and demonstrate all the qualities we value in a good teacher (empathy, enthusiasm and personalisation)?
- How do we measure success when traditional measures do not apply?

Often it is taken for granted that technology can enhance learning and teaching, and discussions often omit why this is the case, how it happens and what specific acts of learning are enhanced (Cukurova and Luckin, 2018). Indeed, as almost anything can constitute a piece of 'technology' (e.g. a pencil, a book, the blackboard, a tablet PC, etc.) and technology is perpetually advancing, importance needs to be placed on how we design contexts that would enable learning to be enhanced, rather than simply focusing on the use of a specific technology.

At one end of the learning design spectrum, educators are now seeking to incorporate MOOCs from universities around the world into traditional on-campus teaching. The richness of experience offered by MOOCs, due to their large learner population on easy-to-use digital media platforms, is being integrated into university modules, topped and tailed by traditional teaching methods, support offered alongside participating in an online MOOC, and followed by an assessment at the end. This 'embedded MOOC' model challenges the notion of what is distinct about each institution.

At the other end of the learning design spectrum, EDUCAUSE's Horizon Report (Alexander *et al.*, 2019), which looks at current and future educational technology trends, highlights that models of education are emerging that offer learners opportunities to go beyond traditional pathways to degree qualifications. Learners are using combinations of formal education with informal online experiences, alongside workplace and extra-curricular experiences. Achievement is evidenced through a combination of formal qualifications and other accreditation methods, such as digital badges and certificates, which provide assurances to prospective employers of skills that have been gained through a range of educational opportunities. The ability to 'build your own degree', through self-paced micro credentials, brings together competing models of education in a modularised and disaggregated manner that enables learners to have more control over their learning journey. Again, this challenges the role of the university, as it is no longer the only academically and professionally valued means of developing knowledge, credibility and employment readiness.

At a time when one in four university students in the USA is taking a formal online course (Seaman *et al.*, 2018), when feedback on assessment is received within minutes from multiple peers around the world in MOOCs, and employers are valuing alternative qualifications, learner-centred approaches to course design are of primary importance. Indeed, there has been a notable shift away from training programmes that support educators in acquiring technical skills, and instead placing the focus on pedagogically-sound course design that harnesses new technological affordances (Alexander *et al.*, 2019). The need to apply design-thinking approaches to developing engaging curricula in multiple modalities and contexts in which learning conversations and debates can take place means that the role of e-learning technologists and instructional designers is in increasing demand. As part of an interdisciplinary team, these education professionals effectively act as expert educational consultants, supporting subject matter experts in implementing technology-rich platforms and developing pedagogically-sound digital learning experiences. As professionals, e-learning technologists made an appearance after the Dearing Report (NCIHE, 1997) which emphasised the focus on the quality of learning and teaching, the need for teacher/lecturer support and development, and the importance of innovation through the use of technology. However, the role is perpetually evolving due to the rapid changes that are brought about by advancement in technologies, as well as political and economic agendas. As such, it is pertinent to further explore the role of such professionals within the field of Education Studies.

Virtual and mixed reality

Computer-simulated environments have been used in education for many years to provide authentic learning experiences. However, virtual, augmented and mixed-reality worlds specifically focus on the intersection between online and offline worlds (Alexander *et al.*, 2019). The lines between digital and physical objects are blurred as they seamlessly co-exist in a single hybrid space. Whereas virtual reality (VR) immerses the user (through their avatar) into a new environment through the wearing of a headset (e.g. Oculus Rift), augmented reality (AR) overlays the physical world with layers of information accessed through digital devices (e.g. smart phones or tablets). Mixed reality (MR) brings these two together (e.g. Microsoft Hololens) and places digital experiences on a continuum of Reality–Virtuality, either more or less physical/virtual (Milgram *et al.*, 1994).

Educationally, mixed-reality worlds can alter how we interact and learn within increasingly digitised contexts. Learners can immerse themselves in mixed-reality environments and learn from first-hand experiences, rather than reading about them or watching a video. For example, this type of technology offers the ability to engage with historical settings, such as attending a gladiator fight in the Roman Colosseum or visiting space and landing on the surface of Mars. It also enables experiences that are completely impossible in the physical world, such as travelling to the molten core of the earth or navigating through a human artery alongside blood cells, as well as a means of safely undertaking high-risk experimentations (e.g. carrying out surgery or mixing chemicals in a chemistry lab).

In a world where learners are constantly straddling both physical and digital environments, these experiences provide a new understanding of authentic learning as they have the potential to transform how learners engage with educational materials and situations in ways that were previously impossible. Indeed, researchers have found that by simply using a VR headset, instead of a traditional desktop PC and mouse, learner recall of information is increased significantly due to learners organising the information spatially and associating salient features of the virtual environment with it (Krokos *et al.*, 2018). Further aided by the fact that learners can repeat their virtual experience, reflection and self-assessment are also critical to experiential learning, but not facilitated by the technology itself (Alexander *et al.*, 2019).

Educational research into VR in education has focused predominantly on researching social interactions in authentic, simulated environments and has also been used as a methodological tool that enables the experimental condition in the virtual environment to remain constant and stable (Bradley and Newbutt, 2018). The majority of AR-related educational research has been done with schoolchildren and university students as the subjects (Bacca *et al.*, 2014), whilst there is much interest in developing such technologies for children with special education needs, such as having a diagnosis of autism or communication difficulties.

Wu *et al.* (2013) emphasise the potential of these technologies to foster a great sense of presence, immediacy, and immersion for learners. Therefore, they encourage educators to view AR as an instructional design concept, rather than a type of technology. They classified the instructional approaches described in the AR literature into three categories:

- Approaches that engage learners in specific 'roles'. Learners individually or collaboratively can interact with components of the virtual world to influence outcomes in that world (similar to online games).
- Approaches based on maximising interactions with the virtually-enhanced 'locations' in which learners find themselves.
- Approaches that emphasise 'tasks' that learners need to undertake.

As such, the focus on learning design and instructional designers comes to the fore once again. However, this time, in order to achieve highly realistic content and environments, Kesim and Ozarslan (2012) state that a multi-disciplinary research approach is required. Hardware and software engineers, working alongside educators and e-learning technologists, would need to engage in multi-sensory content development, drawing on principles from each of their professional disciplines.

Although a highly specialist mix of skills is required to create engaging mixed-reality experiences, initiatives such as Google's 'Expeditions' are shifting the power directly to students. The Expeditions initiative, through which thousands of VR experiences are made freely available to schools, is also making available its Tour Creator software that allows and empowers students to create and publish their own mixed-reality content. Now, not only can children influence what happens in their mixed-reality worlds, through interacting and making choices in the virtual world, they can also generate the digital contexts in which they wish to learn, and they can invite others to them. The new literacies and skills, outlined in previous parts of this chapter, will support them in developing these learner-generated contexts. In turn, this will increase adoption rates of VR in classrooms. However, this type of technological development shifts the power from the teacher to the learner, whilst challenging notions of expertise and quality, and directly opposing them with the advantages derived from increased personalisation.

Questions for discussion

- What is the role of the teacher when learners can generate their own contexts for learning?
- What are the new pedagogies we need to develop to teach and support learners in developing their own mixed-reality worlds?

Conclusion

This chapter presents a number of examples of technological innovations that are challenging the way we conceptualise teaching and learning. Technological developments are rapid and being able to understand their affordances for learning is of key importance to the field of Education Studies for the ongoing development and evolution of the discipline of education. This is not to say that teachers will be replaced by machines. After all, teaching requires high degrees of compassion, making it a truly human profession (Lee, 2018). However, how we define teaching, and education more generally, will shift and change as the context around us becomes more digitised. Irrespective of the technologies, whether they are AI-enabled or offer mixed-reality environments, the examples provided in this chapter raise pertinent questions about the role of the educator, the role of the learner, the value of our education systems and the appropriateness of the curriculum it offers the workforce of the future.

Identifying the right blend of human and artificial intelligence in classroom settings can only be done through more research in this area. The technology itself can increase access to expertise worldwide and can support learners in personalising their experience. However, understanding how it shifts and changes the nature of knowledge and education is of greater importance.

Summary points

- Perceptions and definitions of education, as a discipline, are perpetually evolving as the world around us changes and technology makes further advancements. Understanding and valuing the truly human aspects of professions, and society more generally, will provide a platform from which to explore the evolution of education.
- The rise of digital informal contexts, such as MOOCs, means that learners can choose where, what and how they learn, and are not limited to formal education systems for acquiring knowledge, skills and accreditation.

- The way that technology can enable and shift power directly to learners challenges conventional approaches to teaching that are currently taking place in schools.
- It is important to re-examine today's curriculum offer, at all levels, in order to ensure that current students, who are the workforce of the future, are gaining appropriate skills and knowledge to be able to live and succeed in an increasingly digital society.
- Increasing emphasis on learning design, rather than on technological training, will stimulate the creation of effective digital learning spaces that support high-value educational interactions.
- Collaborative, interdisciplinary approaches to the design of educational technology initiatives will be needed to develop effective learning experiences.

Recommended reading

Alexander, B., Ashford-Rowe, K., Barajas-Murphy, N., Dobbin, G., Knott, J., McCormack, M., Pomerantz, J., Seilhamer, R. and Weber, N. (2019) *Horizon Report: 2019 Higher Education Edition*. Louisville, CO: EDUCAUSE. Available online at: https://library.educause.edu/-/media/files/library/2019/4/2019horizonreport.pdf?#page=7&la=en&hash=5C6DC7ECEEF4803540246E6158E1807A55C703FB (accessed 4 July 2019).

Lacity, M., Scheepers, R., Willcocks, L. and Craig, A. (2017) *Reimagining the University at Deakin: An IBM Watson Automation Journey*. The Outsourcing Unit Working Research Paper Series. Paper 17/04. Available online at: www.umsl.edu/~lacitym/LSEOUWP1704.pdf (accessed 4 July 2019).

Newman, T., Beetham, H. and Knight, S. (2018) *Digital Experience Insights Survey 2018: Findings from Students in UK Further and Higher Education*. JISC. Available online at: http://repository.jisc.ac.uk/6967/1/Digital_experience_insights_survey_2018.pdf (accessed 4 July 2019).

References

Alexander, B., Ashford-Rowe, K., Barajas-Murphy, N., Dobbin, G., Knott, J., McCormack, M., Pomerantz, J., Seilhamer, R. and Weber, N. (2019) *Horizon Report: 2019 Higher Education Edition*. Louisville, CO: EDUCAUSE. Available online at: https://library.educause.edu/-/media/files/library/2019/4/2019horizonreport.pdf?#page=7&la=en&hash=5C6DC7ECEEF4803540246E6158E1807A55C703FB (accessed 4 July 2019).

Aoun, J. E. (2017) *Robot-Proof: Higher Education in the Age of Artificial Intelligence*. Cambridge, MA: MIT Press.

Aravind, V.R. and Refugio, C. (2019) Efficient Learning with Intelligent Tutoring across Cultures. *World Journal on Educational Technology: Current Issues* **11**(1), pp. 030–037.

Bacca, J., Baldiris, S., Fabregat, R., Graf, S. and Kinshuk (2014) Augmented Reality Trends in Education: A Systematic Review of Research and Applications. *Educational Technology & Society* **17**(4), pp. 133–149.

Bersin, J. (2016) Use of MOOCs and Online Education Is Exploding: Here's Why. *Forbes*. Available online at: www.forbes.com/sites/joshbersin/2016/01/05/use-of-moocs-and-online-education-is-exploding-heres-why/#6d1212037649 (accessed 4 July 2019).

Bradley, R. and Newbutt, N. (2018) Autism and Virtual Reality Head-Mounted Displays: A State of the Art Systematic Review. *Journal of Enabling Technologies* **12**(3), pp. 101–113.

Chassignola, M., Khoroshavin, A., Klimovac, A. and Bilyatdinova, A. (2018) Artificial Intelligence Trends in Education: A Narrative Overview. *Procedia Computer Science* **136**, pp. 16–24.

Conole, G. (2013) MOOCs as Disruptive Technologies: Strategies for Enhancing the Learner Experience and Quality of MOOCs. *RED – Revista de Educación a Distancia* **39**.

Cuadrado, L.E.I., Riesco, A.M. and López, F.D.L.P. (2016) ARTIE: An Integrated Environment for the Development of Affective Robot Tutors. *Frontiers in Computational Neuroscience* **10**(77).

Cukurova, M. and Luckin, R. (2018) Introduction: What the Research Says about the Use of Different Technologies to Enhance Learning. In R. Luckin (Ed.), *Enhancing Learning and Teaching with Technology: What the Research Says*. London: UCL IOE Press.

Deakin University (2015) IBM Watson Helps Deakin Drive the Digital Frontier. Melbourne: Deakin University. Available online at: www.deakin.edu.au/about-deakin/media-releases/articles/ibm-watson-helps-deakin-drive-the-digital-frontier (accessed 4 July 2019).

Evans, K., Hodkinson, P., Rainbird, H. and Unwin, L. (2006) *Improving Workplace Learning*. London: Routledge.

Goel, A.K. and Polepeddi, L. (2017) Jill Watson: A Virtual Teaching Assistant for Online Education. Presented to the Learning Engineering for Online Learning Workshop. Cambridge, MA: Harvard University.

Griffin, A. (2017) Saudia Arabia Grants Citizenship to a Robot for the First Time Ever. *The Independent*, 26 October, 2017. Available online at: www.independent.co.uk/life-style/gadgets-and-tech/news/saudi-arabia-robot-sophia-citizenship-android-riyadh-citizen-passport-future-a8021601.html (accessed 4 July 2019).

HM Government (2017) Industrial Strategy: Building a Britain Fit for the Future. Available online at: www.gov.uk/government/publications/industrial-strategy-building-a-britain-fit-for-the-future (accessed 4 July 2019).

Karacı, A., Akyüz, H.İ., Bilgici, G. and Arıcı, N. (2018) Effects of Web-Based Intelligent Tutoring Systems on Academic Achievement and Retention. *International Journal of Computer Applications* **181**(16), pp. 34–41.

Kesim, M. and Ozarslan, Y. (2012) Augmented Reality in Education: Current Technologies and the Potential for Education. *Procedia – Social and Behavioral Sciences* **47**, pp. 297–302.

Krokos, E., Plaisant, C. and Varshney, A. (2018) Virtual Memory Palaces: Immersion Aids Recall. *Virtual Reality* 23(1), pp. 1–15.

Lapowsky, I. (2015) This Robot Tutor Will Make Personalised Education Easy. *Wired*. Available online at: www.wired.com/2015/08/knewton-robot-tutor/ (accessed 4 July 2019).

Lee, K.F. (2018) How Can AI Save Our Humanity? TED-X Conference. Vancouver, Canada. Available online at: www.ted.com/talks/kai_fu_lee_how_ai_can_save_our_humanity?language=en (accessed 4 July 2019).

Luckin, R. (2018) *Machine Learning and Human Intelligence: The Future of Education for the 21st Century*. London: UCL IOE Press.

Marx, R. and Anagnostopoulou, K. (2018) Education and Artificial Intelligence. ICEFIL Annual Conference. Utrecht, Netherlands.

Milgram, P., Takemura, H., Utsumi, A. and Kishino, F. (1994) Augmented Reality: A Class of Displays on the Reality–Virtuality Continuum. *Proceedings of SPIE: Telemanipulator and Telepresence Technologies* **2351**, pp. 282–292.

Morrison, D. (2016) Need-to-Know MOOC News: MOOCs Find Their Niche and Business Model in 2016. *Online Learning Insights*. Available online at: https://onlinelearninginsights.wordpress.com/2016/02/03/need-to-know-mooc-news-the-mooc-business-model-gets-its-teeth-in-2016/ (accessed 4 July 2019).

NCIHE (1997) *Report of the National Committee into Higher Education (Dearing Report)*. London: HMSO.

Onah, D.F.O., Sinclair, J. and Boyatt, R. (2014) Dropout Rates of Massive Open Online Courses: Behavioural Patterns. 6th International Conference on Education and New Learning Technologies (EDULEARN14). Barcelona, Spain.

RT World News (2016) World First: Japanese Robot Enrolls in High School. Available online at: www.rt.com/news/339480-japan-robot-pepper-school/ (accessed 4 July 2019).

Salmon, G. (2000) *E-moderating: The Key to Teaching and Learning Online*. London: Kogan Page.

Seaman, J.E., Allen, I.E. and Seaman, J. (2018) *Grade Increase: Tracking Distance Education in the United States*. Babson Survey Research Group. Available online at: https://onlinelearningsurvey.com/reports/gradeincrease.pdf (accessed 4 July 2019).

Smith, K. (2013) Profits First, Students Last: SUNY's Plan to Use for-Profit Companies to Run MOOCs – Massive Open Online Courses – Threatens Education Quality. *NYSUT.* Available online at: www.nysut.org/news/nysut-united/issues/2013/december-2013-january-2014/profits-first-students-last-sunys-plan-to-use-for-profit-companies-to-run-moocs (accessed 4 July 2019).

Whyte, W. (2015) Does the MOOC Spell the End for Universities? *Oxford University Press Blog*. Available online at: https://blog.oup.com/2015/02/mooc-end-universities/ (accessed 4 July 2019).

World Economic Forum (2015) New Visions of Education: Unlocking the Potential of Technology. Geneva: World Economic Forum. Available online at: www3.weforum.org/docs/WEFUSA_NewVisionforEducation_Report2015.pdf (accessed 4 July 2019).

Wu, H., Lee, S.W., Chang, H. and Liang, J. (2013) Current Status, Opportunities and Challenges of Augmented Reality in Education. *Computers & Education* **62**, pp. 41–49.

Zhenghao, C., Alcorn, B., Christensen, G., Eriksson, N., Koller, D. and Emanuel, E.J. (2015) Who's Benefiting from MOOCs, and Why. *Harvard Business Review*. Available online at: https://hbr.org/2015/09/whos-benefiting-from-moocs-and-why (accessed 4 July 2019).

Section 4

Childhood and youth

Chapter 18

Early Childhood Studies degrees
A twisty road

Ioanna Palaiologou and Zenna Kingdon

Introduction

The field of Early Childhood Studies (ECS) as an academic subject in higher education institutions has grown in the last three decades and still grows, not only as an academic subject, but also as a vocational qualification for people who intend to work with young children from birth to 5 years of age. The introduction of curricula frameworks in Early Childhood Education and Care (ECEC) in the UK has resulted in a re-examination of qualifications for those working in the field. Government initiatives across the UK to have an undergraduate- and even a postgraduate-level qualified ECEC workforce have contributed to the growth of ECS degrees. Subsequently, the picture nationally is comprised of undergraduate and postgraduate degrees that offer either ECEC as an academic subject without leading to a vocational qualification, or ECS degrees that lead to a qualification that will enable graduates to work in the sector by meeting government standards.

This chapter provides a discussion of:

- the historical development of ECS as an academic study;
- an examination of the role of ECS in relation to policy initiatives and development of qualifications in ECEC practice;
- what ECS means in the twenty-first century as an academic subject, the impact of academic research and its role within the wider field of Education Studies.

Historical developments: *dreaming of hope?*

Understanding the development of ECS degrees in the UK needs to be located in the historical development of ECEC. Currently, in the UK, ECEC refers to the statutory provision for children from birth to 5 years (mainly before compulsory schooling age, with the exception of Northern Ireland where compulsory schooling starts at the age of 4) and traditionally has been provided by private, voluntary and independent (PVI) sectors. More recently there has been a movement to include children from the age of 3 to 5 years in state-funded provision, with primary schools now being encouraged to start admitting 2-year-old children, especially from disadvantaged backgrounds. However, the UK's

ECEC presents a peculiar situation due to its history of being divided between education and care, as well as the devolution of the UK's four nations: England, Scotland, Wales and Northern Ireland. Although there are overarching policies such as the Children's Act (1989, revised in 2004) and the Childcare Strategy (1998), in terms of national statutory guidance for quality standards, qualifications and curriculum, each nation has its own legislation and provision for ECEC.

Although progress has now been made to raise quality, the field of ECEC for many years was underdeveloped compared to other levels of formal education, and this was reflected in the quality and level of programmes that existed to train people to work in the field. Calder (1999a) examined the development of qualifications in early childhood education post-1997 and the birth of ECS degrees in UK. He found that, although a number of courses offering qualifications in ECEC existed, at policy level there were limited required qualifications, the quality and the content were variable, and most of the ECEC workforce were unqualified.

These disparities in qualifications mirror the situation prior to the 1990s where the sector for many years was a divided one between care and education. In the 1989 Children Act the term 'day-care services' for the provision of children who were of pre-school age was used to describe what is now ECEC. The day-care services were under the responsibility of the Department of Health (DoH) and these included nurseries, childminders, playgroups, out-of-school childcare and play schemes that were mainly provided by the private sector. The 'care' of children below school age that was provided by one of these sectors at that point was not associated with education, which meant that the qualifications required were minimal. On the other hand, early education was provided by schools for children from the age of 3 (nurseries and reception class) which was the responsibility of the Department for Education (DfE) where the requirement for qualifications differed. The picture was patchy, however, and there were no systemic attempts at policy level to improve or unify the two sectors. Cohen *et al.* (2004), in examining ECEC across England, Scotland and Sweden, concluded that post-1997 there was 'split departmental responsibility between welfare (DoH), responsible for day-care/child-care services and education (DfE) responsible for nursery and compulsory schooling' (ibid.: 55). These disparities between care, education and formal schooling had an impact on how the workforce was structured, resulting in a number of different qualifications, job titles and 'a lack of agreement about roles [that] devalues the nature of work' (Payler and Davis, 2017: 11).

The situation started slowly changing in the 1990s with a commitment from the Conservative government to provide a better start in life for deprived children, and placing education at the heart of that ambition. Investment was made in the education and care of children below school age as an attempt to break the cycle of deprivation, which gave moderate hope to all involved in ECEC. Although research (e.g. Moyles, 1989; Athey, 1990; David, 1993; Goldschmied and Jackson, 1994; Pugh, 1996; Penn, 1997) was emerging at that time about quality in ECEC and the importance of having qualified practitioners in the sector, progress was slow, and the workforce remained underdeveloped, underfunded, varied and in some cases not even regulated (Calder, 1999a, 1999b).

The birth of Early Childhood Studies degrees: *creating hope?*

In such a climate of undervalued and underpaid provision the first two undergraduate degrees in ECS were created in 1992 by Bristol University and Suffolk College. The vision was to 'develop higher education and degree level courses for early childhood workers' (ECSDN, 2019) with the aspiration that ECEC could develop a better future for young children and their families and also meet the standards of other formal schooling in receiving quality funding and developing a graduate workforce. These degrees were not leading to any vocational qualification for their graduates, and the emphasis of the curriculum was on child-related subjects, drawing from a number of disciplines such as Psychology, History of Childhood, Sociology and Pedagogy, with no clear career intentions (Palaiologou and Male, 2016).

Central to these new degrees was the aspiration that a graduate workforce would raise quality in the field for young children and provide their families with better outcomes. A few other HE institutions followed, and by 1996 there were already five, with more planning to develop their own degrees (Calder, 1999a). Within the mission of these new degrees was the intention to develop ECS as an academic subject and at the same time to offer opportunities for a better trained and qualified ECEC workforce.

Although these first degrees were mostly located in Education departments, they lacked official recognition from the Quality Assurance Agency (QAA) that provides the benchmark for undergraduate programmes in HE institutions. Calder (1999a, 1999b) noted that, as the government at the time (post-1997) had no plans to support an undergraduate workforce in ECEC, the ECS degrees varied in their context, purpose and mission.

The demand for specialised reading, however, led to an increase in academic books which explored key and contemporary issues of ECS, examined the nature of such a field of study and addressed key topics that the degrees should cover (e.g. Maynard and Thomas, 2009; Waller and Davis, 2005; Bruce, 2006; Anning *et al.*, 2009, with further editions in the years to follow). The majority of key topics, similar to Education Studies degrees (see Introduction), focused on an interdisciplinary approach, with a number of disciplines such as Psychology, Sociology and the History of Childhood being employed to explore concepts around play, learning, policy and legislation, constructions of childhood, and effective practice. These first ECS degrees thus created a hope that ECEC could gain a place in higher education and claim academic subject status as an autonomous field of study informed by rigorous research, but at the same time offer high-quality skills to a graduate-led workforce. A network of academics who represented these degrees was established (Early Childhood Studies Degrees Network – ECSDN) with the aim of lobbying for recognition of ECS as a subject of study in HE institutions and, at the same time, to promote training and standards for the ECEC workforce that were based on rigorous research. The network's aim was to promote the study of ECEC in HE institutions as much needed and equally as important as other academic subjects. At the embryonic stage of the birth of the ECS degrees, for example, graduates were not considered as qualified candidates for teacher training programmes and the network tried to resolve such issues.

The evolution of ECS degrees: *a glimmer or a glimpse of hope?*

In 1997 and after nearly twenty years of Conservative government there was a change in politics with a Labour government coming into power. Central to its manifesto was a similar ambition to minimise child poverty, again with education being a core component. A series of additional reforms, initiatives and funding started flowing into the ECEC sector, such as the Early Excellence Centres programme that was set up in 1997 aiming to integrate ECEC with support services. Although devolution of the four nations was increasing, the National Childcare Strategy was introduced in 1998 as an overarching policy for the UK to set the targets in relation to the provision for children. Among its core aims was the intention to develop professional standards for ECEC, regulate the sector and create a graduate-led workforce.

These initiatives and radical changes in policy aspiration for a highly trained and qualified ECEC workforce, especially the intention to have a graduate workforce, not only gave hope to the existing ECS degrees, but also resulted in new ones being developed across the country. The new range of degrees not only sought to develop the study of ECEC as an academic subject, but were also linked to vocational opportunities.

By the beginning of the current century many more HE institutions were introducing ECS degrees, either as autonomous bachelor's degrees or in a combination with relevant cognate areas such as Education Studies, Childhood Studies and Psychology. The increasing number of ECS degrees, alongside the lobbying of the ECSDN and the increasing academic research in the field, led to recognition by the QAA, which introduced the first Subject Benchmark (QAA, 2007, revised in 2014) where it was acknowledged that, prior to the existence of these degrees:

> Conceptual development and policy concerns were either split between the subject areas of, for example, sociology, psychology, social policy and health, or were seen as areas of practice outside higher education, and regarded as the province of technical training rather than being seen as an appropriate area for study, research and development. [One of the key aims of ECS degrees is] to offer appropriate education and training to students who either already work in the early childhood studies field, but lack a qualification at degree level, or to those who are interested in studying and working in the field.
>
> (QAA, 2014: 5)

Alongside the government's aspirations to have a graduate-led workforce, an increasing body of academic research was arguing that quality ECEC is dependent upon a highly qualified workforce (e.g. Sylva *et al.*, 2004; NICHD, 2002). This created a hope that the ECS degrees could meet the dual purpose of not only offering specialised child-related education to these graduates, but also providing vocational skills and training to create a highly qualified ECEC workforce.

However, the global economic crisis that began in 2008 was followed by a number of austerity measures in the UK and a slowdown of these initiatives. In 2010 there were government changes, with the Coalition government followed in 2015 by a Conservative government, which meant that these initiatives were re-examined. Although during these years it appeared that there was still a commitment to increasing quality and investment in qualifications for the ECEC workforce, in reality these aims were not met. For example, in 2012 the government commissioned the Nutbrown Report which examined the qualifications of the ECEC sector. The report strongly recommended the creation of a graduate-led workforce, but many recommendations were ignored and the ambition of raising qualifications in ECEC at graduate level has not yet been achieved, especially in the private sector.

Whilst these developments brought an uncertainty in terms of vocational training and skills, as an academic subject ECS degrees have been growing strong and now feature high-quality academic books, specialist journals and a vast body of academic research which examines key concepts, establishing ECS as a university subject in its own right.

The present: *still hoping?*

Currently, a simple search on the UCAS webpage gives about 350 programmes which offer a form of Early Childhood Education Studies in 99 HE institutions across the country, in combination with either an Education Studies or Childhood Studies degree. Across the existing ECS degrees (still mainly located in education departments in HE institutions), although the key focus is child-related education from an interdisciplinary perspective, there is a variation in the content of study and career pathways. However, all bachelor's ECS degrees need to be mapped with the QAA benchmark and offer to the students a curriculum where:

> the ecology of early childhood from conception, and of children [is] in an ecological context. Ecological context is understood as encompassing both time and geographical space, and encompassing the contexts of family and community, and children's and family services. The focus is on the development of the child in context and the implications for practice. Studying children and early childhood ecologically means that it would be inappropriate to specify an age at which early childhood ends because this will differ according to societal and cultural contexts, practices and customs. The attention to child development in an ecological context also situates young children as active participants in the lives and practices of families, societies and cultures.
>
> (QAA, 2014: 6)

In that sense, ECS degrees have a flexibility to develop their own curriculum in terms of their philosophical and ideological underpinnings. The curriculum offered by many ECS degrees in the UK remain interdisciplinary in nature, offering a wide range of child-related topics such as cultural, social, economic, political, international, historical and psychological perspectives of childhood, with a strong emphasis on a children's-rights approach, especially on issues of children's voices and participation. Graduates are expected to develop a set of skills that enable them to seek employment in a number of relevant

ECEC sectors, or move on to the further qualifications that will enable them to seek other occupations such as teaching, social work or educational psychology.

As mentioned above, ECS as a field of study has met its first aim which was to be established as an academic subject in its own right. However, challenges remain in terms of its second aim, to 'encourage professional and practice development and may offer the opportunity for students to meet the requirements of particular statutory or regulatory bodies, through the structure and content of the programme' (QAA, 2014: 6).

The first challenge is that the troublesome issue of relating degrees to ECEC vocational qualifications still exists. In a recent report that examined workforce profiles in ECEC across the UK, Hevey (2017: 4) concluded that devolution has led to 'divergence in policies across the four nations, each leading to a different set of problems and anomalies'. One of the anomalies is the variation in qualifications among those who work, or intend to work, in the sector. In some instances, there is a workforce which is qualified at graduate or postgraduate level, or who have Qualified Teacher Status (QTS), meaning they have met standards and training requirements set by government policy and can work in state-maintained schools with children from 3 to 11. Conversely, there is a workforce across the sector that has a variety of qualifications from a minimum of Level 4 EQF or Level 3 ISCED. These disparities have led to the development of a workforce in ECEC where:

> qualified teachers (with QTS) enjoying significantly better pay, career structures, conditions of service and CPD entitlements than other workers due to the different status of education and care and strong unionisation of the teaching workforce combined with differential patterns of employment across the public/Local Authority and PVI sectors; absence of unionisation amongst the non-teaching workforce; poorly paid and poorly qualified women working in relative isolation in small private and voluntary settings are less likely to join unions.
>
> (Hevey, 2017: 4)

Consequently, on the one hand, studying ECS degrees with the aspiration to join the ECEC workforce leaves its graduates as neither being on the same pay scales nor achieving financial parity with those who have achieved QTS degrees. On the other hand, as a recent study (Silberfeld and Mitchell, 2018) found, although graduates valued their study in the field, they felt having only the ECS degree was not helping them to have employability opportunities, thus creating a need for further study.

Secondly, Payler and Davis (2017) undertook a literature review on research evidence since 2003 that examined issues of professionalisation in the ECEC workforce in relation to the socio-economic and political context of the UK. They concluded that there are two main competing challenges in developing and sustaining quality of workforce professionals. Consequently, they consider that the issue of professionalisation in ECEC is still underdeveloped and suggest that working with young children is demanding and complex in nature, with research strongly suggesting that continuous training is needed to support the ECEC workforce to meet the demands of such complexity. The 'increasing political and economic demands for an "affordable" childcare sector to provide greater capacity at lower costs' (ibid.: 21) means, however, that the demands cannot be met for a graduate qualified workforce, especially in the private sector. For ECS degrees that include a professional route in their curriculum so their graduates can gain professional recognition as an outcome create a disincentive to their seeking a career in the low-paid sector and they tend to look for alternative employment. As explained earlier, one of the aims of the ECS degrees was to develop a high-quality ECEC workforce and these conditions leave this aim unfulfilled.

Conclusion

This chapter has discussed the development of ECS degrees in the UK and began with a twofold aspiration. First, to establish ECS as an academic subject, and second to provide graduates with a set of skills and training that enable them to raise the quality of ECEC provision once they join it. As the aspiration of many ECS degrees across the country was to link them with a clear career pathway to ECEC, their development cannot be seen as distinct from policy and legislation developments in the sector. In the UK since the early 1990s there has been an increase in ECS degrees, but their context, aims and missions vary. Despite these variations, the academic identity of ECS as a subject of study has emerged and it is interdisciplinary in nature, with a strong emphasis on child-related subjects. In terms of the second aim, although ECEC has seen improvement and standards have been raised, due to policy and funding restrictions the sector is still challenging in terms of status of pay and professional recognition. This leaves graduates of ECS degrees pursuing a career in the sector with 'fewer' opportunities compared to graduates from relevant degrees such as those with a QTS route. To conclude, however, ECS degrees have not only been established as an academic subject. They have opened and sustained the debate for high-quality ECEC, the critique of policies and the lobbying for a workforce at graduate level so that standards can be raised, so keeping alive the hope of benefiting the 'ecology of young children and their families'.

Questions for discussion

- What do you think is the role of disciplines such as Psychology, Sociology, Law, History of Education and Childhood in ECS degrees?
- After reading the introduction to the chapter which discusses the development of Education Studies degrees, can you see any similarities and differences between the development of ECS degrees and Education Studies?
- What do you consider should be the main principles of ECS?
- Reflecting on the context of your study, do you consider that suitable opportunities for career pathways exist and, if so, can be furthered?

Summary points

- ECS degrees were developed with the aspiration that they would be established as an academic subject as well as providing a graduate qualified workforce for ECEC.
- The first degrees started in the early 1990s, and their number increased at the start of the twenty-first century as, at the time, the policy was to move to a graduate-led workforce.
- ECS has seen an increase in the publication of academic books, journals and high-quality research which led the subject to be established as an academic subject with recognition from the QAA in 2007.
- Linking ECS degrees directly with a clear career pathway in ECEC is still problematic due to the sector being characterised by low-pay status and variation in qualifications which leads to a number of roles and identities, which jeopardises the development of a clear professional identity in the sector.
- ECS degrees are now offered widely in the UK, although their context, aims and mission vary, with some degrees offering ECS only as an academic subject with no clear intentions to link it with any specific career pathways.

Recommended reading

For a comprehensive guide to ECS:

Waller, T. and Davis, G. (2014) *An Introduction to Early Childhood* (3rd edn). London: Sage.
Powell, S. and Smith, K. (2017) *An Introduction to Early Childhood Studies* (4th edn). London: Sage.

To further your understanding of ECEC workforce qualifications:

Hevey, D. (2017) United Kingdom – ECECC Workforce Profile. In P. Oberhuemer and I. Schreyer (Eds), *Workforce Profiles in Systems of Early Childhood Education and Care in Europe*. Available at: www.seepro.eu/English/Country_Reports.htm (accessed 13 August 2019).

To keep up to date with the developments of ECS degrees:

Early Childhood Studies Degrees Network. Available at: www.ecsdn.org/home/aims/ (accessed 13 August 2019).

References

Anning, A., Cullen, J. and Fleer, M. (2009) *Early Childhood Education: Society and Culture*. London: Sage.
Athey, C. (1990) *Extending Thought in Young Children*. London: Paul Chapman Publishing.
Bruce, T. (2006) *Early Childhood: A Guide for Students*. London: Sage.
Calder, P.A. (1999a) The Development of Early Childhood Studies Degrees in Britain: Future Prospects. *European Early Childhood Education Research Journal* **7**(1), pp. 45–68.
Calder, P.A. (1999b) More Than Degrees of Change: Early Childhood Education and Training. *Early Education* **29**, pp. 45–64.
Cohen, B., Moss, B., Petrie, P. and Wallace, J. (2004) *A New Deal for Children? Reforming Education and Care in England, Scotland and Sweden*. London: Policy Press.
David, T. (1993) Educating Children under 5 in the U.K. In T. David (Ed.), *Educational Provision for Our Youngest Children: European Perspectives*. London: Paul Chapman Publishing.

ECSDN (2019) Early Childhood Studies Degree Network. Available at: www.ecsdn.org/home/our-history/ (accessed 13 August 2019).

Goldschmied, E. and Jackson, S. (1994) *People under Three: Young Children in Day Care*. London: Routledge.

Hevey, D. (2017) United Kingdom – ECECC Workforce Profile. In P. Oberhuemer and I. Schreyer (Eds), *Workforce Profiles in Systems of Early Childhood Education and Care in Europe*. Available at: www.seepro.eu/English/Country_Reports.htm (accessed 13 August 2019).

Maynard, T. and Thomas, N. (2009) *An Introduction to Early Childhood Studies*. London: Sage.

Moyles, J.R. (1989) *Just Playing? The Role and Status of Play in Early Childhood Education*. Milton Keynes: Open University Press.

NICHD (2002) Early Child Care and Children's Development Prior to School Entry: Results from the NICHD Study of Early Child Care. *American Educational Research Journal* 39(1), pp. 133–164.

Nutbrown, C. (2012) *Foundations for Quality: The Independent Review of Early Education and Childcare Qualifications. Final Report*. Runcorn: Department for Education. Available at: www gov.uk/government/uploads/system/uploads/attachment_data/file/175463/Nutbrown-Review.pdf (accessed 13 August 2019).

Palaiologou, I. and Male, T. (2016) The Implementation of Early Years Foundation Stage. In I. Palaiologou (Ed.), *Early Years Foundation Stage: Theory and Practice* (3rd edn). London: Sage.

Payler, J. and Davis, G. (2017) Professionalism: Early Years as a Career. *Early Childhood Research Review*. British Educational Research Association Early Childhood Interest Group and TACTYC: Association for Professional Development in Early Years. www.bera.ac.uk/www.tactyc.org.uk, pp. 9–29.

Penn, H. (1997) *Comparing Nurseries: Staff and Children in Italy, Spain and the UK*. London: Paul Chapman Publishing.

Pugh, G. (Ed.) (1996) *Contemporary Issues in the Early Years: Working Collaboratively for Children* (2nd edn). London: Paul Chapman Publishing.

QAA (2007) *Subject Benchmark Statement Early Childhood Studies*. London: QAA.

QAA (2014) *Subject Benchmark Statement Early Childhood Studies*. London: QAA.

Silberfeld, C. and Mitchell, H. (2018) Graduates' Perspectives on Their Early Childhood Studies Programmes and Employment Opportunities. *Early Years*. Available at: www.tandfonline.com/doi/abs/10.1080/09575146.2018.1490890 (accessed 13 August 2019).

Sylva, K., Melhuish E., Sammons, P., Siraj-Blatchford, I. and Taggart, B. (2004) *The Effective Provision of Pre-school Education (EPPE) Project: Findings from the Pre-school Period*. London: DfES.

Waller, T. and Davis, G. (2005) *An Introduction to Early Childhood*. London: Sage.

Chapter 19

The 'resilient' child

Defining and supporting children's resilience in educational practice

Zeta Brown and Jayne Daly

Introduction

Open your mind to consider and try to understand your perception of the term *resilience*. Sometimes we might see it in setting policy or government documentation, or we might just say the word to ourselves. We usually do not question it because we are likely to believe that the word resilience means to *bounce back*, to *be tough* (Middaugh, 2017), or to have *self-regulation and/or self-determination* (Fite *et al.*, 2017). Some of us might even make connections between the words 'resilience' and 'grit', as others such as Middaugh (2017) have done. This leads us to ask whether to be resilient an individual needs to have good self-confidence and buoyancy with the ability to bounce back.

If the term was not difficult enough to define, other questions arise from considering the extent to which children can be resilient. For instance, is resilience about major changes or challenges in life like destitution, danger or misfortune, or is it about everyday occurrences, such as trying again at an exam or playing a musical instrument when practising is difficult (Masten, 2014)? Does resilience mean that we have strength of mind (Huppert and So, 2013) such that we are able to overcome any form of adversity in life? There are also differences of opinion on the origins of resilience. Is it something we are born with, or can we be supported to develop resilience?

This chapter aims to demystify the term 'resilience' and provide a working definition that recognises its complexities along with the ways it is, and can be, supported in practice.

Individual/group task

Before you read on, consider your definition of resilience. What does resilience mean to you?

Untangling the web: what does resilience mean?

The term 'resilience' is complex and multifaceted. Masten (2014) notes that a simple definition of resilience is not possible and maintains there is not one all-encompassing definition. Luthar *et al.* (2000: 543) state that, whilst resilience is complex, it refers to

... a dynamic process encompassing positive adaptations within the context of significant adversity. Implicit within this notion are two critical conditions: (1) exposure to significant threat or severe adversity; and (2) the achievement of positive adaptation despite major assaults on the developmental process.

In this definition Luthar *et al.* refer to 'significant adversity' and 'critical conditions'. In citing Luthar and colleagues' work, Cefai (2008) states the common threads in most definitions are competence and success in adversity and disadvantage. Terms such as 'bouncing back', 'adversity' and 'disadvantage' appear frequently and consistently in definitions of resilience. However, difficulties remain in how these conditions can be measured. In this chapter we adopt the general definition provided by Southwick *et al.* (2014: 2) who define resilience as 'the ability to bend, but not break, bounce back and perhaps even grow in the face of adverse life experience'. In doing so, we consider the minor and major experiences children encounter where resilience can be identified and supported.

In the literature many question why some people are able to cope with adversity (Southwick *et al.*, 2014). Rutter's (1987) early work stated that children are born with traits that enable them to rebound from adversity. Personality factors of those who are deemed resilient include a proactive approach to problem-solving, positive social relationships, including positive attention from family members, persistence and concentration, autonomy, independence and positive self-esteem and self-concept (Mayr and Ulich, 2009). Dweck's (2012) research provides us with an example of how children can respond differentially to any given scenario and how this can be influenced by their mindset. In one of her examples Dweck (2012) shows how children tackle a puzzle. Some children are enthused by difficult puzzles and see them as a challenge, whereas others would be visibly nervous at the prospect of another task they may fail to achieve. Dweck found that children who were ready for that challenge were of a *growth mindset* status, and those who were perspiring under the pressure and the embarrassment in case they failed had a *fixed mindset*. Dweck's (2012) work is important in this context because in proposing the child's individual mindset as a factor in their development and their experiences of resilience, it helps us to consider the impact any experience can have on a child's mental health and future aspirations (having a 'can do' or an 'I can't' attitude).

Southwick *et al.* (2014: 2) state that there are 'a host of biological, psychological, social and cultural factors that interact with one another to determine how one responds to stressful experiences'. For instance, Masten (2014: 3) suggests that we develop resilience as some kind of *ordinary magic* that can be derived from *'ordinary resources and processes'*. Close supportive relationships with others (not necessarily family members) can help children overcome challenges, and close cultural encouragement and guidance are beneficial in supporting resilience. Supportive relationships give the child a 'sense of hope' (ibid.: 6) in the face of adversity, therefore enabling the child to overcome difficult situations. Children need effective resources to support their development of resilience, but to be 'resilient', children also need to be able to self-regulate, a skill developed from both nature and nurture (Conkbayir, 2017).

The main difficulty with any definition of resilience is trying to generalise the characteristics and qualities of resilience for all children. Children are unique and will have varying levels of resilience dependent on their predisposed characteristics, the experiences they have from birth, support groups throughout their childhood, and every individual experience each child encounters. How then can we determine which children are resilient? Which children have the *grit* and *self-determination* to succeed? Which child will *bounce back* if he/she is reprimanded or does not achieve in a test? Which children need support in developing more resilience?

To provide an example of this we ask you to reflect on your own childhood. You may have considered yourself a resilient child, but were there times in your childhood that you had more or less resilience dependent on the experience you encountered?

Individual/group task

Think back to your time in primary or secondary school. Were there times that you were more or less resilient? Try to think of a time where learning was more difficult for you. For instance, a specific subject, exam or maybe an experience with a specific teacher.

Were you able to 'bounce back' from this experience? What do you think were the reasons for this?

Significant adversity in childhood: its impact on resilience

It is important that we recognise the diversity of experiences encountered in childhood. If you search for articles on resilience in childhood, there are examples that portray a wide variety of experiences. They include individualised, case-specific experiences: for instance, children who have experienced abuse and neglect, illness, bereavement and trauma. The adversity children experience may not be apparent to all and may be known only by the child's immediate family, friends and local community members, such as a teacher. Examples of adverse circumstances may include educational experiences in schools and other settings.

Kwong and Hayes (2017) argue that adverse childhood experiences should not happen to children in the first place and that most exposure to adversities is preventable. However, children are exposed to unhappy situations that cannot be prevented, such as the death of a parent. They warn that adversity in itself can develop into a disease as the child, once exposed to trauma, may develop harmful coping attitudes and behaviours. Kwong and Hayes (2017) comment that, without resilience to fight back, the behavioural and social interactions can spiral out of control, further impacting on the resilient abilities that we have discussed. Keyes (2007) finds that, despite being removed from the adverse situations, some individuals may continue to suffer long-term effects, meaning that they may face depressive futures and mental health problems damaging their ability to flourish through to adulthood. However, Mayr and Ulich (2009) provide a list of longitudinal studies that have found that children who have experienced high-risk adversity can show resilience and develop positively and successfully into adulthood.

Individual/group task

Consider examples of a time in your life where you experienced adverse difficulties. Did this have an impact on your ability to learn something new? Your ability to concentrate? Your ability to be creative? How did you overcome this? How might you transfer your empathy to practice in terms of your understanding of adverse situations that children experience?

The everyday experiences of children: does our education system support children's resilience?

The standards agenda in the school system has dominated education discourse since the 1980s. Originally developed by the Conservative government it instilled a focus on achievement and accountability in schools (see Chapter 1). The entire education system was moved to a neoliberal, marketised system that centralised control of education with the government. It was responsible for the development of the national curriculum and Statutory Assessment Tests (SATs). The publication of SATs results in league tables led to public-facing judgement of school and teacher success.

The dominance of the standards agenda in our education system has endured since its conception almost thirty years ago. The impact of this agenda on children has led to all mainstream children experiencing the same national curriculum and undertaking the same SATs tests to see if they are able to achieve the national average. Each year there are various publications on the proportion of children who do not achieve the national average in SATs tests. There is, however, little information provided to inform parents and the general public on what is meant by 'an average'; of course it is a bell curve distribution that means that not all children can achieve the national average. Instead, children are considered underachieving if they do not achieve the average, and schools and teachers are measured by how many children achieve this average.

Our education system provides a dilemma when we are focused on considering the resilience of children. In our current system the education of children is driven by narrow parameters of success, mainly in literacy and numeracy. It leads us to question whether the experiences children encounter at school support them in developing resilience. It is clear from Masten's (2014) research that children need supportive relationships with others (including teachers) and effective resources to support their development of resilience (including resources at school). However, the system does not take into account (as SATs results do not) the individual and unique qualities and achievements of each child. So what does this mean for the experiences of children in today's education system? Does the standards agenda support children to experience adversity and bounce back? Does it only support the resilience of children who can achieve? Does it depend on the individual's strengths and weaknesses? Does it depend on every experience they have in class, in tests and how they deal with their results?

At present, we cannot say that all children achieve in our national system, nor that all children are ready, willing and able to achieve in national assessment (Brown and Manktelow, 2016). This may lead to children experiencing adversity.

Individual and group task

Consider this dilemma further. Do you believe the standards agenda supports the development of resilience or only supports resilience in those that can achieve? Can you find any evidence in relevant publications for either case?

In 2012, the All Party Parliamentary Group (APPG) published a report on social mobility and sought to investigate why some children achieve while others never reach their full potential. They wanted to find out what could be done to help children succeed in life, regardless of the circumstances of their birth. The report concluded that 'personal resilience and emotional well-being are the missing link to the chain' (Paterson *et al.*, 2014: 10). It recommended that social and emotional skills (known as 'soft skills') should underpin academic skills (hard skills), and that skills such as resilience can be taught. In the report Baroness Claire Tyler suggested that character and resilience are 'about having the fundamental drive, tenacity and perseverance needed to make the most of opportunities and to succeed whatever obstacles life puts in your way' (ibid.: 6). The report linked the development of these 'soft skills' to success in the workplace. In doing so, its recommendations focused on the development of character and resilience from the early years to the transition into the workplace. The recommendations included:

- the development of the Early Years Pupil Premium;
- developing a robust school readiness measure at reception that includes character and resilience;
- incorporating character resilience into initial teacher training and CPD programmes;
- extra-curricular activities to be a formal part of teachers' employment contracts;
- supporting the development of a best practice toolkit for interventions that aid character and resilience in conjunction with the Pupil Premium;
- encouraging the growth of the National Citizenship Service and establishing a recognised National Volunteering Award Scheme;
- seizing the opportunity of the rise in education participation age to re-engage the most disengaged 16- and 17-year-olds by providing character and resilience programmes (ibid.: 8–9).

In 2015 the Department for Education set up a new monetary award scheme for schools to bid for funding to develop excellent character education programmes. This was in response to criticisms from business leaders that school leavers were not prepared with 'soft skills' for work. Secretary of State, Nicky Morgan said, 'the new character awards will help give schools and organisations the tools and support they need to ensure they develop well-rounded pupils ready to go on to an apprenticeship, university or the world of work' (Gurney-Read, 2015: 1). Wang *et al.* (2015: 368) concluded from their study that 'assets and resources' are needed in order to support resilience if it is credible that resilience can be truly curriculum-based and taught as a positive and preventative educational tool. In 2016, the White Paper, *Educational Excellence Everywhere*, set out plans for the next five years in education. Links to resilience are explicit, including a section specifically on building character and resilience in every child. The paper states:

> A 21st century education should prepare children for adult life by instilling the character traits and fundamental British values that will help them succeed: being resilient and knowing how to persevere, how to bounce back if faced with failure and how to collaborate with others at work and in their private lives … These traits not only open doors to employment and social opportunities but underpin academic success, happiness and well-being.
>
> (DfE, 2016: 94)

The paper notes resilience activities that can be seen in many state schools, including activities in sport, art and the Duke of Edinburgh Award, and advocates increased partnerships between local and national businesses, and voluntary and sports organisations. Importantly, it proposes an increase in funding to £1bn over the next four years, so that by 2021 60 per cent of all 16-year-olds can access the National Citizenship Service programme, making it the largest programme in Europe. The paper refers to this programme as 'life changing' and explains that it includes adventure challenges and staying away in university-style accommodation. The paper also details the new 'Educate Against Hate' website that provides practical advice to parents, teachers and school leaders to protect children against extremism and radicalisation and to support building their resilience.

Resilience in education: examples of practice

To develop resilience in children has been considered in education for some time. The *Every Child Matters* agenda introduced by the New Labour government of 2001 stressed to schools their duty to promote and support pupils' wellbeing, and there was increased concern about children's health, behaviour and academic attainment. In this section we present two cases of resilience programmes that have been implemented in the UK.

Case study 1: The UK Resilience Programme

In 2007, three local authorities, South Tyneside, Manchester and Hertfordshire, piloted the UK Resilience Programme (UKRP) which more schools taught after 2007. The programme used the Penn Resilience Program (PRP) curriculum developed by psychologists at the University of Pennsylvania. The original aim of the programme was to reduce adolescent depression. However, it was broadened to include 'building resilience and promoting realistic thinking, adoptive coping skills and social problem-solving in children' (Challen *et al.*, 2011: 8). The programme was used to support Year 7 pupils and originally twenty-two secondary schools across the UK carried out the staff facilitator-led workshops. Professionals including teachers, teaching assistants (TAs) and learning mentors were trained to be facilitators. The programme included encouraging participants to challenge (unrealistic) negative beliefs, to use effective coping mechanisms in adversity, and taught techniques including positive social behaviour, assertiveness and decision-making.

The study concluded that pupils reported a greater understanding of what resilience was and their responses to questions about the study were linked to how they had encountered day-to-day problems and conflict, and dealt with them. By 2009/10 some schools were continuing to deliver UKRP whilst others had to abandon the project for various reasons. This was widely due to staffing levels and staff stress as children divulged the real-life problems they were facing. The evaluation of the project also noted that the impact of the programme on pupils' depression scores, school attendance and grades was short-lived and it recommended that the programme would need to be longer for more lasting results. Whilst overall this project showed success in terms of an increase in pupil wellbeing, particularly in relation to mental health, there was also the issue that the project had a negative impact on staff and children alike due to its sensitive nature (Challen *et al.*, 2011).

Case study 2: The Headstart programme

Headstart is a current long-term programme funded by the Big Lottery (2017–2021) trialling a broad range of initiatives for improving resilience and emotional wellbeing in 10–16-year-olds in six locations in England. In Wolverhampton, it includes implementing the SUMO-based resilience programme in schools and a range of activities in the community including relax and craft, dance, active bodies … active minds, and flourishing families (Royle, 2017).

Headstart Wolverhampton commissioned the University of Wolverhampton to evaluate aspects of the programme not covered by the Wellbeing Measurement Framework (WMF) in 2017. The evaluation contained a number of strands aimed at investigating young people's resilience, wellbeing and self-efficacy. Here we focus on the education and community card sort strand. The project investigated children's perspectives on their resilience, but without using the term 'resilience' because of the complexity in defining the term. In total, fifty-five children were asked to sort a set of statements (using Q-methodology) onto a distribution grid based on whether they agreed or disagreed with statements on their daily lives. Statements included: *I can work things out for myself*; *people often ask me to help them*; *I have never worried about anything really*; and *I've had support from my family*. There were also two statements included that related to the child's Headstart experiences. The findings showed that all of the children included in the card sort believed they and/or their peers had benefited from attending Headstart activities. This was especially the case for children who appeared to have had less support from their family. Additional findings relating to the children's perspectives on their resilience included:

- All of the children had experienced worries and had experienced adversity in their lives, including those who felt well supported by their families.
- The degree of family support consistently seemed to influence the child's perception of themselves and their resilience.
- Children who had limited family support did not seek to independently 'deal' with anxiety in their lives, but sought support elsewhere, usually from friends and Headstart.
- Children valued support they received from others more than their own resilience, especially when the child did not feel supported by their family.

These additional findings show that all of these children had experienced adversity and worries in their lives and had sought support from accessible support groups, including Headstart. This in itself is a recognisable resilient behaviour.

Moving forward: how can we further support children's resilience?

This chapter has detailed the complexity of defining resilience and the many questions we have around the concept of resilience in childhood. We have emphasised the need to consider children as unique individuals who have predisposed characteristics, have varying adverse experiences and have various support groups. In considering how we further support children's resilience we need to look again at the dominance of the standards agenda in the UK. Cefai (2008: 21) noted the need for focus on children's strengths rather than weaknesses in education:

> [the resilience perspective] … shifted the focus from deficit and disadvantage to growth and strength development. It asks 'what makes children in difficulty achieve and be successful?' rather than 'what prevents children in difficulty from succeeding?' Through the study of children and young people who managed to strive and be successful at school despite negative circumstances in their lives, the resilience perspective has led to a reconsideration of the ways in which schools can foster success in children and young people. It suggested that we may be more effective in supporting children's and young people's development and well-being by focusing on their strengths rather than their weaknesses.

We have provided two examples of resilience programmes carried out in the UK. There is evidence that resilience programmes can support children. However, they need continuous funding, staff time and resources to be effectively implemented. As seen in the UK Resilience Programme, discussing resilience can be a sensitive subject; however, the Headstart programme indicates that providing such a programme can benefit all children, especially those with limited family support. It seems important from the Headstart evaluation that resilience programmes are embedded into community as well as education settings. These are, however, separate programmes that are add-ons to the existing educational system. As the inclusion agenda emphasises (see Chapter 7), there are always going to be difficulties with continuity and consistency of any objectives if they are seen as extra to the existing education system. We would advocate that the standards agenda objectives are reconsidered in light of thoroughly considering the development of children's resilience and the experiences children have that could affect their resilience. For instance, do SATs support children's resilience or negatively affect their mental health (Ecclestone and Lewis, 2014)? Are we celebrating moments of resilience (large and small) with and for children? Are we giving children the opportunity to try again and bounce back in the face of adversity and/or failure? It would be wholly beneficial for children if their resilience was seen as as important as their academic successes at school.

Summary points

- Resilience is complex and multifaceted.
- Resilience should be considered in all children's experiences – minor and major.
- Children are unique and will have varying levels of resilience dependent on their predisposed characteristics, the experiences they have from birth, their potential support groups throughout their childhood, and every individual experience each child encounters.
- Children encounter a diverse range of experiences including for some significant adversity.
- Children will not respond to the same experiences in the same way (including school experiences). This depends on factors including their resilience.
- The dominance of the standards agenda could lead to some children experiencing adversity.
- Resilience has become a buzzword in education and programmes have been developed to support the development of resilience, but it is not always well understood.
- Standards agenda objectives need to be reconsidered to prioritise developing and supporting children's resilience.

Recommended reading

Brown, Z. and Daly, J. (2017) The Complexities of Childhood Resilience. In Z. Brown and S. Ward (Eds), *Contemporary Issues in Childhood: A Bio-Ecological Approach*. Abingdon: Routledge

Cefai, C. (2008) *Promoting Resilience in the Classroom: A Guide to Developing Pupils' Emotional and Cognitive Skills*. London: Jessica Kingsley Publications.

Southwick, S.M., Bonanno, G.A., Masten, A.S., Panter Brick, C. and Yehuda, R. (2014) Resilience Definitions, Theory, and Challenges: Interdisciplinary Perspectives. *European Journal of Psychotraumatology* **5**(10), pp. 1–19.

References

Brown, Z. and Manktelow, K. (2016) Perspectives on the Standards Agenda: Exploring the Agenda's Impact on Primary Teachers' Professional Identities. *Education 3–13* **44**(1), pp. 68–80.

Cefai, C. (2008) *Promoting Resilience in the Classroom: A Guide to Developing Pupils' Emotional and Cognitive Skills.* London: Jessica Kingsley Publications.

Challen, A., Noden, P., West, A. and Machin, S. (2011) *UK Resilience Programme: Final Report.* London: DfE.

Conkbayir, M. (2017) *Early Childhood and Neuroscience. Theory, Research and Implications for Practice.* London: Bloomsbury.

DfE (2016) *Educational Excellence Everywhere.* London: DfE.

Dweck, C. (2012) *Mindset: Changing the Way You Think to Fulfil Your Potential.* New York: Robinson.

Ecclestone, K. and Lewis, L. (2014) Interventions for Resilience in Educational Settings: Challenging Policy Discourses of Vulnerability and Risk. *Journal of Education Policy* **29**(2), pp. 195–216.

Fite, R.E., Lindeman, M.I.H., Rogers, A.P., Voyles, E. and Durik, A.M. (2017) Knowing Oneself and Long Term Goal Pursuit: Relations among Self-Concept Clarity, Conscientiousness and Grit. *Personality and Individual Differences* **108**, pp. 191–194.

Gurney-Read, J. (2015) Lessons in 'Grit and Resilience' Recognised by New Award. *The Telegraph*, 7 January 2015, p. 1

Huppert, F.A. and So, T.C. (2013) Flourishing across Europe: Application of a New Conceptual Framework for Defining Well-Being. *Social Indicators Research* **110**(3), pp. 837–861.

Keyes, C. (2007) Promoting and Protecting Mental Health as Flourishing. *American Psychologist* **62**(2), pp. 95–108.

Kwong, T.Y. and Hayes, D.K. (2017) Adverse Family Experience and Flourishing amongst Children Ages 6–17 years: 2011/12: National Survey of Child Health. *Child Abuse and Neglect* **70**, pp. 240–246.

Luthar, S., Cicchetti, D. and Becker, B. (2000) The Construct of Resilience: A Critical Evaluation and Guidelines for Future Work. *Child Development* **71**(3), pp. 543–562.

Masten, A.S. (2014) *Ordinary Magic: Resilience in Development.* New York: Gilford Press.

Mayr, T. and Ulich, M. (2009) Social-Emotional Well-Being and Resilience of Children in Early Childhood Setting – PERIK: An Empirically Based Observation Scale for Practitioners. *Early Years* **29**(1), pp. 45–57.

Middaugh, D.J. (2017) True Grit. *Nursing Management* **26**(5), pp. 347–348.

Paterson, C., Tyler, C. and Lexmond, J. (2014) *Character and Resilience Manifesto.* London: All Parliamentary Group on Social Mobility. Available at: www.educationengland.org.uk/documents/pdfs/2014-appg-social-mobility.pdf (accessed 12 June 2019).

Royle, K. (2017) Resilience Programmes and Their Place in Education: A Critical Review with Reference to Interventions in Wolverhampton. *Journal of Education and Human Development* **6**(1), pp. 53–65.

Rutter, M. (1987) Psychological Resilience and Protective Mechanisms. *American Journal of Orthopsychiatry* **57**, pp. 316–331.

Southwick, S.M., Bonanno, G.A., Masten, A.S., Panter Brick, C. and Yehuda, R. (2014) Resilience Definitions, Theory, and Challenges: Interdisciplinary Perspectives. *European Journal of Psychotraumatology* **5**(10), pp. 1–19.

Wang, J.L., Zhang, D.J. and Zimmerman, M.A. (2015) Resilience Theory and Its Implications for Chinese Adolescence. *Psychological Reports* **117**(2), pp. 354–375.

Chapter 20

Health education and behaviour

Bethan Mitchell

Introduction

Health education draws together a number of different disciplines such as health psychology, public health, philosophy, policy, science and sociology. These are considered in the models of health that are used by practitioners for individual and collective interventions. Some of the models centre on the idea that individuals can control their health through lifestyle choices, whereas others acknowledge the powerful role of societal structures.

Health education has many faces and can be considered as educating *for* health, or educating *about* health. This chapter focuses on how different models of health influence how we teach health education. There is an emphasis on Education Studies and how theories of learning and knowledge can help us to deliver health education. Specifically, the chapter focuses on social learning theories and how these support more social and collective approaches in health education. The chapter draws from the idea of learning networks to explore how this approach to health education can help us to conceptualise how these fields interact, and how new approaches in education, such as network learning through actor-network theory, can add to the criticality of health education.

Models of health

WHO defines health education as: 'any combination of learning experiences designed to help individuals and communities improve their health, by increasing their knowledge or influencing their attitudes' (World Health Organization, 2019: 1). This definition emphasises the need for education to go beyond knowledge transfer and to affect health behaviours. Health education is sometimes criticised for being too focused on 'healthism', in other words promoting dominant ideas in health uncritically, and targeting the individual without considering social factors (Leahy and McCuaig, 2014). Other criticisms of health education include the organisations involved in the dissemination of information. Powell (2014) argues that health education can become corporatised by big organisations providing resources for school teachers relating to health education. Although this might seem benign, the agenda of profit-making organisations may not always be aligned to public values. Powell argues that the idea of individual choice and how this affects lifestyles promotes a neoliberal stance in relation to health, promoting values such as competition, entrepreneurialism and consumerism which may be incommensurate with social justice and health equality. For example, keeping a food diary may be helpful to individuals with regard to their nutritional intake, but it propagates the idea that health comes down to individual choice. As this chapter will illustrate, there are different ways to conceptualise health that consider both individuals and collectives.

The biomedical model presents health as a binary of either illness or good health. The individual is viewed as a passive recipient to disease, and is therefore treated by professionals, rather than having the power to influence their own health. In the last fifty years there has been a move away from the biomedical model towards the acceptance of other factors that may influence health, such as environmental and social circumstances (Larkin, 2013). Health psychology challenges the biomedical model by emphasising the agency of individuals and the role of behaviour, drawing from a biopsychosocial model of health (Ogden, 2012). Along with this is the notion of wellbeing and 'salutogenesis' as being pivotal to health. Salutogenesis is a holistic view of health and wellbeing, focusing on physical and mental wellness rather than illness and disease. These models of health suggest that individuals are empowered to control aspects of their health through lifestyle choices.

The salutogenic approach to health education is sometimes positioned as the opposite to a biomedical, disease-prevention approach. However, salutogenesis is more about approaching health education in a different way (Quennerstedt et al., 2014). For example, conceptualising the person's health as a whole rather than fragmenting the body and creating a dualism between mind (psychic) and body (somatic). This is also related to an upstream model of health, where practitioners are seeking to prevent health issues at source, rather than heroically rescuing ill patients at the end (Antonovsky, 1996). The idea of health improvement and promotion stems from these ideas (Tannahill, 2008). Instead of concentrating on treatment when a person becomes ill, the approach aims to prevent illness and promote wellbeing through lifestyle choices. Sometimes this translates as the prevention of risk, for example encouraging people to quit smoking, reduce alcohol intake, eat a healthy diet and participate in regular physical activity. In schools, the emphasis on young people is geared more towards prevention: second-hand smoke, childhood obesity and sex education. However, health education is not confined to risk and lifestyle.

A pathogenic approach to health education brings with it the idea of health as the norm, and any deviance as illness or a departure from morally correct behaviour. In schools this translates as correct/incorrect behaviour, as health education creates a governmentality of risk. In other words, the role of the health education teacher is to control health behaviours by teaching right behaviours from wrong. In this context, education becomes instrumental, where the shared goals of good health are assumed, regardless of social circumstances. Health education then becomes reductionist, with a focus on outputs rather than process (Quennerstedt et al., 2014). It can be argued that pathogenic approaches reinforce a neo-liberal agenda of individualism by focusing on lifestyles and self-help. Wider arguments in education have been made in this regard, claiming that there is more to education than a good output. This relates to the concept of 'technical validity', which is concerned with whether things are being done correctly, with normative validity, and questions whether what we are measuring is meaningful, or just easy to measure (Biesta, 2007). For example, the measurement of body mass index (BMI) can be considered as an abstract measurement to pass judgement about whether individuals are eating healthily and taking enough physical activity, rather than ensuring communities have access to nutritionally balanced foods and the means to cook.

The concept of health and lifestyle choices was further developed in health policy through the introduction of 'nudge theory', which is based on behavioural economics (Thaler and Sunstein, 2009). Recently, advances in behavioural medicine (Marteau *et al.*, 2006) and behaviour-change approaches (Michie *et al.*, 2011) have provided a framework for individual and collective interventions, as well as research regarding how interventions work at individual and population levels. The Social Determinants of Health Model (Dahlgren and Whitehead, 2006) considers health and wellbeing in the context of health inequalities. Assets-based approaches have also challenged pathogenic and biomedical approaches to health by guiding health and wellbeing towards health promotion and health improvement (Tannahill, 2008).

The tensions in health education around individualism and social influences on health can be confusing to work with. It is clear from the overview of health education outlined above that there are different ways of thinking about health: individuals as passive (biomedical model), individuals as agentic (biopsychosocial model), and individuals as part of society (social determinants of health). This draws interesting parallels with learning theories, where pedagogical approaches are shaped through notions of the self (Burgoyne, 2002). For example, if teachers consider learners to be passive, they may favour a pedagogical approach that is transmitted and didactic; if the teacher considers learners as 'agentic' and possessing the ability to participate in their own knowledge construction, then a more constructivist pedagogy will be applied. The reverse can also be considered: if constructivist pedagogies are employed, learners will be encouraged to participate.

Education Studies provides a way of critically examining health education through social theories of learning. An Education Studies approach emphasises inequalities and social justice by drawing from sociological, political, geographical and philosophical disciplines. Social justice is a key element in health education, as can be demonstrated through health inequalities and the links between health and social deprivation as outlined by Marmot *et al.* (2010). Such an interdisciplinary approach can be very complex, as navigating the language and traditions of these disciplines requires flexible thinking. Education Studies has a long tradition of drawing from these different and sometimes incommensurate fields, and much can be learned and translated to health education.

Health behaviours are influenced by a variety of factors, including health beliefs and social influences. It is therefore important, in order to bring about meaningful change, for individuals to be convinced and persuaded by the evidence presented in health. For example, the early research into tobacco use was counteracted by research funded by tobacco manufacturers; this led to a slowing down on action against tobacco, as beliefs were influenced by the desire to smoke. In other words, a lot of people didn't want to believe that smoking was bad for their health because they wanted to continue smoking (Proctor, 2012). Of course, there are many examples of people making informed decisions about their lifestyle, choosing to engage in risky behaviours despite being knowledgeable about how it might be detrimental to health.

Health education, then, needs to target beliefs in order to bring about change. Campaigns need to capture the imagination; leaflets and text-based resources are usually accompanied by other media to facilitate this. From a health-inequalities perspective, health is influenced by societal structures, and social determinants of health need to be considered. An understanding of health education, therefore, requires an understanding of the underpinning of education in general: how people learn and change. This is often overlooked in favour of transmitting information, cascade models and dissemination of health policy messages. In order to achieve change through learning, it is necessary to scrutinise the ways in which we view education, the language we use to describe knowledge and learning, and how this can restrict the way we approach health education.

In summary, health models promote thinking about the rational decisions of individuals (some take social class into consideration), but this creates a particular configuration of beliefs and attitudes. A collective view of learning, through social theory, creates a different perspective of health behaviours and how to influence them. It is still important to understand the psychological models as these relate to individual behaviour, but it is important to understand that this restricts the way in which we think about learning and change. Education and social theories need to be considered in addition as these configure learning in different ways and provide a broader understanding about how we can help change behaviours. In particular, socio-material theories can highlight the connectivity of people and objects which make up the lifestyles and societies that influence health.

Health education as social learning

Education Studies can inform health education and ensure that learning theories are congruent with concepts of health. For example, when we talk about knowledge as something we can acquire, we are unwittingly assuming that knowledge has the form of something that can be accumulated. In education there are other ways of conceptualising knowledge. For example, knowledge can be considered as intrinsically attached and associated with its disciplinary context. So, for example, the knowledge that is valued in philosophy does not take the same form as that in the health sciences. Knowledge in one field holds a different meaning in another and cannot be unproblematically transferred. There is always a process of movement and translation that takes place. There is also the issue of the type of knowledge: some knowledge is propagated by experts, people who have experience of the field and who are involved in specialist communities whose knowledge is perhaps more valuable than that of those who are on the periphery. For example, teachers are not health psychologists, so how can they work with individuals in this capacity? Health educators come from different disciplines; so how do we foreground and value their strengths, and what connections do we have for other specialisms? In this sense, the networks start to emerge.

Social theories of learning follow the idea that learning is relational and collective, rather than individualised. For example, Lave and Wenger's (1991) notion of Communities of

Practice suggests that professionals start at the periphery of a specialism and move towards mastery by engaging with the appropriate social groups and adopting the language and customs of that group. When a professional leaves a profession to teach, the periphery becomes the target, and other communities emerge. It could be argued that educators move towards the core of the teaching profession, but in order to do that, the educator must be an educator of some form of specialism. This is sometimes difficult for other professions to understand, as every other professional strives towards the centre of their own mastery. The goal is to settle and master, but the educator is a nomad between worlds.

Another way to think about professional learning is through actor–network theory (ANT). This is not like social networks or telephone networks, but alludes to the connections and associations that occur when a professional becomes involved in a different field, much like a teacher of health education. Although teachers will associate with some of the same networks, health educators will connect with health education. ANT is a social and material theory of learning, and so takes on social collectives as a mixture of people and things.

ANT: a socio-material approach to learning

ANT can bring a number of insights to health education, particularly in relation to the separation of politics and science that has made it increasingly difficult to apply evidence-based or evidence-informed interventions against a backdrop of 'fake news'. By examining connections, ANT enables a shift of focus from the individual as the centre of power and agency, towards more collective and relational descriptions of the diverse array of entities that are held together under the phrase 'health education'. For example, the biological, physical, embodied interpretations of health are entwined with politics, society and philosophy to challenge the presentation of norms and values.

ANT provides a way of challenging the dichotomy between science and nature. Drawing from Latour's (2005) concept of networks, health education can be considered as an assemblage of connected people and objects that form a network. Health education, as a discipline, creates its own knowledge. For example, different topic areas such as tobacco control, alcohol reduction and physical activity are adopted by different members of the workforce and target different audiences. Tobacco control has a prevention strategy aimed at young people, and a quit strategy aimed at addicts. Sexual health and drug-taking may be brought together under the banner of blood-borne viruses. Members of the workforce are committed to different areas of interest, as are journals and special interest groups. For example, professionals might consider themselves aligned with youth and supporting the youth agenda.

For health professionals, health education might be an intuitive transition; but for teachers there may be more to consider. In ANT terms, teachers are enrolling into new networks, forging connections between health research, policy, and education theory. Part of the difficulty of connecting with new networks is the difference between disciplines, particularly science and politics, which makes health education sometimes difficult to navigate and to form connections with.

Health education as a discipline: science and politics

Science and politics have a tradition of being addressed in different terms and in different ways, and by different people who move in different circles. In health education, there is a need to view these as part of each other (Leahy, 2014); science informs policy, but policy has an influence as to what is researched and foregrounded. The Behaviour Change Wheel (Michie *et al.*, 2011) attempts to draw these together in terms of influencing behaviours through policy and individual interventions. The rise of a post-truth society has led to fake news (Ferguson *et al.*, 2017), which has influenced the public perception of health and wellbeing, making it even more important for practitioners to understand science and policy research.

In health education it is important to look at the whole picture and not to separate science and politics. For example, the obesity epidemic is so termed as a combination of scientific data and policy decisions: research shows that obesity is a serious issue that affects morbidity and mortality (Abarce-Gómez *et al.*, 2017), and therefore many interventions are state-funded. However, dealing with these issues separately can create problems. Science is used to make politics credible; however, science itself is political (Latour, 1987). The funding for research comes from different sources that have a stake in the outcomes; scientific papers are written in a particular form and by scientists with sets of values that influence their work (for example, integrity, scientific rigour and representation).

Not all health interventions are based purely on scientific evidence, and they can be deeply influenced by theories, models and underlying philosophical concepts. This chapter has described how health models (biomedical, biopsychosocial, sociological) and education approaches (knowledge transfer, constructivism and social learning) shape interventions by assuming the degree of individual agency and societal structures. For example, nudge theory assumes the position of libertarian paternalism (Thaler and Sunstein, 2009). Adopted from the field of behavioural economics, libertarian paternalism allows for free choice (libertarian) combined with a gentle nudge in the right direction for healthy life-style choices, much as a parent might guide a child (paternalism). Nudge claims to address the dual process mechanism of health decisions. It is recognised that many health behaviour models rely on reflective, rational decision-making, and that aspects such as impulsivity and habit are often not accounted for (Ogden, 2012). The latter originate from automatic behaviours, where a choice is made impulsively rather than balancing the pros and cons. The nudge approach claims to account for more of the automatic processes that affect health decisions by developing environmental prompts: for example, placing a pair of trainers by the front door in readiness for a run, or having a bowl of fruit in an easily accessible position. On a wider scale, nudge approaches can be about supermarket displays where health foods are made more prominent, so customers have free choice, but the healthy choices are easier to make. Critiques of nudge are aimed at the apparently oxymoronic position of the two underpinning philosophies: how can one be guided and yet claim to have free choice? Further critiques examine the notion of free choice in a more Foucauldian sense (Jones *et al.*, 2011), and question the exclusion of seemingly effective interventions such as coercion to change behaviour (Michie *et al.*, 2011).

Foucault has been drawn upon for critique in health education to challenge how the self is conceptualised. For example, the neoliberal emphasis on risk and lifestyles can lead to placing the blame on individuals, when other health-influencing factors such as society and the environment may have a greater emphasis.

Professionalism and practice

What does health education mean for teachers? Are teachers expected to become experts in health in order to deliver health education? Health professionals have access to information and updates through journals and professional networks, whereas teachers engage with their own professional networks on the periphery of health. Research can be confusing, with evidence-based practice requiring long periods of waiting for results to be verified and published. Because of the nature of health promotion and improvement, it is not always considered ethical to wait for long periods of time before taking action (Tannahill, 2008). As well as knowledge of the health issues themselves, teachers are required to think critically about how health messages come across. With supermarkets and corporations increasingly providing resources for teachers, there is a danger of the corporatisation and marketisation of health, where values of consumerism and competition are promoted in the interests of market penetration (Powell, 2014).

The approaches taken from a health perspective (based on biomedical, biopsychosocial, and social models) combined with pedagogy (knowledge-transfer, constructivism, social theories of learning) ultimately configure how health messages are delivered. Health messages are often couched in terms of risk mitigation and protection, especially when directed at children. In addition to this are the underlying philosophies that shape interventions, for example individual responsibility in a neoliberal context (Leahy, 2014).

From a schools perspective, health education relates to something quite specific: educating school children about health issues. Personal, Social, Health and Economic (PSHE) in England, Personal and Social Education in Wales, Curriculum for Excellence in Scotland and Personal, Social and Health Education in Ireland, provide guidance for schools regarding health issues. A lot is expected of teachers. They are expected to be scholarly, and academically critical; to manage the behaviour of others; to develop skills for teaching, as well as orating, and organising materials such as timetables; and to consider the social needs of the pupils. Therefore, teacher training requires an education that incorporates criticality through philosophy; social activism, inclusion and empowerment through sociology; growth and development through biology and psychology; understanding qualitative and quantitative research; and navigating policy.

Conclusion: health education in the future

In light of political changes and access to information, social media and fake news, health education is in flux and appropriate interventions need to be flexible. Social learning theories can support social approaches to health, enabling a more in-depth critique of the assumptions that are made about individuals and the level of control that individuals and societies have over health outcomes. Teachers also need to consider the complex networks that different disciplines connect with, particularly in the ways that science and policy are enacted.

Questions for discussion

- How can health models and learning theory be brought together to teach health education?
- How can non-health professionals critique health research?
- How can teachers decide on health messages and the process of delivery?

Summary points

- Health models, combined with pedagogical approaches, influence the way health education is taught.
- It is important for teachers to deliver health education critically and not to deliver health messages on face value.
- Teachers need to be aware of the disciplinary rifts between science and politics in order to bring about meaningful change.

Recommended reading

Ogden, J. (2019) *Health Psychology* (6th edn). London: McGraw-Hill.

References

Abarce-Gomez, L., Abdeen, Z.A., Hamid, Z.A., Abu-rmeileh, N.M., Acosta-Cazares, B., Acuin, C., Adams, R.J., Aekplakorn, W., Afsana, K. and Aguilar-Salinas, C.A. (2017) Worldwide Trends in Body-Mass Index, Underweight, Overweight, and Obesity from 1975 to 2016: A Pooled Analysis of 2416 Population-Based Measurement Studies in 128·9 Million Children, Adolescents, and Adults. *The Lancet* **390**(10113), pp. 2627–2642.

Antonovsky, A. (1996) The Salutogenic Model as a Theory to Guide Health Promotion. *Health Promotion International* **11**(1), pp. 11–18.

Biesta, G. (2007) Why 'What Works' Won't Work: Evidence-Based Practice and the Democratic Deficit in Educational Research. *Educational Theory* **57**(1), pp. 1–22.

Burgoyne, J. (2002) Learning Theory and the Construction of Self: What Kinds of People Do We Create through the Theories of Learning That We Apply to Their Development? In M. Pearn (Ed.), *Individual Differences and Development in Organizations*. Hoboken, NJ: John Wiley and Sons.

Dahlgren, G. and Whitehead, M. (2006) *European Strategies for Tackling Social Inequities in Health: Levelling up Part 2*. Copenhagen: World Health Organization.

Ferguson, R., Barzilai, S., Ben-Zvi, D., Chinn, C.A., Herodotou, C., Hod, Y., Kali, Y., Kukulska-Hulme, A., Kupermintz, H., McAndrew, P., Rienties, B., Sagy, O., Scanlon, E., Sharples, M., Weller, M. and Whitelock, D. (2017) *Innovating Pedagogy 2017*. Milton Keynes: Open University Innovation Report 6.

Jones, R., Pykett, J. and Whitehead, M. (2011) Governing Temptation: Changing Behaviour in an Age of Libertarian Paternalism. *Progress in Human Geography* **35**(4), pp. 483–501.

Larkin, M. (2013) *Health and Well-Being across the Life Course*. London: Sage.

Latour, B. (1987) *Science in Action: How to Follow Scientists and Engineers through Society*. Cambridge, MA: Harvard University Press.

Latour, B. (2005) Reassembling the Social: An Introduction to Actor-Network-Theory. Oxford: Oxford University Press.

Lave, J. and Wenger, E. (1991) *Situated Learning: Legitimate Peripheral Participation*. Cambridge: Cambridge University Press.

Leahy, D. (2014) Assembling a Health[y] Subject: Risky and Shameful Pedagogies in Health Education. *Critical Public Health* **24**(2), pp. 171–181.

Leahy, D. and McCuaig, L. (2014) Disrupting the Field: Teacher Education in Health Education. In K. Fitzpatrick and R. Tinning (Eds), *Health Education: Critical Perspectives*. Abingdon: Routledge.

Marmot, M., Allen, J., Godblatt, P., Boyce, T., McNeish, D., Grady, M. and Geddes, I. (2010) *The Marmot Review: Fair Society, Healthy Lives*. London: The Strategic Review of Health Inequalities in England Post-2010.

Marteau, T., Dieppe, P., Foy, R., Kinmonth, A.L. and Schneiderman, N. (2006) Behavioural Medicine: Changing Our Behaviour. Online. Available at: www.ncbi.nlm.nih.gov/pmc/articles/PMC1382526/ (accessed 1 June 2019).

Michie, S., van Stralen, M.M. and West, R. (2011) The Behaviour Change Wheel: A New Method for Characterising and Designing Behaviour Change Interventions. *Implementation Science* **6**(42).

Ogden, J. (2012) *Health Psychology: A Textbook*. London: McGraw-Hill Education.

Powell, D. (2014) The Corporatization of Health Education Curricula. In K. Fitzpatrick and R. Tinning (Eds), *Health Education: Critical Perspectives*. Abingdon: Routledge.

Proctor, R.N. (2012) The History of the Discovery of the Cigarette-Lung Cancer Link: Evidentiary Traditions, Corporate Denial, Global Toll. *Tobacco Control* **21**(2), pp. 87–91.

Quennerstedt, M., Öhma, M., Fitzpatrick, K. and Tinning, R. (2014) Salutogenic Approaches to Health and the Body. In K. Fitzpatrick and R. Tinning (Eds), *Health Education: Critical Perspectives*. Abingdon: Routledge.

Tannahill, A. (2008). Beyond Evidence – to Ethics: A Decision-Making Framework for Health Promotion, Public Health and Health Improvement. *Health Promotion International* **23**(4), pp. 380–390.

Thaler, R.H. and Sunstein, C.R. (2009) *Nudge: Improving Decisions about Health, Wealth, and Happiness*. London: Penguin.

World Health Organization (2019) *Health Topics: Health Education*. Online. Available at: www.who.int/topics/health_education/en/ (accessed 1 June 2019).

Professionalism and employment

Chapter 21

Work-based learning

Catherine A. Simon

Introduction

Placements and work-based learning have a significant role in Education Studies degrees. They are also often closely linked to university key performance indicators relating to employability and further study. This is because, as with many of the social sciences, Education Studies is both career- and practice-orientated, bringing together the professional and the academic, theory and practice, so as to enhance understanding of educational processes and contexts. The Quality Assurance Agency (QAA) benchmark for Education Studies sets out the role of learning in the workplace: 'Knowledge, understanding and critical analysis to inform current and future professionals [...] may be achieved through learning in the workplace' (QAA, 2015: 6).

Whilst a significant number of students of Education Studies pursue traditional careers in classroom teaching, this is far from the full picture. The QAA acknowledges that Education Studies provides access to careers in the broad range of formal and informal contexts where education occurs including 'educational settings such as administration, post-16 learning, children's services, community development' (QAA, 2015: 7). The range of placements and work-based learning openings available via higher education (HE) institutions providing Education Studies degrees reflects this diversity. Professional education careers may include education-focused departments or teams within local authorities, community education, education administration, cultural settings or national or local charities (Simon, 2017: 33). Indeed, many professional education roles can be found within HE institutions themselves, including library and support services, academic services, curriculum development, employability, widening participation outreach services, and education administration.

Although contexts may vary, they do contain areas of commonality in terms of the skills and competencies required by professional educators. These include:

- Interpersonal skills
- Organisation and administration

- Professionalism
- Resilience
- Reflection
- Team working

This list is not exhaustive, but developing such skills through observation and practice self-evidently enhances employability and career orientation. Work-based learning enables the opportunity for students to 'try out' and 'try on' potential career options and to relate professional experiences to critical understandings of educational contexts and processes gained through other aspects of the degree. In this way, work-based learning supports the development of professional and career identity. Bringing the university into the workplace also has significant advantages for employers and settings, such that learning is two-directional – from workplace to student and student to workplace. Work-based learning thus has the potential to influence practices and culture in the receiving organisation. It is the nature of the placement, however, that influences what and how students learn.

This chapter explores the character of placements and work-based learning in Education Studies. It draws on theoretical models such as expansive and restrictive models (Fuller and Unwin, 2004), considers the nature of learning and construction of knowledge, and outlines some of the key aspects of preparation for the learning experience. Throughout the chapter work-based learning is located within current political, social, economic and technical contexts of the workplace and HE.

Work-based learning and higher education

In 2018 the QAA published 'Advice and Guidance: Work-Based Learning' (QAA, 2018). Work-based learning is defined as:

> … learning through work, learning for work and/or learning at work. It consists of authentic structured opportunities for learning which are achieved in a workplace setting or are designed to meet an identified workplace need. This type of learning typically has a dual function of being designed to meet the learning needs of the employees, developing their knowledge, skills and professional behaviours, and also meeting the workforce development needs of the organisation. Work-based learning is, therefore, learning which is distinguished from work-related or simulated learning activity that has not been formulated or commissioned by, or in partnership with employers to address a current workforce need.
>
> (QAA, 2018: 1)

> … work-based learning for higher education courses describes courses that bring together higher education providers and work organisations to create learning opportunities.
>
> (QAA, 2018: 2)

The guiding principles, whilst not mandatory, offer 'a concise expression of the fundamental practices of the HE sector, based on the experience of a wide range of providers' (QAA, 2018: 4). These are listed as follows:

1. Work-based learning courses and opportunities are designed and developed in partnership with employers, students and other stakeholders (where appropriate) and contain learning outcomes that are relevant to work objectives.
2. Work-based learning consists of structured opportunities for learning and is achieved through authentic activity and is supervised in the workplace.
3. Work-based learning opportunities are underpinned by formal agreements between education organisations, employers and students.
4. Education organisations and employers consider any specific issues in relation to the workplace environment and deal with them appropriately, including informal agreements where appropriate.
5. Work-based learning is delivered through a meaningful partnership between students, employers and the education organisation.
6. Work-based learning opportunities enable students to apply and integrate areas of subject and professional knowledge, skills and behaviours to enable them to meet course learning outcomes.
7. Parties understand and respect the respective roles, responsibilities and expectations of the education organisation, employer and student, and appropriate training and support is provided where required.
8. Education organisations and employers acknowledge individuals have unique needs within the education organisation and in the workplace, and collaborate to ensure opportunities are inclusive, safe and supported.
9. Work-based learning opportunities are designed, monitored, evaluated and reviewed in partnership with employers. (QAA, 2018: 4)

What is assumed here is that placements and work-based learning are to the mutual benefit of both the HE institution and the employer. More specifically, they offer a bridge between HE and the world of work. Lester and Costley (2010) for example refer to 'negotiated work-based learning': in other words, learning that is negotiated between the learner, university and the employer. The UK government over recent decades has found ways of incentivising universities to develop their provision in this area (Major, 2016). Of particular note is the recent introduction of degree-level apprenticeships where employers are encouraged to lead on curriculum design and work in partnership with HE to define and deliver programmes. In this way the workplace itself becomes the locus of learning in addition to the university seminar room and lecture theatre. It is important to note at this juncture that the 'work' element of work-based learning does not have to be paid employment. Indeed, on most Education Studies degrees, students engage in placements in an unpaid capacity, emphasising the mutual benefits of work placements. Depending on the nature of placements, some institutions may enter into financial arrangements with employers in recognition of their support for students. This is most typical for students in schools whilst undertaking initial teacher training.

Questions for discussion

Look at Education Studies degrees at a number of universities. Choose five.

- How many offer placements?
- How visible is the offer of placements and work-based learning?
- Are placements available across all levels of the degree (Levels 4–6)?
- Are placements available in education settings other than schools or early years settings?
- How important was the offer of placements and work-based learning to you in your own selection of an Education Studies degree?
- Why?

The following section explores some of the theoretical models of work-based learning with particular reference to Education Studies.

Theoretical models of work-based learning

For Lester and Costley (2010) work-based learning is any learning that is situated in the workplace or arises out of work-based concerns. Traditional models of work-based learning for students have emerged from disciplinary approaches, most often with specific connections to professionals where subject knowledge is applied to the workplace through placements and training, as in the case of teaching, medicine and law. The emphasis placed on the university–workplace partnership will, however, differ. Where it is weighted towards the university the workplace becomes the 'test-bed of subject-based and professionally-related knowledge' (Portwood, 2007: 8). Where the workplace is given primacy, it is the role of the university to translate and transpose work-based knowledge. Needless to say, understanding what constitutes knowledge in these contexts is far from straightforward.

Billet (1994) proposed a model of work-based learning based on 'authentic' activities within the workplace with the intent of gaining expertise. This 'situated learning' (Lave and Wenger, 1991) is by nature social, in that it involves social interactions within the community of practice. In this model, learning is given primacy over teaching. The goals for learning are the forms of knowledge considered necessary for vocational/professional expertise. Two forms of knowledge are evident here: propositional knowledge – *knowing that* – and procedural knowledge – *knowing how*. When combined, they contribute to the development of expertise. A further element recognised by Billet is disposition – those attitudes, values and interests that influence an individual's tendencies to put their capabilities into practice (Billet, 1994). Dispositions, therefore, determine whether an individual values a particular form of knowledge enough to put in the effort and engage in the activities required to gain it. Dispositions are, by nature, socially influenced and subject to what is valued in specific situations (Billet, 1994).

The participatory nature of work-based learning is therefore essential in building the necessary knowledge and experience associated with the field of work. Through observation, access to experts and the opportunity to engage in workplace practices, students are able to try out and try on their chosen profession within the boundaries of a predetermined placement. The placement 'curriculum' assists the student to build on the theoretical knowledge and understanding gained at the university in a supportive way. In some educational settings this may follow a structured, linear process of induction. In others it may be an immersive experience supported by a work-based mentor. Both practices involve work-based supervisors getting to know students, their pre-existing knowledge, experiences, capabilities and dispositions, in order to make the most out of the placement.

Expansive and restrictive models of learning

Fuller and Unwin's (2004) study of learning in the workplace resulted in a framework for understanding the barriers and opportunities for learning experienced by workers (see Table 21.1). Although not exhaustive the list of features was intended to provide a typology

Table 21.1 Expansive-restrictive continuum (adapted from Fuller and Unwin, 2004: 7)

Expansive	Restrictive
Participation in multiple communities of practice inside and outside the workplace	Restricted participation in multiple communities of practice
Primary community of practice has shared 'participative memory': cultural inheritance of workforce development	Primary community of practice has little or no 'participative memory': no or little tradition of apprenticeship
Breadth: access to learning fostered by cross-company experiences	Narrow: access to learning restricted in terms of tasks/knowledge/location
Gradual transition to full, rounded participation	Fast – transition as quick as possible
Vision of workplace learning: progression for career	Vision of workplace learning: static for job
Organisational recognition of and support for employees as learners	Lack of organisational recognition of and support for employees as learners
Workforce development is used as a vehicle for aligning the goals of developing the individual and organisational capability	Workforce development is used to tailor individual capability to organisational need
Widely distributed skills	Polarised distribution of skills
Technical skills valued	Technical skills taken for granted
Knowledge and skills of whole workforce developed and valued	Knowledge and skills of key workers/groups developed and valued
Team work valued	Rigid specialist roles
Cross-boundary communication encouraged	Bounded communication
Managers as facilitators of workforce and individual development	Managers as controllers of workforce and individual development
Chances to learn new skills/jobs	Barriers to learning new skills/jobs
Innovation important	Innovation not important
Multi-dimensional view of expertise	Uni-dimensional top-down view of expertise

of pedagogical, organisational and cultural factors that contribute to workplace development and learning environments. For Fuller and Unwin, it is those characteristics associated with the expansive model of learning which provide stronger and richer learning environments. The conceptual model highlights that approaches to work organisation, job design and skills influence the barriers and opportunities for learning in the workplace, and that the configuration of informal and formal learning and the control and distribution of knowledge and skills explains the uneven nature of work-based learning environments.

For students of Education Studies engaged in work-based learning there is the added dimension of learning beyond the workplace to be considered. This inevitably includes learning as part of the university degree, but also via other external environments, for example across a number of placements provided throughout the course, or through engagement with practitioners via local, national or international associations or interest groups. Participation in such learning environments allows for personal reflection on career and skills development, a broadening of understanding in terms of professional contexts, and appreciation of the current socio-political/economic debates regarding the educational workforce.

There are links here with Nottingham's (2012) threefold typology of work-based learning: discipline-centred, employer-centred and learner-centred. In a discipline-centred model curriculum design is linked to the work-based skills and competencies required by the learner. Acquisition of such skills is often supported by a mentor, as in the case of initial teacher training. By contrast, the employer-centred model focuses on workforce development priorities, for example through accredited continued professional development. Finally, in the learner-centred model the interests of the learner take centre stage. Negotiating the complex boundaries between the university, workplace and career objectives becomes an important skill for students engaged in educational placements.

Questions for discussion

- Consider a workplace environment with which you are familiar. How does the expansive-restrictive framework help you understand the learning opportunities available to you?
- Using Nottingham's typology, how would you define the learning focus of your placement – discipline-centred, employer-centred and/or learner-centred?

Learning in educational placements

Experiential learning was defined by Kolb (1984: 41) as 'the process whereby knowledge is created through the transformation of experience. Knowledge results from the combination of grasping and transforming experience.' Kolb represented this as a cyclical process: see Figure 21.1. The learner engages in all four modes of realising experience

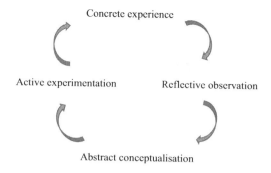

Concrete experience

Active experimentation

Reflective observation

Abstract conceptualisation

Figure 21.1 Kolb's learning cycle

through visiting and revisiting the points in the cycle, thereby gaining concrete experience, reflecting on that experience, endeavouring to make sense of the experience, and finally, trying out ways of putting the new learning and understanding into practice. As the cycle is repeated, so understanding is reviewed and refined.

Learning and reflection

Central to the notion of experiential learning is reflection. Education Studies courses offering placements and work-based learning allow for opportunities for student reflection. Reflection is understood in a number of ways: reflection *on, in* and *for* learning. Kolb's reflective observation permits the student an opportunity to stand back from the learning environment and consider the learning that has taken place. It is through reflection-*on*-action that experience is transformed into learning, whereas reflection-*in*-action reveals that learners know more than they are at first able to articulate (Simon, 2017: 34). However, an important use of reflection as a means of enhancing the placement experience is reflection-*for*-action: using the available time prior to the placement experience to consider how one might approach a given situation or apply skills and theoretical knowledge in such a way as to gain practical experience and achieve predefined learning objectives. The cycle begins again with reflection-in-action which permits the reframing of unanticipated responses thereby challenging preconceived or underlying/institutional assumptions. This in turn produces new ideas (Simon, 2017: 34).

Constructs of professionalism

It is also worthy of note that, as well as assisting with professional development and career identity, placements and work-based learning also enable students to explore concepts of professionalism more fully. A professional education career for students of Education Studies can be many and various, as indicated earlier in this chapter. How notions of professionalism are constructed and enacted within and across those careers, and by whom, describes a complex picture for the 'pre-professional'. In England for example, teachers are governed by the *Teachers' Standards* (DfE, 2011). These standards set out the minimum professional standards expected of all teachers employed in England and reflect a global approach to improving outcomes for teachers and their students. Borrowed from the world of business, 'performativity' as a measure of standards is embedded within notions of teacher professionalism, and in many instances across the education sector more widely. Accountability sits alongside performativity and to such an extent that in education discourse these two concepts often go hand-in-hand. For Kennedy (2016: 148) there is 'a tension between the use of standards to support professional growth and bottom–up accountability, and their use as a top-down, hierarchical and managerial means of ensuring compliance and performativity'. Sachs (2001) makes a distinction between 'managerial' professionalism which values efficiency and compliance and 'democratic' professionalism which emphasises social justice and equity. With particular regard to teaching, Whitty (2006b) proposed four models of professionalism:

> *Traditional* – where teachers are regarded as trusted members of society;
> *Managerial* – where the state specifies expectations of teachers;
> *Collaborative* – where teachers collaborate with other professionals rather than only with teachers;
> *Democratic* – where teachers are acknowledged agents of change to promote equity and justice for their pupils.

Such models of teacher/educational professionalism are not exhaustive but point to the complex landscape students will encounter as they engage with placements. Part of the reflective process for students on placement would be to consider what model of educational professionalism they hold to (if any) and to which mode(s) they wish to aspire. Using the workplace as an opportunity to discuss professionalism with practitioners is a revealing and challenging exercise.

Questions for discussion

- Would you describe teachers, teaching assistants, youth workers, or education officers within the arts or cultural industries as 'professionals'? Why/why not?
- Explore some of the models of professionalism introduced in this chapter. Which sits best with your own aspirations to become a teacher/educational professional?

Role of research: bringing the workplace into the university and the university into the workplace

One significant aspect of work-based learning is the contribution to research. Bringing the university into the workplace permits opportunities for enquiry that not only assists student learning but also enables small-scale projects in partnership with employers. An example here might be students undertaking an evaluation of a new initiative or resources for the classroom, researching and creating new activities for a creative arts project, or capturing data for a longer-term project for a local authority. Occasionally employers and schools approach university education departments with ideas for potential projects that can be developed into dissertation research at level 6, such as exploring how outdoor spaces at a school are utilised by children, or best practice in partnering mentors and young people in a youth centre. Of course, appropriate procedures for ethics and safe working practices must be adhered to. These are often managed and supported by university research officers and academic staff. The emphasis here is on the employer organisation being *partners* in research rather than *objects* of student enquiry. The objective is for purposeful knowledge and skills production and a strengthening of the employer/university partnership.

Preparation for placement

Activity

Having read the chapter thus far, consider your answer to the following questions:

* What type of placement are you looking for?
* What specific areas of interest are there for you?
* What type of setting will help you fulfil the academic requirement of your module/course?
* What types of experience will help you develop your knowledge of work-related practices?
* What skills, competencies and personal characteristics will you take into your placement?

(Adapted from Simon, 2017: 35)

Answers will depend on a range of factors including your past history and experiences, perceptions of your current skills, your future career aspirations and your personal values and beliefs (Simon, 2017: 34). They will also help you identify your personal and professional aims for the placement. If you have already engaged in placements, then answering these questions in the light of previous feedback will also help you to define your learning and professional goals. Both the university and your placement should have clearly defined expectations and responsibilities; these are usually provided in a placement handbook. Take the opportunity to read through before you visit your setting and discuss them together with your tutor and the work-based mentor. Consider what to do if things go wrong on placement: who to contact, procedures for reporting illness, problems with transport or general concerns. If working with children or vulnerable adults you must be clear about safeguarding procedures and who is the safeguarding officer.

Sourcing the placement may be part of your assessment, or placements may be allocated to you. In either event it is essential that you make contact with the placement before the initial start date. It may be necessary to visit in order to go through an induction process. This is the opportunity to discuss any specific needs you may have, to demonstrate you have all the necessary documentation in place such as a DBS (Disclosure and Barring Service) certificate and driving licence and that health and safety and safeguarding processes (if applicable) are explained. Time of arrival and departure, dress codes and rules regarding mobile phones, data storage and social media should also be explained.

It is useful to keep a journal during the course of your placement so as to record your thoughts, ideas, responses and observations. Consider how you will make notes during your working day so as not to distract from your activities or those around you.

Conclusion

The central role of placements and work-based learning for students of education is testament to the breadth of career options available across the education sector. Equipping students for the world of work or further study is the core business of HE institutions in the twenty-first century. University league tables are constructed on measures including the 'destination of leavers' survey. The success of students entering further study or graduate employment in schools and the wider education sector is testament to the close relationship between the study of education including placement opportunities and professional employment. In the most recent figures, 86 per cent of female and 94 per cent of male UK education graduates entered professional employment in the UK (HESA, 2018).

However, university placements should not be classed as mere work experience. Students must navigate complex spaces as emergent academics and novice professionals bringing together theory, practice and critical enquiry. In this way placements encourage critical reflection and personal and professional development.

Summary points

- The chapter has explored the central role of placements and work-based learning for students of Education Studies.
- It has provided an overview of work-based learning and its theoretical underpinnings.
- Concepts of professionalism and the role of research have also been discussed.
- The chapter concludes with practical pointers for preparation for placements and work-based learning.

Recommended reading

Hordern, J. and Simon, C.A. (2017) (Eds) *Placements and Work-Based Learning in Education Studies.* Abingdon: Routledge.

References

Billet, S. (1994) Situating Learning in the Workplace: Having Another Look at Apprenticeships. *Industrial and Commercial Training* **26**(11), pp. 9–16.

DfE (2011) *Teachers' Standards*. London: DfE. Available at: https://assets.publishing.service.gov.uk/government/uploads/system/uploads/attachment_data/file/665520/Teachers Standards.pdf (accessed 19 May 2019).

Fuller, A. and Unwin, L. (2004) Expansive Learning Environments. In H. Rainbird, A. Fuller and A. Munro (Eds), *Workplace Learning in Context*. London: Routledge.

HESA (2018) *Higher Education Leavers Statistics: UK, 2016/17 Outcome by Subject*. Cheltenham: HESA. Available at: www.hesa.ac.uk/news/28-06-2018/sfr250-higher-education-leaver-statistics-subjects (accessed 29 July 2019).

Kennedy, A. (2016) Standards and Accountability in Teacher Education. In The Teacher Education Group, *Teacher Education in Times of Change*. Bristol: Policy Press.

Kolb, D. (1984) *Experiential Learning: Experience as the Source of Learning and Development*. Englewood Cliffs, NJ: Prentice Hall.

Lave, J. and Wenger, E. (1991) *Situated Learning: Legitimate Peripheral Participation*. Cambridge: Cambridge University Press.

Lester, S. and Costley, C. (2010) Work-Based Learning at Higher Education Level: Value, Practice and Critique. *Studies in Higher Education* **35**(5), pp. 561–575.

Major, D. (2016) Models of Work-Based Learning: Examples and Reflections. *Journal of Work-Applied Management* **8**(1), pp. 17–28.

Nottingham, P. (2012) An Exploration of How Differing Perspectives of Work Based Learning within Higher Education Influence the Pedagogies Adopted. Unpublished thesis. London: Birkbeck, University of London.

Portwood, D. (2007) Towards an Epistemology of Work-Based Learning: Eliciting Clues from Work-Based Learning Projects. In D. Young and J. Garnett (Eds), *Work-Based Learning Futures. Proceedings from the Work-Based Learning Futures Conference*. Buxton, April 2007.

QAA (2015) *Subject Benchmark Statement: Education Studies*. Gloucester: QAA. Available at: www.qaa.ac.uk/docs/qaa/subject-benchmark-statements/sbs-education-studies-15.pdf?sfvrsn=959cf78110 (accessed 20 July 2019).

QAA (2018) *UK Quality Code: Advice and Guidance: Work-Based Learning*. Gloucester: QAA. Available at: www.qaa.ac.uk/quality-code/advice-and-guidance/work-based-learning (accessed 20 July 2019).

Sachs, J. (2001) Teacher Professional Identity: Competing Discourses, Competing Outcomes. *Journal of Education Policy* **34**(3), pp. 411–423.

Simon, C.A. (2017) Preparing for Your Placement. In J. Hordern and C.A. Simon (Eds), *Placements and Work-Based Learning in Education Studies*. Abingdon: Routledge.

Whitty, G. (2008) Changing Modes of Teacher Professionalism: Traditional, Managerial, Collaborative and Democratic. In B. Cunningham (Ed.), *Exploring Professionalism*. London: Institute of Education, University of London.

Chapter 22

Professionalism and education

Jim Hordern and Kendra McMahon

Introduction

This chapter examines issues of professionalism in education, discussing broader changes in educational occupations globally but with particular reference to the context of teaching in England. First, we examine what we mean by professions, professionalism and 'professionalisation' in education, discussing the role of governments, representative bodies and educational institutions in developing professionals and their role in society. Secondly, we consider some prominent models of professionalism in education, highlighting more descriptive models based on sociological and historical study and some more normative approaches which emphasise particular views of teacher professionalism. Next, we discuss issues of teachers' professional knowledge and expertise, before finally addressing the development of teaching standards and the importance of values in teaching. Throughout the chapter we aim to raise questions about educational professionalism that you can consider as part of your study of education, and suggest some further readings for further exploration of the key themes.

Professions and professionalisation

Education has been described as a 'pre-theoretical human practice' (Carr, 2003: 254), suggesting that educational activity has been an element of human social activity throughout history. As societies have industrialised, educational work has become formalised, with the development of schools and other educational institutions in which students can undertake courses of study and gain qualifications. While the central pedagogical relationship between teacher and student remains vitally important, the roles of educational practitioners have become increasingly organised and structured. Educators generally work within organisations (such as schools and colleges) in which their work is managed, controlled and evaluated. In some countries these educators are employed directly by educational institutions, but they may also be employed by states or governments, they may be self-employed or working for smaller private or charitable organisations. In most countries, therefore, educational work has become increasingly seen as an occupational activity, sometimes considered alongside other similar 'human service' occupations such as social workers, psychologists or other public service occupations. Establishing education as an 'occupation' suggests that researchers can draw upon sociological studies of work to develop insights into the roles and responsibilities of educational practitioners.

Not all occupations are necessarily *professions*, however. There has been considerable debate about whether educational practitioners are professionals, and what kind of professionals they could or should be. Most sociological analysis of the professions considers occupations to be professions when they exercise a degree of authoritative control over an area of work (Freidson, 2001), or what Abbott terms a 'jurisdiction' (Abbott, 1988). Professionals typically maintain their control over an area of work by deciding who is accredited as a practitioner and by deciding what counts as appropriate knowledge for their profession. This has also often involved developing programmes of study in partnership with universities and higher technical institutions.

A degree of 'self-governance', when the professionals control their own affairs, allows the profession to negotiate relationships with other occupations and the state and to further 'professionalise' their occupation. Self-governance is often handled through representative bodies who accredit the initial education and ongoing development of practitioners, and these bodies can also sometimes act as (or with) trade unions. In England, the recent establishment of the Chartered College of Teaching can be seen as a move towards a representative professional body. There are some differences here between professions in the Anglophone world (i.e. the UK and USA) where professionals have tended to have to secure their control over a jurisdiction continuously, and the continental European countries where professionals have often been guaranteed their jurisdiction by the state (and underpinned by legislation). Some occupations have also clearly 'professionalised' over time as a consequence of greater public requirements for their expertise, and a recognition of the need for transparent accountability for their work. For example, Foray and Hargreaves (2003: 15) document the rise of medical expertise and the growth of a 'scientific epistemic culture' as a consequence of societal demands for better healthcare.

Since the 1980s at least, however, there has been considerable criticism of some professions. These criticisms have often stemmed from a suspicion that professionals are primarily self-interested and act to preserve their privileges through 'professional closure', rather than always work in the interests of their customers or clients. Larsson (1978) argued that occupations are often engaged in 'professional projects', seeking to establish and defend their own interests and privileges. This more sceptical view of professionals has seeped into public consciousness. In the United Kingdom various reforms were undertaken in the 1980s and 1990s that aimed to make entry to the professions easier, and to reduce the control that professionals had over specific areas of work (Ackroyd, 1996). This broader context affects the professional aspirations of any occupational group.

So where does teaching fit within the landscape of professionalism? Barber (2005) outlined the trajectory of teaching professionalism in England as involving the following phases:

(i)   uniformed professionalism, when teachers had autonomy, but lacked a secure knowledge base (before the 1980s);
(ii) uniformed prescription, when the government increasingly took control of teacher education and the curriculum (during the Thatcher governments of the 1980s);

(iii) informed prescription, when government and researchers started to invest more in 'evidence-based' approaches to teaching (the New Labour period in the 1990s and 2000s);

(iv) informed professionalism, where teachers gain greater autonomy, again on the basis of a robust form of 'knowledge-rich' professional expertise (gradually over the last ten years).

Barber's (2005) work has been criticised for a degree of historical inaccuracy (Whitty, 2006a). However, the idea that teacher professionalism is strongly influenced by relations with the state is widely supported, with some arguing that teachers in England have taken on a 'governmental' type of professionalism in recent years (Beck, 2008). It has been suggested that the government has 'demanded' a specific type of professionalism through the imposition of a set of Teacher Standards that emphasise certain kinds of behaviour (Evans, 2011). Such an approach could be seen to limit teacher autonomy and hold teachers in the 'prescription' phase indefinitely.

Taking the longer view, it could be argued that the professionalism of educational practitioners is closely intertwined with the development of national education systems, and the role of the state within such projects. In England, the creation of the welfare state after the Second World War led to the development of public service professions in health, social services and education (Green, 1990). This could be understood as educational practitioners entering into a partnership with the state to secure the 'jurisdiction' of educational work, and this might mean having to accept radical change to professional work when new governments take charge and new policies are introduced. 'Professional closure' may thus be more difficult for public service professions such as teaching than it is for medicine or law, as the autonomy of teachers is limited by the extent to which the state allows them discretion in their work. However, it is also important to remember that in England and elsewhere there are many qualified teachers within independent schools located outside the public sector. Furthermore, recent reforms to the education system in England which offer greater autonomy for schools may lead to fewer teachers in state education seeing teaching as a public service profession. The professionalism of teaching may also involve the development of forms of knowledge and expertise that are specific to teaching itself, irrespective of state involvement. We return to this issue briefly below.

Questions for discussion

- Do teachers and other educational practitioners have control over their own work? How much control should they have? Should others (governments, parents, employers) have a say?
- Is teaching similar to other occupations and professions? Which ones and why?
- How different is educational professionalism in the different nations of the United Kingdom?

Prominent models of professionalism in education

The nature of teacher professionalism can be described, as in Barber's account of historical changes above, or it can be set up as an ideal to be achieved or standard to be adhered to; there are both descriptive and normative models of teacher professionalism. Descriptive accounts of the realities such as Barber's can be challenged by authors with different interpretations and perspectives on how things are. Normative models of what teacher professionalism *should be* are certainly contested according to different views of the purposes of education and what it means to teach and thus what it means to be a teacher. This section will explore some descriptive and normative models, though the distinction blurs – you may wish to consider to what extent they describe your experiences of teaching and your view of how things should be.

One aspect to consider is the scope of teachers' work the model addresses: is it focused entirely on classroom practice and limited to the academic outcomes of their pupils or does it encompass wider aspirations for social change and community engagement? Hoyle (1974) influentially conceived this dimension as a continuum with a 'restrictive' view of professionality at one end and 'expansive' view of professionality at the other. So a restricted professional is reliant upon their experiences, intuition and has a classroom-based perspective, whereas in extended professional values the theory underpinning practice has a wider vision of what education involves. This expansive-restrictive continuum has been adapted by Menter *et al.* (2010) who identify four models of what it means to be a teaching professional and place these at different points. At the restricted end of the continuum is the 'effective teacher model'. This has an economically-driven view of the purpose of education and has dominated government discourse about education in England. It regards being a teaching professional as having a set of technical accomplishments such as the ability to maintain an orderly classroom and producing measurable outcomes in terms of children's academic attainment. Menter *et al.* (2010) argue that this model restricts teacher professionalism rather than enhancing it as it limits the scope of teacher autonomy and judgement.

Further along the continuum of Menter *et al.* (2010) is the reflective teacher. Being a reflective teacher means that a teacher draws on educational theory and social awareness to evaluate and to continuously change their practice. This model is expansive in that it places responsibility on teachers to identity and use relevant theory, such as theories of learning and research, to make judgements about how to improve practice. Reflection is a thoughtful process driven by both personal values and immediate concerns. Some authors (e.g. Pollard, 2014: 84) emphasise that this should not be done in isolation, and that teachers working together on issues in professional communities of practice leads to more significant change (Wiliam, 2011). The connection made between theory and practice to develop the individual means that the reflective teacher is a model often used in university-based initial teacher education programmes. The model of the 'enquiring teacher' in which teachers are engaged in research is considered by Menter *et al.* (2010) to be more expansive in that it may involve teachers working with others, such as university lecturers, and thus encountering a wider range of ideas. Sometimes teachers work in collaboration with university researchers to identify wider problems of practice and work on developing solutions together, for example how to assess children's science enquiry skills (Davies *et al.*, 2017). In this model teachers are producers as well as users of knowledge; this is not the same as teachers only participating in research by carrying out 'interventions' that have been designed by others.

At the 'extended' end of the spectrum, Menter *et al.* (2010) place the model of the 'transformative teacher' whose responsibilities extend beyond the classroom to contribute to social change, by changing the life chances of pupils themselves or by preparing the pupils to contribute to change. The conception of teaching as an 'activist' profession (Sachs, 2003) emphasises teachers working to reduce inequality and to support social justice by challenging the status quo. This is a very different view of a teacher from the 'effective professional' focused on delivering a prescribed curriculum to their class. It might involve challenging curriculum content, assessment processes or the ways in which resources are allocated to and within education systems, thus it requires wider knowledge and a preparedness to identify where policy as well as practice is at odds with values.

Arguably, in a democratic society, there should be limits to teacher autonomy and the views of a wider range of stakeholders – parents, children, potential employers and society in general – should inform how taxes are spent on education. In the 1980s, under the Thatcher government, a dominant view was that teachers had failed, and therefore needed to be made more accountable for their work. Decisions on curriculum and assessment that were previously made by teachers and schools (and in the case of secondary education shaped by exam boards) were taken on by the central government. In England the Office for Standards in Education (Ofsted) was established to judge how well schools implemented these statutory frameworks, meaning that headteachers were held accountable for the performance of their schools and they in turn intervened more directly in the work of teachers. In this 'managerial professionalism' (Whitty, 2006b), teachers in England expect to be set performance targets and to have their work judged at an annual performance review. However, schools can and do opt to include teachers in setting school policy and deciding on pedagogical approaches, and many schools have collaborative processes for developing a 'whole school approach', for example to behaviour management. Teachers have also been required to collaborate with others beyond teaching; close communication with social workers and the police is built into safeguarding policies and teachers need to draw on the expertise of educational psychologists and others such as occupational therapists to support children with special educational needs and disabilities. Although these requirements may have stemmed from a managerial approach, they have created more 'collaborative professionalism' (Whitty, 2006b).

However, collaboration only with other professionals can be subject to the same criticism of elitism and excluding the voices of stakeholders (such as parents) as traditional professionalism. In response, Whitty (2006b) proposed a 'democratic professionalism' in which teachers engage with a wide range of viewpoints, including those of children. This vision of democratic professionalism draws on the model of 'activist professionalism' proposed by Judith Sachs (2003) in which teachers work to create networks and alliances with others such as community organisations in pursuit of a more just society. There are clear resonances here with Menter *et al*.'s (2010) 'transformative teacher'.

Questions for discussion

- What examples of these models of professionalism have you noticed in schools and early years settings?
- Which models of professionalism are most aligned with your view of the role of teachers?

Professional knowledge

Questions of teachers' professional knowledge and expertise are central to debates about their professionalism. As Barber's (2005) analysis demonstrated, the development of a knowledge base for teaching can be seen as a route to greater autonomy (and therefore professionalism). However, the need for a specific knowledge base for teaching has often been questioned. Seldon (2013), for example, suggests that subject expertise (e.g. in Maths or History) accompanied by certain behaviours and attitudes are the central requirements of good teachers. Others might suggest that a moral or ethical commitment to the wellbeing of learners is the most important characteristic of teaching (Heilbronn, 2010). Still others have focused on identifying the specific forms of curriculum and pedagogic knowledge that teaching requires. The work of Shulman (1987), for example, has been ground-breaking in advancing the notion of 'pedagogical content knowledge' as a specific category of teachers' knowledge that can arguably only be developed through engagement with the challenge of making subject knowledge meaningful to students in pedagogical contexts. In this respect it parallels the work of German *Didaktik* theorists, who have stressed the importance of teachers' expertise in translating content into something meaningful for students.

Winch *et al*. (2015) provide a helpful overview of how different types of knowledge interrelate in teaching. They identify 'situated understanding', 'technical knowledge' and types of 'critical reflection' as characteristic elements of teacher knowledge. These are often connected, respectively, with conceptions of teachers as 'craftworkers', 'technicians' and 'reflective practitioners', conceptions which may also be reflected in assumptions about teacher education and national education policies (Hordern and Tatto, 2018). Winch *et al*. (2015) suggest that good teaching requires all of these types of knowledge, and that once teachers have developed the capacity to critically reflect through scholarly engagement with research (and potentially by becoming active researchers themselves) their understanding and application of their 'situated' and 'technical' knowledge is transformed. In a sense, they understand their teaching practice differently and are able to make more critically reflective and appropriate forms of professional judgement.

The important work of Winch *et al*. (2015) raises further questions for teacher professionalism, however. Their overview of teacher knowledge leads us to ask what forms of scholarly work and research teachers should engage with in order to become critic-ally reflective expert practitioners. And who should decide what counts as good schol-arship or research? Teachers, governments or professional researchers? From the point of view of Barber (2005), government could play a key role, and others have suggested that specific forms of 'gold standard' research such as Randomised Controlled Trials should be prioritised for funding. The current government in England has emphasised the role of the Educational Endowment Foundation (EEF) as a gateway to the types of evi-dence that teachers should make use of in their teaching practice. This has parallels in the United States, where the federal government has set up a process for selecting and foregrounding 'what works' for teaching practice (Paine, 2017). However, these moves towards selecting the types of research considered important for teaching do not neces-sarily advance teacher autonomy or control over their work. Arguably, the development of a centralised knowledge base that fits with policy prescription *reduces* teacher autonomy and control, making teaching ever more dependent on whatever is considered a priority by governments and their preferred researchers. Teaching can therefore be shaped as an activity in accordance with policy priorities or particular assumptions about education and educational knowledge.

While recent governments in England have taken a prescriptive approach to teachers' knowledge, this is not necessarily the case in other nations of the UK. In Scotland, for example, reforms to the curriculum and teacher education have arguably strengthened the influence of teacher educators and teachers, albeit still within a partnership with government. There is an acknowledgement that teachers' expertise is best developed when teachers have greater autonomy (Menter and Hulme, 2011). Recent reforms in Wales are plotting a similar trajectory, in contradistinction to England. These developments may well result in forms of teacher professionalism that can become more 'transformative' and critically reflective, acknowledging that the 'evidence-based' approaches need to be balanced with a recognition of the complex nature of teaching practice. The reforms also suggest that there is a recog-nition that there may well be aspects of teacher knowledge and practice that *only teachers themselves* can define and make judgements about, and this calls into question any claims that systematic empirical research is in itself a 'gold standard' form of educational know-ledge. A knowledge-rich teacher professionalism may require more than just governmental prescription or what is sometimes termed 'adaptive expertise' (Darling-Hammond, 2006). It is likely to require a capacity to make well-grounded ethical educational judgements about curriculum, pedagogy and assessment in complex and varied educational contexts.

Questions for discussion

- What do teachers need to know to teach well? How do views differ on this?
- Do teachers need to take account of educational research findings? Why? What about philosophical perspectives on teaching? Are they relevant?

Professional standards and values?

In England, Qualified Teacher Status (QTS) is currently awarded by the Teaching Regulation Agency on behalf of the Secretary of State for Education. So unlike in the traditional model of professionalism in which a professional body controls entry into the profession, QTS is awarded by the government. The award of QTS is made when it is judged that a set of competences have been demonstrated; these competences are listed in the *Teachers' Standards* (DfE, 2011). It is worth noting that QTS is not currently (in 2019) a requirement to teach in academies, free schools and independent schools in England, although most schools do employ teachers with QTS.

On the face of it, it seems reasonable that prospective teachers should be competent and that it should be possible to list features that make up a shared understanding of what 'good practice' entails. Indeed, it is helpful for those aspiring to be teachers and those mentoring them to understand the areas they will need to learn about; standards can act as a curriculum and they can also provide useful focus points for discussion and feedback during teacher education. Individual standards might be considered in relation to the models of professionalism discussed earlier. For example, Teaching Standard 8 requires teachers to: 'Fulfil wider professional responsibilities' and 'develop effective professional relationships with colleagues, knowing how and when to draw on advice and specialist support' (DfE, 2011: 13), apparently supporting a collaborative model of professionalism (Whitty, 2006b). Similarly, embedded within Teaching Standard 4 is a requirement for teachers to be reflective professionals: 'all teachers reflect systematically on the effectiveness of lessons and approaches to teaching' (DfE, 2011: 11), although as the focus of that reflection is on planning and teaching well-structured lessons this is more in line with restricted than extended professionality (Hoyle, 1974).

However, the conception of professionalism as a set of standards is problematic. One issue is that definitions of 'good teaching' are contested (Heilbronn, 2010) and that attempting to construct a set of standards implicitly denies this and asserts a monologic view that closes down critical debate and dialogue. As discussed in the previous section, the professional knowledge of teaching is not a simple matter. Vanassche and Kelchtermans (2015) suggest that the problem is not necessarily the content of any set of standards, but that the existence of a set of standards provide one lens which comes to be the accepted way of looking at teaching, which means that other perspectives may be unseen. For example, the role of emotion, teacher passion and teachers' deep care for children (Gu, 2007) is a dimension of teaching that is not easily captured in a set of standards.

A further issue is that standards are inherently generalisations and these cannot capture the complexity of teaching in every context (Heilbronn, 2010). Therefore they need to be interpreted. An assessor will have to make a judgement on whether or not a standard has been met in a particular school or early years setting. Furthermore, the interpretation of standards may involve value-based decisions. Orchard *et al.* (2016) exemplify this through a look at Standard 7 in part 1: 'maintain good relationships with pupils, exercise appropriate authority, and act decisively when necessary' (DfE, 2011: 10), arguing that, in practice, the complex moral and value-based issues around behaviour management are generally ignored and that instead meeting this standard usually takes the form of implementing whatever behaviour management approaches are being used in the school.

The emphasis on demonstrable outcomes is a feature of managerial professionalism (Whitty, 2006a) in which the work of teachers is controlled and monitored by others with more authority. However, teachers may internalise these requirements and judge themselves against them. Ball (2008: 51) describes this as performativity.

> Performativity invites and incites us to make ourselves more effective, to work on ourselves to improve ourselves and to feel guilty or inadequate if we do not. But it operates with a framework of judgement within which what improvement is determined for us, and 'indicated' by measures of quality and productivity.

Standards can be seen as one such framework of judgement. Ball (ibid.) goes on to explain that teacher professional identities are deeply affected by performativity. When looked at from this perspective, translating into practice the requirement for reflection in the *Teachers' Standards* (DfE, 2011) becomes more problematic. It may involve creativity, but it also becomes a process of compliance as teachers strive to improve their practice in a particular way (Perryman *et al.*, 2017). Finnish educator and policy advisor Pasi Sahlberg (2012) notes that standards-based approaches rightly focus on educational outcomes of pupil learning and school performance, but argues that alongside this has been the mistaken belief that setting high standards will, of itself, improve educational outcomes. Sahlberg locates the standards approach within an infectious global educational reform movement (GERM), in which international comparison of pupil achievement in the 'basics' of literacy and numeracy drives a culture of performance-based testing and managerialism, narrows the curriculum and reduces teacher innovation.

Questions for discussion

- Should there be a set of standards that must be met in order to become qualified to be a teacher?
- To what extent do you think an individual teacher's values should be shared by others in the profession?

Conclusion

This chapter has briefly examined some of the key themes in discussion of educational professionalism, with a particular focus on teaching. Our primary examples have come from the context of school teaching in England, but the themes themselves are central to debates about educational occupations in many countries around the world. The relationship between occupations, their clients, governments and other occupations is always changing. This is as true of teaching and the education professions as it is of other occupations. The nature of work itself continues to change, and therefore what it means to educate may well change considerably in the future, with advances in technology and expertise. However, it is worth bearing in mind that point made by Carr (2003), namely that education is a human practice that is fundamental to human relationships and that existed before organised scientific thought. The ethical and values-based dimension of teacher professionalism may therefore be vitally important, whatever educational science offers in terms of better understanding of more helpful and insightful ways to teach.

Summary

- Professions can be analysed in terms of their self-governance, relationship to the state, and degree of control of knowledge and qualifications.
- In England, educational occupations professionalised in the twentieth century, in parallel with the development of the welfare state, and have been strongly influenced by government education policy.
- Models of teaching professionalism highlight 'restrictive' and 'expansive' dimensions, the need for teachers to collaborate with other professionals, and the role of teachers in educational and social change.
- Educational knowledge is multifaceted, and teachers may need situated understanding, technical knowledge and the capacity to critically reflect to work professionally.
- Using professional standards in education may help develop shared understanding of professionalism, but may not fully capture professional values. Standards could also be used to control teachers' work, and thus reduce professional autonomy.

Recommended reading

Cunningham, B. (Ed.) (2008) *Exploring Professionalism*. London: Institute of Education, University of London.

Evans, L. (2011) The 'Shape' of Teacher Professionalism in England: Professional Standards, Performance Management, Professional Development and the Changes Proposed in the 2010 White Paper. *British Educational Research Journal* **37**(5), pp. 851–870.

Menter, I., Hulme, M., Elliot, D. and Lewin, J. (2010) *Literature Review on Teacher Education in the 21st Century*. Edinburgh: The Scottish Government.

References

Abbott, A. (1988) *The System of Professions: An Essay on the Division of Expert Labour*. Chicago: University of Chicago Press.

Ackroyd, A. (1996) Organization contra Organizations: Professions and Organizational Change in the United Kingdom. *Organization Studies* **17**(4), pp. 599–621.

Ball, S. (2008) Performativity, Privatisation, Professionals and the State. In B. Cunningham (Ed.), *Exploring Professionalism*. London: Institute of Education, University of London.

Barber, M. (2005) The Virtue of Accountability: System Redesign, Inspection, and Incentives in the Era of Informed Professionalism. *Journal of Education* **185**(1), pp. 7–38.

Beck, J. (2008) Governmental Professionalism: Re-Professionalising or De-Professionalising Teachers in England? *British Journal of Educational Studies* **56**(2), pp. 119–143.

Carr, D. (2003) Rival Conceptions of Practice in Education and Teaching. *Journal of Philosophy of Education* **37**(2), pp. 253–267.

Darling-Hammond, L. (2006). Constructing 21st-Century Teacher Education. *Journal of Teacher Education* **57**, pp. 300–314.

Davies, D.J., Earle, S., McMahon, K., Howe, A. and Collier, C. (2017) Development and Exemplification of a Model for Teacher Assessment in Primary Science. *International Journal of Science Education* **39**(14), pp. 1869–1890.

DfE (2011) *Teachers' Standards: Guidance for School Leader, School Staff and Governing Bodies.* London: Department for Education. Online. Available at: www.gov.uk/government/publications/teachers-standards (accessed 20 May 2019).

Evans, L (2011) The 'Shape' of Teacher Professionalism in England: Professional Standards, Performance Management, Professional Development and the Changes Proposed in the 2010 White Paper. *British Educational Research Journal* **37**(5), pp. 851–870.

Foray, D. and Hargreaves, D. (2003) The Production of Knowledge in Different Sectors: A Model and Some Hypotheses. *London Review of Education* **1**(1), pp. 7–19.

Freidson, E. (2001) *Professionalism: The Third Logic.* London: Polity.

Green, A. (1990) *Education and State Formation.* Basingstoke: Macmillan.

Gu, Q. (2007) *Teacher Development: Knowledge and Context.* London: Continuum.

Heilbronn, R. (2010) The Nature of Practice-Based Knowledge and Understanding. In R. Heilbronn and J. Yandell (Eds), *Critical Practice in Teacher Education: A Study of Professional Learning.* London: Institute of Education.

Hordern, J. and Tatto, M.J. (2018) Conceptions of Teaching and Educational Knowledge Requirements. *Oxford Review of Education* **44**(6), pp. 686–701.

Hoyle, E. (1974) Professionality, Professionalism and Control in Teaching. *London Educational Review* **3**(2), pp. 13–19.

Larsson, M.F. (1978) *The Rise of Professionalism: A Sociological Analysis.* London: University of California Press.

Menter, I. and Hulme, M. (2011) Teacher Education Reform in Scotland: National and Global Influences. *Journal of Education for Teaching* **37**(4), pp 387–397.

Menter, I., Hulme, M., Elliot, D. and Lewin, J. (2010) *Literature Review on Teacher Education in the 21st Century.* Edinburgh: The Scottish Government.

Orchard, J., Heilbronn, R. and Winstanley, C. (2016) Philosophy for Teachers (P4T): Developing New Teachers' Applied Ethical-Decision Making. *Ethics and Education* **11**(1), 42–54.

Paine, L. (2017) Framing Education: Cautionary Tales from the USA of the Relationship between Education Studies and Teacher Education. In G. Whitty and J. Furlong (Eds), *Knowledge and the Study of Education: An International Exploration.* Didcot: Symposium.

Perryman, J., Ball, S.J., Braun, A. and Maguire, M. (2017) Translating Policy: Governmentality and the Reflective Teacher. *Journal of Education Policy* **32**(6), pp. 745–756.

Pollard, A. (2014) *Reflective Teaching in Schools* (4th edn). London: Bloomsbury.

Sachs, J. (2003) Teacher Professional Standards: Controlling or Developing Teaching? *Teachers & Teaching: Theory and Practice* **9**(2), pp. 175–186.

Sahlberg, P. (2012) How GERM is Infecting Schools around the World. Online. Available at: https://pasisahlberg.com/text-test/ (accessed 20 May 2019).

Seldon, A. (2013) Teaching is Like Parenting: You Don't Need to Have a Qualification. Online. www.theguardian.com/commentisfree/2013/oct/28/teaching-qualification-nick-clegg-course (accessed 20 May 2019).

Shulman, L. (1987) Knowledge and Teaching: Foundations of the New Reform. *Harvard Educational Review* **57**(1), 1–22.

Vanassche, E. and Kelchtermans, G. (2015) The State of the Art in Self-Study of Teacher Education Practices: A Systematic Literature Review. *Journal of Curriculum Studies* **47**(4), pp. 508–528.

Whitty, G. (2006a) Teaching Professionalism in a New Era. Paper presented at the first General Teaching Council for Northern Ireland Annual Lecture, Belfast, March 2006.

Whitty, G. (2006b) Changing Modes of Teacher Professionalism: Traditional, Managerial, Collaborative and Democratic. In B. Cunningham (Ed.), *Exploring Professionalism*. London: Institute of Education, University of London, pp. 28–49.

Wiliam, D. (2011) *Embedded Formative Assessment*. Bloomington, IN: Solution Tree Press.

Winch, C., Oancea, A. and Orchard, J. (2015) The Contribution of Educational Research to Teachers' Professional Learning: Philosophical Understandings. *Oxford Review of Education* **41**(2), pp. 202–216.

Notes on contributors

Prof Kyriaki Anagnostopoulou is Head of the School of Education, Bath Spa University, and Professor of Higher Education. As an education specialist with extensive leadership experience, Kyriaki has worked for over twenty-two years in the field of higher education and digital innovation. Her work has informed institutional, national and international policy and practice, and has spanned from developing strategic direction through to implementation. Kyriaki has presented at over fifty national and international conferences, has taken part in a number of Global Education Dialogues and, in 2018, she was awarded a prestigious National Teaching Fellowship.

Dr Brendan Bartram is Reader in Education at the University of Wolverhampton. He was awarded a National Teaching Fellowship by the Higher Education Academy in 2012. His research and publications cover a wide range of issues related primarily to higher education (HE) practice, pedagogy and policy. Much of this work has involved a comparative dimension, examining such themes as international student mobility, behaviour, support and motivation. Outside of HE, his book – *Attitudes to Modern Language Learning: Insights from Comparative Education* – examined secondary language learning in the UK, USA, Australia, Germany and the Netherlands.

June Bianchi is an artist, senior lecturer, and researcher in arts education at Bath Spa University. June's pedagogy and practice are based within the Artist, Researcher, Teacher model and she promotes wider participation, engagement and empowerment through the arts within her exhibitions, publications and educational practice. She has developed international arts educational research projects and partnerships across statutory and voluntary educational, cultural and community sectors in the UK, continental Europe, USA, South and East Asia, and Africa.

Dr Zeta Brown is Reader in Education for Social Justice at the University of Wolverhampton, and is leader of the 'Children, Young People and Families' research cluster for the University's Education Observatory. She is an executive member and currently Chair of the British Education Studies Association (BESA). Zeta's research predominantly focuses on agendas and policies in early and primary education.

Prof Charlotte Chadderton is Professor of Education in the School of Education, Bath Spa University. She conducts research in the field of social justice in education with a particular focus on race (in)equality and the way in which different kinds of inequalities are produced and reproduced in educational spaces and by educational processes.

She has written widely on issues of race in education and research, and her book, *Judith Butler, Race and Education*, was published by Palgrave Macmillan in 2018.

Dr Rita Chawla-Duggan is Senior Lecturer in the Department of Education, University of Bath where she teaches and supervises across all levels: PhD, EdD (professional doctorate), undergraduate and full- and part-time Masters – including the Department's overseas MA Education study centre provision in India and Qatar. Her research interests include culture and pedagogy in early years and quality education. She has researched and worked with colleagues in India for the past twenty years; and has also researched early years and primary curricula implementation in England, Japan and Ghana.

Prof David Coulby has published widely, and occasionally deeply, in the fields of international education and interculturalism. His main research theme is the sociology and history of knowledge and culture, though current interests also include the political and economic decline of Europe and the impact of climate change on curricular systems.

Prof Denise Cush was Professor of Religion and Education at Bath Spa University until 2015. The first female professor of RE in the UK, she was a member of the Commission on Religious Education, 2017–2018, and Deputy Editor of the *British Journal of Religious Education* from 2011 to 2018. She taught religious studies at school and university levels, and RE in both primary and secondary teacher education. She is known for *Buddhism*, a textbook for A level, the *Routledge Encyclopaedia of Hinduism*, and many other publications on RE, Buddhism and paganism. In 2016 she was awarded an Honorary Doctorate from the University of Uppsala, Sweden.

Jayne Daly is Senior Lecturer at the University of Wolverhampton, teaching on a range of courses including the BA in Early Childhood Studies. Her career in early childhood and education began over thirty years ago. She has worked within the public care, health and education sectors, and from 2007 in further and higher education. She is currently engaged in doctoral research for a PhD in Education. Her research interests include childhood resilience, quality early years leadership, children's creative development and the impact of higher education on the life of the mature female learner.

Prof Christine Eden was Assistant Dean of the School of Education at Bath Spa University for many years, and is now an Emerita Professor of Education. She has a background in Sociology and Education Studies and is interested in understanding how the implementation of policy reproduces or challenges inequalities. She has published *Gender, Education and Work: Inequalities and Intersectionality, Key Issues in Education Policy* with Stephen Ward and contributed to a number of student textbooks in Education Studies.

Dr Tom Feldges is a research associate at the Institute of Education Studies of the Humboldt University in Berlin (Germany). After having worked and taught in UK higher education for more than ten years he is now researching the possibility of an experience-based theory of education (Bildung) with a value-based focus. Tom has published on various aspects of education and subjectivity and has recently edited a book in the Routledge Education Studies series, *Philosophy and the Study of Education*.

Prof David Hicks was formerly Professor in the School of Education at Bath Spa University and has a particular interest in issues of sustainability and climate change.

His most recent books are: *Sustainable Schools, Sustainable Futures: A Resource for Teachers* (2012) and *A Climate Change Companion: For Family, School and Community* (2016). His informative website is at www.teaching4abetterworld.co.uk.

Dr Jim Hordern is Lecturer in the Department of Education at the University of Bath. His research interests are in educational knowledge and practice, particularly in professional, vocational and higher education. Before becoming an academic he worked in English language teaching and further education, for local authorities and the Learning and Skills Council.

Dr Zenna Kingdon is Senior Lecturer at the University of Wolverhampton, with expertise in primary education, pre-school education and pedagogic theory. Her research interests focus on play and in particular role-play and exploring the concept of flourishing in early childhood.

Dr Kendra McMahon is Reader in Education at Bath Spa University. A former primary school teacher and deputy-head, she researches science education with an emphasis on developing support for teachers and has published academic and professional texts on the teacher assessment of science and on talk in science lessons. She is currently working on how initial teacher education might respond both critically and constructively to the emerging Science of Learning. Kendra's teaching includes undergraduate modules on science education and on teaching and professionalism.

Dr Bethan Mitchell is a lecturer in Education Studies for the School of Education at Bath Spa University and formerly worked at NHS Health Scotland, overseeing national health improvement programmes. Her particular area of interest is professional education and actor-network theory.

Dr Cathal Ó Siochrú is Senior Lecturer in the Psychology of Education at Liverpool Hope University. In addition to lecturing he has extensive experience with curriculum development and has developed psychology courses and psychology of education courses for a number of different universities. His research interests include student beliefs about knowledge, student and staff views on the choice between seen vs unseen exams, and student engagement. Cathal's most recent output is *Psychology and the Study of Education: Critical Perspectives on Developing Theories*, an edited volume which explores both the insights and applications that psychology can offer in a range of educational contexts.

Dr Ioanna Palaiologou is an Academic Associate at UCL Institute of Education and a child psychologist with specialism in child development and learning theories. Her research interests focus on early childhood education, child development, play and learning and digital technologies.

Dr Richard Riddell is an educationist who has worked for over forty years in and with state schooling in England. Following teaching in comprehensive schools in Oxfordshire and Berkshire, including four years as a head of department, he was a senior local authority officer for over twenty years. He held appointments in Wiltshire, Nottinghamshire, the County of Avon and the City of Bristol, where he was Director of Education for seven years. After leaving Bristol, he worked first as a consultant advising local authorities and (the then) learning and skills councils. He was then Head of Education for three years at the international NGO Amnesty International. Since 2009, he has worked part-time as a senior lecturer in Education Studies at Bath Spa University, combining this with research and being a school governor. His books include *Schools for Our Cities* (2003), *Aspiration, Identity and Self-Belief – Snapshots of Social Structure* (2010) and *Equity, Trust and the Self-Improving Schools System* (2016).

Dr Catherine A. Simon is Programme Leader for the Education Studies Undergraduate Programme at the School of Education, Bath Spa University where she is also a Teaching Fellow. Her professional experience includes teaching secondary history and RE and, latterly, primary years education. She has taught in schools throughout the UK and spent seven years working for Service Schools Education in Germany. Her research interests are concerned with education policy, school systems and leadership and management.

Prof Stephen Ward is Emeritus Professor of Education, formerly Dean of the School of Education and subject leader for Education Studies, at Bath Spa University. A founder member of the British Education Studies Association, he was Chair in 2006–2007. He has published books on the primary curriculum, primary music teaching and Education Studies. His research interests are education policy and university knowledge.

Dr Jo Winwood is Senior Lecturer in Special Educational Needs, Disability and Inclusion Studies at the University of Wolverhampton, teaching at undergraduate and postgraduate levels. She worked previously in mainstream and special schools. Her particular area of interest is the role of the Special Educational Needs Co-ordinator (SENCO) and her doctoral thesis examined this issue. She has worked internationally, supporting the development of inclusion for all children and young people.

Index

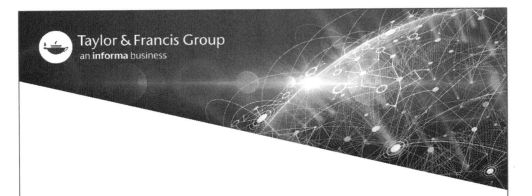

Taylor & Francis eBooks

www.taylorfrancis.com

A single destination for eBooks from Taylor & Francis
with increased functionality and an improved user
experience to meet the needs of our customers.

90,000+ eBooks of award-winning academic content in
Humanities, Social Science, Science, Technology, Engineering,
and Medical written by a global network of editors and authors.

TAYLOR & FRANCIS EBOOKS OFFERS:

A streamlined
experience for
our library
customers

A single point
of discovery
for all of our
eBook content

Improved
search and
discovery of
content at both
book and
chapter level

REQUEST A FREE TRIAL
support@taylorfrancis.com

Printed in Great Britain
by Amazon

66251581R00160